Lecture Notes in Computer Science   11686

Founding Editors

Gerhard Goos
Karlsruhe Institute of Technology, Karlsruhe, Germany
Juris Hartmanis
Cornell University, Ithaca, NY, USA

Editorial Board Members

Elisa Bertino
Purdue University, West Lafayette, IN, USA
Wen Gao
Peking University, Beijing, China
Bernhard Steffen
TU Dortmund University, Dortmund, Germany
Gerhard Woeginger
RWTH Aachen, Aachen, Germany
Moti Yung
Columbia University, New York, NY, USA

More information about this series at http://www.springer.com/series/7409

Panos Panagiotopoulos · Noella Edelmann ·
Olivier Glassey · Gianluca Misuraca ·
Peter Parycek · Thomas Lampoltshammer ·
Barbara Re (Eds.)

Electronic Participation

11th IFIP WG 8.5 International Conference, ePart 2019
San Benedetto Del Tronto, Italy, September 2–4, 2019
Proceedings

Springer

Editors
Panos Panagiotopoulos [ORCID]
Queen Mary University of London
London, UK

Olivier Glassey [ORCID]
University of Lausanne
Lausanne, Switzerland

Peter Parycek
Danube University Krems
Krems, Austria

Barbara Re
University of Camerino
Camerino, Italy

Noella Edelmann
Danube University Krems
Krems, Austria

Gianluca Misuraca
European Commission
Joint Research Centre
Sevilla, Spain

Thomas Lampoltshammer
Danube University Krems
Krems, Austria

ISSN 0302-9743 ISSN 1611-3349 (electronic)
Lecture Notes in Computer Science
ISBN 978-3-030-27396-5 ISBN 978-3-030-27397-2 (eBook)
https://doi.org/10.1007/978-3-030-27397-2

LNCS Sublibrary: SL3 – Information Systems and Applications, incl. Internet/Web, and HCI

This Springer imprint is published by the registered company Springer Nature Switzerland AG
The registered company address is: Gewerbestrasse 11, 6330 Cham, Switzerland

Editorial

Welcome to EGOV-CeDEM-ePart 2019! The conference presents the merger of the IFIP WG 8.5 Electronic Government (EGOV), the IFIP WG 8.5 Electronic Participation (ePart), and the E-Democracy and Open Government Conference (CeDEM). The conference is dedicated to the broader area of electronic government, open government, smart governance, e-democracy, policy informatics, electronic participation and other social innovation, and digital society applications. Scholars from around the world have been attending this premier academic forum for a long time, which has given EGOV a worldwide reputation as one of the top two dedicated conferences in the broader domain of digital government.

EGOV-CeDEM-ePart 2019 was held during September 2–4, 2019, in San Benedetto Del Tronto, and was hosted by the University of Camerino, Italy. The University of Camerino has a seven-decade long history, starting in 1336 when it was founded as Studium Generale. Today, the university is ranked first among the small-scale Italian Universities. The University of Camerino is responsible for research and training in multiple areas and the local organization belongs to the Computer Science Division. This is a vibrant and young research group that is part of the School of Science and Technology with a research background in modeling, analysis, verification, and deployment of distributed systems.

The call for papers attracted completed research papers, work-in-progress papers reporting on ongoing research (including doctoral papers), project and case descriptions, as well as workshop and panel proposals. The submissions were assessed through a double-blind review process with at least two reviewers per submission. This conference of eight partially intersecting tracks presents advances in the socio-technological domain of the public sphere demonstrating cutting-edge concepts, methods, and styles of investigation by multiple disciplines. The papers were distributed over the following tracks:

- General E-Government and Open Government track
- General E-Democracy and eParticipation track
- Smart Cities (Government, Communities and Regions) track
- AI, Data Analytics, and Automated Decision Making track
- Social Media track
- Social Innovation track
- Open Data: Social and Technical Aspects track
- Digital Society track
- Practitioners' track

The current volume contains 13 completed research papers presented at the General e-Democracy and e-Participation track, the Social Media track, the Digital Society track, and the Social Innovation track. Another 27 completed research papers presented at the conference can be found in the LNCS EGOV proceedings (vol. 11685).

The volume begins with eParticipation Developments and a decade overview of the ePart conference by Marius Rohde Johannessen and Lasse Berntzen. Such important milestones allow community reflections on how eParticipation has evolved as a research area within an interdisciplinary conference. In a case study of participatory budgeting in Helsinki, Titiana-Petra Ertiö, Pekka Tuominen, and Mikko Rask discuss how an effective combination of offline and online engagement can make such exercises more effective and inclusive. Tiago Silva, António Tavares, and Mariana Lameiras provide an overview and adoption models of social media channels for local government engagement in Portugal. Labeled as 'trendy cities', they observe how the local government's use of social media varies based on demographic characteristics, administrative capacity, and geographical location. Michael Sachs and Judith Schossböck design and apply a user identification framework for eParticipation platforms. They conclude that purposefully built digital engagement platforms can be of higher quality and relevance than public spaces when sufficient legitimizing mechanisms mitigate user concerns.

The section on Digital Transformations begins with a promising exploration of chatbots in public services by Colin van Noordt and Gianluca Misuraca. Even such novel applications seem to follow a known pattern: while immediate benefits to providing information can be realized, more complicated uses like transactions will require organizational change. Shefali Virkar, Noella Edelmann, and a group of colleagues present an extensive study of informal knowledge sharing networks within the public sector. They identify internal workflows and culture as important reasons to explain why some organizations have made more progress than others. From a design perspective, Helena Korge, Regina Erlenheim, and Dirk Draheim present a qualitative study of proactive business event services in the Estonian company registration portal. They demonstrate how better user experience can be achieved with consideration to small changes like notifications and data reuse.

Continuing with two contributions in the area of Crisis and Emergency Management, Sofie Pilemalm examines how response capabilities during the early stages of emergencies can be enhanced by engaging early respondents using digital tools. Reflections are offered on the co-production of emergency response and its impact on different groups. On a related note, Monika Magnusson, Geir Ove Venemyr, Peter Bellström, and Bjørn Tallak Bakken report on the Swedish-Norwegian CriseIT project that developed a platform for crisis management training. A design science approach is adopted to draw the components of the system and discuss how they individually and altogether can facilitate and improve training.

Moving on to the ever-important User Perspectives, Bettina Distel and Ida Lindgren provide a critical reflection of citizens as 'users' in e-government research. By unboxing the concept of the 'user-citizen' as an active entity, they provide a value perspective that can inform future research and design. Mapping citizen roles to their motivations emerges as an important factor in the case studies of open agriculture data hackathons reported by Arie Purwanto, Anneke Zuiderwijk, and Marijn Janssen. Participants in such events were found to be motivated both by instinct and extrinsic reasons which are important to consider when designing such events. In a study of digital divides in Brazil, Marcelo Henrique de Araujo and Nicolau Reinhard find that mobile phones have become a substitute device for computer use in more marginalized groups, hence reinforcing digital exclusion patterns. This is important for considering mobile accessible policies that will stimulate multiuse device skills in the digital economy. Marie Anne Macadar, Gabriela Viale Pereira, and Fernando Bichara Pinto integrate eParticipation studies with the capability approach by Sen and Nussbaum. This analysis illustrates the increasing digital engagement inequalities in a development context.

Closing the volume, the editors would like to thank the many people that make large events like this conference happen. Our gratitude goes to over 100 members of the Program Committee and dozens of additional reviewers for their great efforts in reviewing the submitted papers. We particularly express our gratitude to the local organizing team from the University of Camerino for the organization and management of the conference.

July 2019

Panos Panagiotopoulos
Noella Edelmann
Olivier Glassey
Gianluca Misuraca
Peter Parycek
Thomas Lampoltshammer
Barbara Re

Organization

Conference Lead Organizer

Marijn Janssen — Delft University of Technology, The Netherlands

General E-Government and Open Government Track

Ida Lindgren (Lead) — Linköping University, Sweden
Hans Jochen Scholl — University of Washington, USA
Gabriela Viale Pereira — Danube University Krems, Austria

General E-Democracy and eParticipation Track

Panos Panagiotopoulos (Lead) — Queen Mary University of London, UK
Robert Krimmer — Tallinn University of Technology, Estonia
Peter Parycek — Fraunhofer Fokus, Germany,
and Danube-University Krems, Austria

Smart Cities (Government, Communities and Regions) Track

Manuel Pedro Rodríguez
Bolívar (Lead) — University of Granada, Spain
Karin Axelsson — Linköping University, Sweden
Nuno Lopes — DTx: Digital Transformation Colab, Portugal

AI, Data Analytics and Automated Decision Making Track

Habin Lee (Lead) — Brunel University London, UK
Euripidis Loukis — University of Aegean, Greece
Tomasz Janowski — Gdansk University of Technology, Poland,
and Danube University Krems, Austria

Social Media Track

Noella Edelmann (Lead) — Danube University Krems, Austria
Sarah Hoffmann — University of Agder, Norway
Marius Rohde Johannessen — University of South-Eastern Norway, Norway

Social Innovation Track

Gianluca Misuraca (Lead)	European Commission's Joint Research Centre, Spain
Marijn Janssen	Delft University of Technology, The Netherlands
Csaba Csaki	Corvinus Business School, Hungary

Open Data: Social and Technical Aspects Track

Efthimios Tambouris (Lead)	University of Macedonia, Greece
Anneke Zuiderwijk	Delft University of Technology, The Netherlands
Ramon Gil-Garcia	University at Albany, USA

Digital Society

Thomas Lampoltshammer (Lead)	Danube University Krems, Austria
David Osimo	The Lisbon Council, Spain
Martijn Hartog	Delft University of Technology, The Netherlands

Practitioners' Track

Peter Reichstädter (Lead)	Austrian Parliament, Austria
Morten Meyerhoff Nielsen	United Nations University, Portugal
Francesco Mureddu	The Lisbon Council, Belgium
Francesco Molinari	Politecnico di Milano, Italy

Chair of Outstanding Papers Awards

Gabriela Viale Pereira	Danube University Krems, Austria

PhD Colloquium Chairs

Gabriela Viale Pereira (Lead)	Danube University Krems, Austria
J. Ramon Gil-Garcia	University at Albany, SUNY, USA
Ida Lindgren	Linköping University, Sweden
Anneke Zuiderwijk	Delft University of Technology, The Netherlands
Evangelos Kalampokis	University of Macedonia, Greece

Program Committee

Suha Alawadhi	Kuwait University, Kuwait
Laura Alcaide	University of Granada, Spain
Charalampos Alexopoulos	University of the Aegean, Greece
Karin Axelsson	Linköping University, Sweden
Peter Bellström	Karlstad University, Sweden

Tomasz Janowski	Gdansk University of Technology, Poland, and Danube University Krems, Austria
Marijn Janssen	Delft University of Technology, The Netherlands
Marius Rohde Johannessen	University of South-Eastern Norway, Norway
Yury Kabanov	National Research University Higher School of Economics, Russia
Muneo Kaigo	University of Tsukuba, Japan
Evangelos Kalampokis	University of Macedonia, Greece
Eleni Kanellou	National Technical University of Athens, Greece
Evika Karamagioli	University of Paris 8, France
Divya Kirti Gupta	Indus Business Academy, India
Bram Klievink	Delft University of Technology, The Netherlands
Elena Korge	Taltech University, Estonia
Robert Krimmer	Tallinn University of Technology, Estonia
Toomas Kästik	Estonian Business School, Estonia
Thomas J. Lampoltshammer	Danube University Krems, Austria
Habin Lee	Brunel University, UK
Azi Lev-On	Ariel University, Israel
Katarina Lindblad Gidlund	Midsweden University, Sweden
Ida Lindgren	Linköping University, Sweden
Ralf Lindner	Fraunhofer, Germany
Helen Liu	The University of Hong Kong, SAR China
Euripidis Loukis	University of the Aegean, Greece
Rui Pedro Lourenço	INESC Coimbra, FEUC, Portugal
Luis Luna-Reyes	University at Albany, SUNY, USA
Bjorn Lundell	University of Skövde, Sweden
Truls Löfstedt	Linköpings Universitet, Sweden
Cristiano Maciel	Universidade Federal de Mato Grosso, Brazil
Christian Madsen	IT University of Copenhagen, Denmark
Agnes Mainka	HHU Düsseldorf, Germany
Keegan Mcbride	Tallinn University of Technology, Estonia
John McNutt	University of Delaware, USA
Ulf Melin	Linköping University, Sweden
Sehl Mellouli	Laval University, Canada
Tobias Mettler	University of Lausanne, Switzerland
Morten Meyerhoff Nielsen	Tallinn University of Technology, Estonia
Andras Micsik	SZTAKI, Hungary
Yuri Misnikov	University of Leeds, UK
Gianluca Misuraca	European Commission, JRC-IPTS, Spain
Francesco Molinari	Politecnico di Milano, Italy
Josémaría Moreno-Jiménez	Universidad de Zaragoza, Spain
Vadym Mozgovoy	UNIL, IDHEAP, Switzerland
Francesco Mureddu	Lisbon Council, Portugal
Karine Nahon	University of Washington, USA, and Interdisciplinary Center at Herzliya, Israel
Morten Nielsen	The Open University, UK

Maria Nikolova	New Bulgarian University, Bulgaria
Vanessa Nunes	UnB, CIC, Brazil
Adegboyega Ojo	Insight Centre for Data Analytics, National University of Ireland, Ireland
Michele Osella	Istituto Superiore Mario Boella, Italy
David Osimo	The Lisbon Council, Portugal
Kerley Pires	United Nations University, Portugal
Jenny Palm	Lund University, Sweden
Panos Panagiotopoulos	Queen Mary University of London, UK
Darcy Parks	Linköping University, Sweden
Peter Parycek	Danube University Krems, Austria
Luiz Paulo Silva	UNIRIO, Brazil
Manuel Pedro Rodríguez Bolívar	University of Granada, Spain
Vasilis Peristeras	International Hellenic University, Greece
Sofie Pilemalm	Linköping University, Sweden
Vigan Raca	Ss. Cyril and Methodius University in Skopje, Republic of North Macedonia
Peter Reichstaedter	The Austrian Parliament, Austria
Nicolau Reinhard	University of São Paulo, Brazil
Harald Rohracher	Linköping University, Sweden
Athanasia Routzouni	University of the Aegean, Greece
Boriana Rukanova	Delft University of Technology, The Netherlands
Michael Räckers	WWU Münster, ERCIS, Germany
Mariana S. Gustafsson	Linköping University, Sweden
Michael Sachs	Danube University Krems, Austria
Rodrigo Sandoval Almazan	Universidad Autonoma del Estado de Mexico, Mexico
Günther Schefbeck	The Austrian Parliament, Austria
Hans J. Scholl	University of Washington, USA
Margit Scholl	TH Wildau, Germany
Hendrik Scholta	University of Münster, ERCIS, Germany
Harrie Scholtens	European Institute of Public Administration, The Netherlands
Johannes Scholz	Graz University of Technology, Austria
Judith Schossboeck	Danube University Krems, Austria
Erich Schweighofer	University of Vienna, Austria
Johanna Sefyrin	Linköping University, Sweden
Tobias Siebenlist	Heinrich Heine University Düsseldorf, Germany
Andrzej M. J. Skulimowski	AGH University of Science and Technology, Poland
Simon Smith Charles	University in Prague, Czech Republic
Mauricio Solar	Universidad Tecnica Federico Santa Maria, Chile
Maddalena Sorrentino	University of Milan, Italy
Witold Staniszkis	Rodan Systems, Poland
Leif Sundberg	Mid Sweden University, Sweden
Iryna Susha	Örebro University, Sweden

Jakob Svensson	Malmö University, Sweden
Øystein Sæbø	University of Agder, Norway
Fredrik Söderström	Linköpings Universitet, Sweden
Efthimios Tambouris	University of Macedonia, Greece
Ella Taylor-Smith	Napier University, UK
Luis Terán	University of Fribourg, Switzerland
Peter Teufl	IAIK, Graz University of Technology, Austria
Lörinc Thurnay	Danube University Krems, Austria
Jolien Ubacht	Delft University of Technology, The Netherlands
Nuno Vasco	DTx: Digital Transformation CoLAB, Portugal
Marco Velicogna	Consiglio Nazionale delle Ricerche (CNR), Italy
Natasa Veljkovic	Faculty of Electronic Engineering in Nis, Serbia
Gabriela Viale Pereira	Danube University Krems, Austria
Shefali Virkar	Danube University Krems, Austria
Wilfred Warioba	Commission for Human Rights and Good Governance, Tanzania
Elin Wihlborg	Linkoping University, Sweden
Maria Wimmer	Universität Koblenz-Landau, Germany
Chien-Chih Yu	National ChengChi University, Taiwan
Pär-Ola Zander	Aalborg University, Denmark
Thomas Zefferer	A-SIT Plus GmbH, Austria
Saleem Zoughbi	International Adviser, Palestine
Anneke Zuiderwijk	Delft University of Technology, The Netherlands
Stefanos Gritzalis	University of the Aegean, Greece

Additional Reviewers

Eiri Elvestad	University of South-Eastern, Norway
Zoi Lachana	University of the Aegean, Greece
Michalis Avgerinos Loutsaris	University of the Aegean, Greece
Vasiliki Diamantopoulou	University of the Aegean, Greece
Thodoris Papadopoulos	University of the Aegean, Greece
Enrico Ferro	Istituto Superiore Mario Boella, Italy
Aggeliki Androutsopoulou	University of the Aegean, Greece
Zoi Lachana	University of the Aegean, Greece
Anna-Sophie Novak	Danube University Krems, Austria
Hong Joo Lee	Catholic University of Korea, South Korea
Truong Van Nguyen	Brunel University London, UK
Maria Karyda	University of the Aegean, Greece
Amal Marzouki	Université Laval, Canada
Vasiliki Diamantopoulou	University of the Aegean, Greece
Changwoo Suh	Brunel University London, UK
Amal Ben Rjab	Université Laval, Canada

Contents

User Perspectives

eParticipation Developments

A Decade of eParticipation Research

An Overview of the ePart Conference 2009–2018

Marius Rohde Johannessen[✉] and Lasse Berntzen

School of Business, University of South-Eastern Norway, Vestfold, Norway
{Marius.johannessen, lasse.berntzen}@usn.no

Abstract. The first ePart conference was organized in Linz in 2009, co-located with the longer-running eGov conference, which at the time was in its 7th year. Since then, we have seen ten conferences focusing on eParticipation research. In this paper, we summarize these ten years by examining authors, keywords and prominent themes of the conferences. Our starting point is two early papers on eParticipation, which aimed to provide an overview and agenda for the field. We show how the eParticipation community addressed this agenda, and how the agenda has changed over a decade of eParticipation research.

Keywords: ePart · eParticipation research · Review · Overview

1 Introduction

In 2009, the ePart conference was organized in Linz, Austria for the first time. ePart was derived from and co-located with the eGov conference, which in 2009 was already in its 8th year. The first year, DEXA was the organizer, but from 2010 the conference moved to the International Federation for Information Processing (IFIP), under technical committee 8 – Information Systems, as part of working group 8.5: Information Systems in Public Administration[1]. The conference arguably emerged from the EU FP6 Demo-Net[2] project, as many of the Demo-Net participants were active in establishing ePart. Demo-Net aimed at integrating what was then a fragmented group of individuals working on eParticipation-related themes. A total of 23 papers mention Demo-Net in text or references, 17 of these published in the first three years of the conference.

The preface to the first "electronic participation" proceedings states the purpose of the conference as "reviewing research advances in both social and technological scientific domains, seeking to demonstrate new concepts, methods and styles of eParticipation. ... It aims to bring together researchers from a wide range of academic disciplines." [1]. The focus on eParticipation as a multidisciplinary field is emphasized throughout the history of the conference.

In 2015, ePart was no longer a stand-alone conference, as it merged back together with the eGov conference as a separate track. However, ePart still had separate

---

[1] http://ifiptc8.dsi.uminho.pt/index.php/wgroups#wg81-5.

[2] https://cordis.europa.eu/project/rcn/79315/factsheet/en.

© IFIP International Federation for Information Processing 2019
Published by Springer Nature Switzerland AG 2019
P. Panagiotopoulos et al. (Eds.): ePart 2019, LNCS 11686, pp. 3–14, 2019.
https://doi.org/10.1007/978-3-030-27397-2_1

proceedings. In addition to the general eGovernment and eParticipation tracks, 2015 introduced new tracks for deliberation, policy modelling and policy informatics as well as a track for evaluation of eParticipation initiatives, reflecting current changes in the focus of eParticipation research [2].

In 2018, the eGov/ePart conference again merged, this time with Danube University Krems' CeDeM conference. From 2018, name of the conference is "eGov/ CeDeM/ePart", still with separate proceedings for eParticipation. The 2018 conference had the following tracks: General, social media, policy modelling/informatics and social innovation. The purpose of the conference remains the same, but topically we can argue that it has seen an increasing focus on technology in recent years:

> "*e-government and open government, e-democracy and e-participation, smart governance, artificial intelligence, data analytics and automated decision-making, digital collaboration and social media, policy modelling and policy informatics, social innovation, and open data, linked data and the semantic web*" [3].

So far, we have seen ten editions of ePart (2009-2018), with 150 full papers presented by 262 different authors. The conference locations have been scattered around Europe, with Austria as the only country to organize the conference twice. Since the beginning, accepted full papers have been published in the Springer *Lecture Notes in Computer Science* book series, under the title "Electronic participation".

This paper aims to analyse how the ePart conference has evolved over the past decade. We do so in order to provide a status and overview of a decade of research, but also to point forward to future eParticipation research themes. In a time of fake news, polarization and attacks on democracy in several countries, eParticipation research is more important than ever, as long as we stay relevant and address current issues and topics in society.

The paper is structured as follows: Sect. 2 summarizes the themes that early eParticipation research from the conference as well as related journals papers identified as important for the field. Section 3 describes the methodology of the paper. In Sect. 4, we present our findings related to tracks, keywords and themes, authors and impact. Finally, we present our conclusions about how the conference has evolved and point to some future research directions for eParticipation.

2   Defining the eParticipation Research Agenda

From 2008 and onwards several papers were published aiming to identify the emerging field of eParticipation. In this section, we briefly go through the main findings from these, in order to identify the research directions laid out in the early days. This provides us with a frame for the findings presented in Sect. 4.

In the paper "the shape of eParticipation", Sæbø, Rose and Flak [4] perform a literature review of eParticipation, mapping the fields' actors, activities and outcomes. They define eParticipation activities as eVoting, online discourse, online decision making, eActivism, eConsultation, eCampaigning and ePetioning. Their review shows that the field is a mix of various fields and disciplines, notably political science, public administration, Information Systems and sociology. In terms of theory use, eParticipation had not developed a set of common theories at the time, and many papers were mainly empirical with little attention to theory. Methods-wise, surveys, case studies and various forms of content analysis were commonly applied. They pointed to six avenues of research for future eParticipation research: *Normative* - The why - objectives and goals/purpose of eParticipation – from a research and practice perspective. *Instrumental* - The how – frameworks, methods and standards to research, create and implement eParticipation.

Descriptive - describing and summarizing initiatives – ongoing case studies, country studies etc. *Evaluation methods* – Find a common set of methods to evaluate initiatives *Technology* – specific technologies were mostly black boxed in 2008, *Theory/methods* – Agree on specific theories and methods.

The following year, Macintosh, Coleman and Schneeberger [5] published a paper at the first ePart conference, where they identified the research gaps that eParticipation should address in the coming years. They also found six areas where research should be focused, some overlapping and some different from that of Sæbø, Rose and Flak:

Breadth of research field – eParticipation research was made up from many disciplines, but there were few multidisciplinary studies. IS people study IS questions, and public policy scholars focused on public policy. *Research design* – Immature and little agreement on relevant methods. Few studies of citizen-initiated participation and the lack of true multidisciplinary approaches led to fragmented research lacking a holistic approach. *Technology design* – a socio-technical approach to design of eParticipation tools and processes, and research on how to analyse vast amounts of non-structured dialogue-data from a wide range of sources. *Institutional resistance* – Resistance from politicians and government, as eParticipation can be seen to change or at least affect the balance of power. Lack of support from policy makers was identified as a major barrier to eParticipation. *Equity* –the digital, civic and social divides, which cause some people to participate and others to refrain from doing so. *Theory* – A general discussion of benefits and risks of eParticipation in the context of established democratic theories, and theory development to analyse key concepts such as deliberation, power structures and the many facets of the political game.

If we merge these two early attempts at defining the eParticipation research agenda, we can sum them up as follows:

Why and how to conduct eParticipation research? What should be the objectives of eParticipation from a research and practitioner perspective? Which frameworks, methods and standards can be applied to reach these goals?

Theory and methods, especially theoretical development and methods allowing for a true multidisciplinary approach, is mentioned as important by both papers.

Technology and context. While Sæbø, Rose and Flak argue that technology has been black boxed, Macintosh, Coleman and Schneeberger argue for a sociotechnical approach. The balance between technology and context emerges as the sweet spot to aim for.

Evaluation of issues such as resistance, various divides and the effect of eParticipation initiatives.

Descriptive studies, case studies and country comparisons in order to keep track of initiatives that are being implemented.

In 2012, Government Information Quarterly published two studies building on these earlier papers, and examining how the field had progressed since 2009/2009. Susha and Grönlund [6] conclude that there had been some progress, as the field had some "in-house" theory development. However, there was still theoretical immaturity in how eParticipation applies democracy theory, and on combinations of the research themes (stakeholders, environment and applications/tools).

Medaglia's literature review [7] also showed some progress, and pointed to future challenges: Contextual factors were limited to underlying technological issues, while policy, legal issues and the wider social context was largely ignored. He also called for method plurality, as most studies were surveys, case studies or content analyses, and as the field is about participation, especially called for more studies involving eParticipation actors directly. As with Susha and Grönlund, Medaglia also calls for more research on actors other than government (e.g. citizens and other stakeholders).

Summing up, these two "mid-term" reviews showed some progress, but also called for more studies of context compared to technology, as well as continued methodological and theoretical development. In the findings and discussion, we will examine how these issues have evolved towards 2018 within the confinement of the ePart conference.

3 Research Approach

We collected data for this paper from the Digital government Research library[3] (DGRL) V14.5, the ten volumes of proceedings from the Springer Lecture Notes in Computer Science series' "Electronic participation" and their affiliated Bookmetrix statistics, as well as Google scholar for citation analysis. This provided us with a total of 150 publications published over the ten previous editions of the ePart conference. In addition to the Springer proceedings, the conference has also published work in progress papers on Trauner and later IOS Press, and CeDeM, which merged with eGov/ePart in 2018, has a long series of proceedings. As we in this paper are interested only in completed research in the ePart conference, Trauner/IOS and CeDeM pre-2018 has been excluded from the analysis. Later work summing up eParticipation more broadly should consider including these sources as well.

The data was manually coded into an MYSQL database. In this process, we were able to flush out some minor errors in the data set, such as errors in author names. We created individual tables for "paper title", "author", "and keyword", and used these to create joins between authors, papers and keywords. We left abstracts in the Endnote database, and browsed for identification of research methods and theories.

---

[3] http://faculty.washington.edu/jscholl/dgrl/ .

For the sections on keywords, methods and theories, we also used Nvivo12 and its word search functionality to search the paper abstracts for theory and methods. Nvivo generates both word clouds and word trees, which are useful in creating an overview of the situation. While this did not provide a comprehensive list, it did provide some insights about theory and method use which can form the basis for future studies.

Finally, we performed a citation analysis using the "publish or perish" tool[4] to query Google scholar for citation data on the 150 papers. We chose to use Google scholar rather than web of science, as Google scholar have proven to be an accurate and relevant source for social science citation analysis [8]. There is not room to include all the data in this article, but interested readers can download the data from our University's open data archive[5].

This combination of data allows us to examine if there is a core of eParticipation researchers, the themes and topics addressed over time, the theories and methods being used as well as the impact of the conference over the past decade. The paper structure is inspired by Scholl's review of the eGov conference [9] and Carvalho, Meyerhoff Nielsen and Rohman's review of Icegov, another conference aimed at eGovernment and eParticipation research [10].

4 Findings

4.1 Tracks and Keywords – What Is the Conference Concerned with?

Each year the proceedings have been divided into 3–4 different tracks (or sections in the first years before there were official tracks in the call for papers). When grouping tracks with similar content, we end up with 11 different topics (Table 1), which have changed over time. Tools, platforms and techniques, as well as case and country studies were prominent in the first editions of the conference. These have disappeared as tracks, but are still common in papers submitted for other tracks, and can be seen as a response to the call for studies of this type.

Tracks related to the field more broadly, such as foundations, research gaps, outlook, reviews and reflection, have featured throughout the conference. Focus has moved from establishing the field towards reflecting on our status. Social media and various forms of citizen engagement (consultation, deliberation) were popular in the middle years, with social media making a comeback in 2018. In 2015 a new topic, policy modelling, appeared – perhaps as a response to the growing importance of data analytics, open data and big data. eVoting in 2010, methodological issues in 2017 and social innovation in 2018 have been once-only tracks. However, social innovation returns as a track for 2019, so this could be a new direction for eParticipation, broadening the field to cover society rather than the narrower citizen-politician relation. eVoting also has a conference of its own, which might explain why we have only seen this track once.

Overall, the tracks seem to cover a lot of the themes and issues called for by the early eParticipation publications.

---

[4] https://harzing.com/resources/publish-or-perish.

[5] https://usn.figshare.com/.

Table 1. Overview of conference tracks

	Tools	Case	Evaluation	Field	Voting	Argument	Social media	Engagement	Policy mod.	Method	Innovation
2009	▓				▓						
2010		▓									
2011		▓	▓								
2012	▓							▓			
2013			▓				▓				
2014							▓	▓			
2015				▓		▓		▓			
2016							▓		▓		
2017										▓	
2018							▓				▓

Using Nvivo 12, we created a word cloud that included specialisations of words (grouping similar words, such as "talk" and "whisper"), and the most common words identified were *events, artefacts, participation, countries, content, status, active, citizens, political, process* and *system*. This shows broadly what the papers at the conference have been covering, and reveals a broad range of issues, but may also indicate a somewhat narrow focus on events (cases, places etc.) and artefacts (which includes tools, frameworks, methods and services). Examining the title and content of papers strengthen the impression that artefacts and events have been the centre of a lot of research.

The authors published in the Springer proceedings have used 390 different keywords, but many appear only once or a few times, and there is little standardisation as many can be seen as synonymous. In addition, a lot of themes and issues seem to appear once or twice, and then disappear, which indicates that authors are testing a variety of approaches, tools and themes.

We created a list of frequently used keywords by only including those that were used more than four times each year. This narrowed the list down from 390 to 16, which includes eParticipation, eGovernment, Internet and ICTs. Excluding these, we get the list in Table 2. Most of the keywords appeared in the first years of the conference, and have been used on and off throughout. The exception is argument visualization, which seems to have fallen out of popular use after 2012, and policy-making, which has not been a popular keyword after 2013. Mostly, this list reflects what has been defined as core activities in eParticipation: engagement with citizens (deliberation, consultation, participation), activities (argument visualization, petitions), the "why and how" question (democracy, policymaking and public policy), methods (case study, genre theory) and evaluation of eParticipation initiatives and tools. Social media as the most frequently appearing keyword could indicate the importance of social media for democracy and participation over the past decade.

Table 2. Keywords used five times or more

	Argument viz.	Case study	Participation	(e)deliberation	(e)consultation	(e)petiotns	evaluation	Genre theory	(e)democracy	Policymaking	Public policy	Social media
2009			■	■					■			
2010	■			■			■					■
2011		■										■
2012			■									■
2013		■					■			■		
2014	■							■				■
2015			■									
2016		■			■		■					■
2017							■	■				
2018			■		■		■	■				

4.2 Method and Theory Use

The papers cited in section two all point to the importance of methodological and theoretical development. While we did not have the resources to do a full manual evaluation of this, we were able to extract some information using Nvivo's text search tool and word tree feature. We assumed that papers with a strong emphasis on method or theory would use these in title, keywords and/or abstract content, so we searched these items for words commonly used to describe theory and method. Papers mention several theories and methods, but overall, our impression is that theoretical and methodological development is not a major concern of most papers presented at ePart.

"(Literature) review" is a common phrase, and the word three shows it is used for examining social media, frameworks, methods, urban planning, campaigning, opinion mining, the public sphere, policy and heritage. Mostly in one or two papers, but the public sphere is found in 8 different papers, supporting earlier research saying that the public sphere is frequently used for theoretical grounding of eParticipation.

"Theory" provides only 15 hits. The word tree shows the following theories applied: Diffusion of innovation, technology acceptance, genre theory, democratic theory, institutional theory, social network theory, online deliberation theory, policy networks theory and framing theory. While this shows theoretical width, the limited number of hits shows that many theories are used once or a few times, with few papers building on earlier research presented at the conference (ref. next sections on authors and citations).

"Method" reveals references to mixed methods, both on/offline and quantitive/ qualitative. Other methods include surveys, technology acceptance, opinion mining, content analysis, policy analysis and case study. Many of the hits refer to development of methods for participation rather than research methods.

4.3   Authors and Countries – Is There an ePart Core?

262 different authors, 81 female and 181 male, have been published in the Springer proceedings of ePart. Of these, 202 only had one accepted paper during the ten years. 38 authors had two accepted papers, while 22 authors had three or more accepted papers (Table 3). Based on this, only about 23% of the participants in the conference are returning authors, with even fewer authors being regular participants. If we include those who swap between eGov and ePart proceedings, as well as those in the work in progress series, the number of returning authors increases somewhat, but the ePart core remains relatively small.

Table 3. ePart community as defined by number of publications. Based on Scholl, 2009

Publications per author	Number of publications	Cumulative count	Percentage	Cumulative percentage
10 or more	4	4	1,53	1,53
5 to 6	5	9	1,91	3,44
3 to 4	13	22	4,96	8,4
2	38	60	14,5	22,9
1	202	262	77,1	100

If we focus on the authors with three or more contributions, we find several teams co-authoring papers. The University of the Aegean has ten papers, Koblenz six, Macedonia five, Örebro three and Agder one. An outlier here is a team of Japanese scholars, who have co-authored four papers (Table 4).

Table 4. Teams of co-authors

University of Aegan -10 papers	University of Koblenz – 6 papers
Euripidis Loukis	Maria Wimmer
Yannis Charalabidis	Sabrina Scherer
Aggeliki Androutsopoulou	
University of Macedonia – 5 papers	**Nagoya inst. of Technology – 4 papers**
Efthimios Tambouris (6)	Tadachika Ozono (4)
Eleni Panopoulou (5)	Shun Shiramatsu (4)
Konstantinos Tarabanis (7)	Toramatsu Shintani (4)
Örebro University – 3 papers	**University of Agder – 1 paper**
Joachim Åstrøm	Øystein Sæbø
Martin Karlsson	Marius Johannessen

These teams, however, seem to work mostly in isolation. We examined the citations to earlier ePart proceedings, and found that most teams cite their own previous work, but citations building on other people's ePart publications are less common, except for the citations of the top three cited papers (see next section). Figure 1 shows two examples of co-author networks, visualising how these mostly consist of members from a single university.

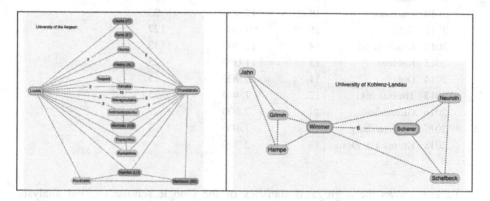

Fig. 1. Examples of co-citation networks

If we look at the countries and institutions represented at ePart, we see that a majority is from Europe (including Russia). Eastern European are a notable absence, with only Hungary and Slovenia being present once each. Even though the conference is always held in Europe, there have also been several authors from the US (21), Brazil (8) New Zealand (3) and Australia (3).

129 different institutions have been represented at the conference, with 13 institutions having been represented by more than five different authors: University of Macedonia (9), ITMO St. Petersburg (7), Örebro University (7), Nagoya Institute of Technology (6), University of Koblenz-Landau (6), National University of Ireland (6), University of Twente (5), NTU Athens (5), Brunel University (5), University of the Aegean (5), University of Agder (5), Danube University Krems (5) and the University of Geneva (5).

4.4 Impact

Table 5 presents and overview of the conference locations, number of published full papers, downloads (from Springer), citations and tracks for each year. The numbers are from Springers Bookmetrix service. Citation numbers are higher in reality if you examine each paper in for example Google Scholar, but the number is included for the purpose of comparison. Numbers were collected 27th February 2019. It seems as if there was a dip in interest between 2013 and 2014, with the number of downloads being cut almost in half. However, 2015-17 saw a rise again, although not to the same levels as in the early years of the conference. The number of papers also went down from 2011 to 2012. While the cause is not known, it can be speculated that this at least partially is a consequence of less funding for democracy research from EU FP7 to H2020. Informal talks with experienced researchers in eParticipation and other fields studying democracy supports this speculation.

Table 5. Overview of ePart conferences

Year	City	# of papers	Paper downloads	Citations, Bookmetrix
2009	Linz	16	14.000	138
2010	Lausanne	19	17.000	92
2011	Delft	26	97.000	127
2012	Kristiansand	14	12.000	33
2013	Koblenz	13	11.000	23
2014	Dublin	11	5.900	15
2015	Thessaloniki	12	7.400	25
2016	Guimarães	14	7.500	29
2017	St. Petersburg	13	7.100	3
2018	Krems a.d. Donau	13	2.300	

Table 6 shows the aggregated statistics of the Google scholar citation analysis created with the *Publish or Perish* Citation analysis tool. The 150 papers in the Springer proceedings have received 1972 citations, with a H-index of 20 (20 papers have been cited at least 20 times, and Hc-index of 15. The Hc-index adds age-related weighting to each paper, giving less weight to older papers.

Table 6. Aggregated Google scholar statistcs

Papers	Citations	Cites/year	Cites/paper	Authors/paper	H-index	Hc-index
150	1972	197,2	13,15	2,58	20	15

25 papers have yet to receive any citations in Google scholar. Of these, only six are published before 2017, so it is likely that more of the recently published papers will receive citations as time goes by. In other words, most papers published at the ePart conference receive citations. 53 papers have 10 or more citations, 38 have more than 15, and if we examine citations per year, we see that 10 papers have more than five citations per year.

It is difficult to compare these numbers with other conferences publishing eParticipation research, as neither ICEGOV, EGOVIS, DG.O or the HICSS egov-track seems to be indexed by Google scholar. Using the Publish or Perish tool to search for these conferences only provides hits on papers that are self-archived in Researchgate and other indexed self-archiving repositories. This could be taken as an argument that even with self-archiving as an option, the decision to publish proceedings with an established publisher such as Springer contributes to the impact of the conference when measured in number of citations.

Table 7 shows the top 10 cited papers of the ePart conference, all of which published between 2009 and 2012. Topic-wise, six of the papers are related to «web 2.0» and new technologies - social media, opinion mining and crowdsourcing, while three examine the state of the field in terms of research gaps and models, and summing up the European eParticipation agenda. The final paper in the list examines e-voting.

Table 7. Top ten cited papers

Citations	Authors	Title	Year	Cites/Year
230	Van Effing, Hillegersberg, Huibers	Social media and political participation: are Facebook, Twitter and YouTube democratizing our political systems?	2011	28.75
164	Macintosh, Coleman, Schneeberger	eParticipation: The research gaps	2009	16.40
85	Grönlund	ICT is not participation is not democracy– eParticipation development models revisited	2009	8,50
81	Sæbø,Rose, Nyvang	The role of social networking services in eParticipation	2009	8,10
81	Ladner, Pianzola	Do voting advice applications have an effect on electoral participation and voter turnout? Evidence from the 2007 Swiss Federal Elections	2010	9.00
70	Sæbø	Understanding TwitterTM Use among Parliament Representatives: A Genre Analysis	2011	8,75
58	Andersen, Medaglia	The use of Facebook in national election campaigns: politics as usual?	2009	5,80
53	Panopoulou, Tambouris, Tarabanis	eParticipation initiatives in Europe: learning from practitioners	2010	5,89
41	Maragoudakis, Loukis, Charalabidis	A review of opinion mining methods for analyzing citizens' contributions in public policy debate	2011	5,13
39	Charalabidis, Triantafillou, Karkaletsis	Public policy formulation through non moderated crowdsourcing in social media	2012	5,57

5 Conclusion and Future Work

Summing up this review of the past ten years of ePart, we can draw some tentative conclusions and suggestions for the future. Impact-wise, the conference seems to do quite well in terms of reach (downloads and citations), indicating that the Springer proceedings is a worthwile investment. However, the core of participants is fairly small, so we should try to attract more researchers to become part of the community.

Many of the calls made by early research have been met, at least to some extent. There is research on the themes and topics being called for, the how and why of eParticipation, technology and tools, evaluation of initiatives and an ever growing list of case studies covering different countries. However, theory and methodological development is not as strong, and there is still little connection between the themes stakeholders/environment/tools. The papers at the conference are stronger when it comes to practical issues; systems, tools, frameworks and methods for participation.

Moving forward, we should perhaps call for more collaboration between participants, so we can improve theoretical development and loosen what seems to be institutional silos working together independently from each other. Further, as the same keywords appear over time, it might be time for some discussions on future themes. Policy informatics has emerged as a new area, but there is so far little evidence for example of research into the current political climate of right-wing populism, polarization and other contemporary issues.

Finally, we have some suggestions for future work based on this research: IOS/Trauner, CeDeM and Springer proceedings should be included in an extended study of the wider eParticipation community, perhaps also including other conferences. We only briefly examined the theory and method use, and future studies should do a comprehensive review of this area. Finally, we call for future studies of the entire field, to build on the comprehensive reviews of 2008, 2011 and 2012.

References

1. Macintosh, A., Tambouris, E.: Preface. In: Macintosh, A., Tambouris, E. (eds.) Electronic Participation 2009. Springer, Berlin (2009)
2. Tambouris, E., et al.: Preface. In: Tambouris, E., Panagiotopoulos, P., et al. (eds.) Electronic Participation 2015. Springer, Berlin (2015)
3. Edelmann, N., Parycek, P., Misuraca, G.C., Panagiotopoulos, P., Charalabidis, Y., Virkar, S.: Preface. In: Edelmann, N., Parycek, P., Misuraca, G.C., Panagiotopoulos, P., Charalabidis, Y., Virkar, S. (eds.) Electronic Participation 2018. Springer, Berlin (2018)
4. Sæbø, Ø., Rose, J., Skiftenes Flak, L.: The shape of eParticipation: characterizing an emerging research area. Gov. Inf. Q. **25**, 400–428 (2008)
5. Macintosh, A., Coleman, S., Schneeberger, A.: eParticipation: the research gaps. In: Macintosh, A., Tambouris, E. (eds.) ePart 2009. LNCS, vol. 5694, pp. 1–11. Springer, Heidelberg (2009). https://doi.org/10.1007/978-3-642-03781-8_1
6. Susha, I., Grönlund, Å.: eParticipation research: systematizing the field. Gov. Inf. Q. **29**, 373–382 (2012)
7. Medaglia, R.: eParticipation research: moving characterization forward (2006–2011). Gov. Inf. Q. **29**, 346–360 (2012)
8. Harzing, A.-W.: A preliminary test of Google Scholar as a source for citation data: a longitudinal study of Nobel prize winners. Scientometrics **94**, 1057–1075 (2013)
9. Scholl, H.J. (Jochen): Profiling the EG Research Community and Its Core BT - Electronic Government. Presented at the (2009)
10. Carvalho, N.R., Nielsen, M.M., Rohman, I.K.: A decade of international conference on theory and practice of electronic governance. In: Proceedings of the 11th International Conference on Theory and Practice of Electronic Governance, pp. 230–235. ACM (2018)

Turning Ideas into Proposals: A Case for Blended Participation During the Participatory Budgeting Trial in Helsinki

Titiana-Petra Ertiö[1]([✉]) [iD], Pekka Tuominen[2], and Mikko Rask[1] [iD]

[1] Faculty of Social Sciences, Centre for Consumer Society Research,
University of Helsinki, Helsinki, Finland
{titiana.ertio,mikko.rask}@helsinki.fi
[2] Faculty of Social Sciences, Media and Communication Studies,
University of Helsinki, Helsinki, Finland
pekka.tuominen@helsinki.fi

Abstract. Balancing between online-offline stages of participatory procedures is a delicate art that may support or hinder the success of participatory democracy. Participatory budgeting (PB), in particular, is generally rooted in online platforms, but as our case study on the City of Helsinki PB trial suggests, face-to-face events are necessary to engage targeted and often less resourceful actors in the process. Based on a longer-term participant observation, covering the PB process from its early to ideation phase to the current stage of proposal development for the final vote, we argue that the process has thus far been successful in blending online-offline components, largely supported by the active support of borough liaisons who have served as navigators between the different stages. From the point of view of co-creation, different stages of the PB process (ideation, co-creation) call for different strategies of online-offline participation. Effective mobilization of marginalized actors and interactions between public servants and citizens seem to benefit from face-to-face processes, while city-wide voting and discussion can effectively occur in the online platform.

Keywords: Participatory budgeting · Co-creation · Technology · Civic participation

1 Introduction: Participatory Budgeting, Co-creation, and Participatory Technologies

Currently, cities seek ways to increase transparency in their operations and service delivery, while at the same time ensure that taxpayer euros are put to work where they are most needed. Whether addressed as civic engagement [1], democratic innovation [2] or hacking the budget [3], participatory budgeting (PB) has reached diffusion in several countries across the globe. PB facilitates structures that enable citizens to propose ideas, develop them into proposals together with public servants, gain support and vote on proposals they consider important for their communities.

© IFIP International Federation for Information Processing 2019
Published by Springer Nature Switzerland AG 2019
P. Panagiotopoulos et al. (Eds.): ePart 2019, LNCS 11686, pp. 15–25, 2019.
https://doi.org/10.1007/978-3-030-27397-2_2

Indeed, the "travel of participatory budgeting" has been intensive. Cabannes and Lipietz [4] identify three phases of PB evolution. The years 1989 to 1997 were a period of experimentation, when the concept was invented in Porto Alegre, and introduced to few other Brazilian cities. In the next phase, variations of PB were generated and it has spread to more than 130 Brazilian municipalities. Since the beginning of 2000s, a phase of expansion and profound diversification followed. During that time, PB travelled throughout Latin America to Europe and North America, and most recently, Asia including China. Overall, more than 3,000 instances of PB across 40 countries have been identified [4].

Diversification of the PB has resulted in different underpinning logics and models. Cabanne and Lipietz [4] distinguish political, technocratic and governance oriented PB. They also refer to the different organizational underpinnings, including territorially, thematically and actor-based models. Sintomer et al. [5] have identified six different PB models - participatory democracy, proximity democracy, participatory modernisation, multi-stakeholder participation, neo-corporatism, community development - based on the different contexts, normative frames, procedures, dynamics of collective action, relationships between conventional politics and participatory instruments, as well as strengths, weaknesses and challenges encountered.

Despite such differences, however, there are also commonalities in PB that make it look like a rather coherent tool, perhaps also explaining the attraction of cities worldwide to test and integrate it into municipal planning and decision making. First, PB calls for direct democratic participation of citizens. In particular, PB has proved to be effective in empowering less resourceful citizens and societal groups. Second, PB combines online and offline activities to create effective participatory platforms for the development of new urban ideas and solutions. Unlike some other democratic innovations (e.g. mini-publics), PB has effectively stimulated new technologies and services. Third, PB represents, in many ways, a recent turn of the public sector from a legal authority and service provider to an arena of co-creation, where "co-creation replaces public service monopolies and public-private competition with multi-actor collaboration and in so doing, it transforms the entire perception of the public sector" [6: 4]. Co-creation also facilitates the implementation of those PB proposals that receive most votes, unlike other government crowdsourcing initiatives [7].

The prospect of combining PB and technological innovations includes both design and usage. Holston and colleagues [8: 576-7] performed a review of IT tools that support participatory democracy and citizens' engagement; the authors concluded that none of the solutions they reviewed includes the features needed for instrumenting participatory budgeting online and hence IT solutions are "limited and scattered". The authors developed a prototype called AppCivist-PB that includes a feature themed Citizen Assembly, which enables citizens to organize themselves in small groups and develop PB proposals. Interestingly, the authors emphasized the fact that the feature was inspired by the face-to-face meetings. Similarly, Gilman [1] illustrates a case of PB using a crowdsourced platform called Citizinvestor: residents identified the community need, donated funds to purchase trash cans, and were also involved in their installations. The use of the crowdsourced platform falls under what the author defines as civic tech, "leveraging digital tools to improve democratic governance toward more transparency, inclusion, and participatory outcomes" [1: 2]. Thus, online participation on PB platforms integrate some of the offline practices like the face-to-face meetings but also gauges which existing tools can be used to the same end as customed solutions. In contrast, when it comes to the tools and technologies used for civic engagement, Firmstone and Coleman [9] argue that the engagement process is more important than the tools used to reach citizens.

Addressing the issue of digital skills is important to account for the time and effort devoted to develop PB proposals [10]. Many of the PB studies have focused on the deliberative aspects as well as the characteristics of participants who contributed in PB [2], but their interplay with technology has received less attention. Studies reviewed by Goodwin [2] show that the use of technology indeed increased the number of people who vote on PB proposals as was the case in New York and Vallejo; further, those studies also showed that highly-educated women participated more often and the percentages of Asian voters increased over time [2: 137-138].

Questions related to the choice of online and offline activities, the technology employed and the digital skills needed to participate impact who can participate and how. Evidence is scarce when it comes to PB instruments, but for instance, the study conducted by [11] shows just how complex the phenomenon is. The authors did not find any differences in demographics related to gender, income or political orientation but highly educated and non-immigrants participated more often in both online and offline participation activities. Younger, highly educated and non-immigrants were more prevalent online than offline [11]. These results suggest that combining different types of participations across different activities helps public managers to broaden civic engagement.

Stortone and De Cindio [12: 178] identify two problems of online citizen participation. First, the authors argue that the ICTs employed to engage citizens are "top-down", proprietary solutions designed to suit the purposes of the owners. Second, political representatives find it difficult to design effective and appropriate participatory processes regardless of the technology employed. The authors go further to argue that participatory budgeting addresses some of the issues around the advisory nature of citizen involvement, because proposals that receive vast support are actually implemented rather than only having an advisory nature. In a typical participatory budgeting process, citizens both contribute ideas and are involved in the final decisions.

More recently, such concerns have been addressed in the form of open-source software tailored for PB. The Decidim digital platform [13] is a free and open-source platform designed for cities and other organizations that promote participatory democracy. Decidim is particularly scalable to participatory budgeting activities and has been used by several municipalities, including the City of Helsinki. One of the main features of the Decidim platform is organized around the PB stages: idea generation, proposal development, voting - all supported by deliberative features to comment and collaborate online. For the purposes of this paper, we will not detail the entire architecture of the Decidim platform, but rather we are interested in the interplay between the online and offline activities.

This article responds to Stortone and De Cindio's [12: 179] call to evaluate the impact of participatory budgeting on citizen participation as a whole, both online and offline. We hope to contribute to this call with an elevated understanding of the benefits of blending online and offline engagement as it unfolded in the case of proposal development stage of the Helsinki participatory budgeting trial in 2018-2019. As more cities employ technology to engage the public on the one hand and participatory budgeting on the other, civic managers will find it useful to know how to integrate online and offline activities. Further, we are interested in understanding how the different online and offline aspects of PB contribute to its role as an instrument of co-creation, an important theoretical development that has received less attention than PB's deliberative nature. We formulate our research question as follows: How do online and offline activities blend during the early stages, the ideation stages, and proposal development stages of the PB process, to support meaningful co-creation?

This paper is organized as follows. Section 2 presents the background to the participatory budgeting trial in Helsinki, elaborating also on the methods used to collect the data. Then, in Sect. 3, we present the results of our study and discuss the findings against our theoretical background. The last section concludes with an argument on hybrid participation to support meaningful co-creation within participatory budgeting processes.

2 Helsinki's Participatory Budgeting Process. Data and Methods

The City of Helsinki has set a budget of 4.4 million Euros to fund projects proposed by citizens through PB. This budget is divided in a general budget for the entire city plus budgets for seven separate districts that cover the entire municipality; districts' funds are set according to the number of residents. The participatory budgeting process in Helsinki is structured in the following sequential phases: (1) citizens generate ideas, (2) evaluation of ideas proposed against eligibility criteria (see below) by public officials in city departments, (3) development of ideas into proposals in co-creation workshops, (4) the city departments estimate the budget for proposals, (5) citizens vote on the proposals they wish to see implemented, and (6) implementation of the proposals. The PB process stresses ample opportunities for discussion and co-creation: among citizens, between citizens, public officials, and other stakeholders, both on the platform as well as face-to-face [14: 24-31].

Establishing a successful balance between online and offline activities results in a complex PB process [12]. This section examines how the online-offline blend is elevated while moving chronologically from the launch of Helsinki PB to its current phase of proposal development. While a considerable part of the PB process depends on the work on the digital platform OmaStadi [15] to document the ideas and proposals, Helsinki's PB process also emphasizes strongly face-to-face interaction at regular intervals. The following analysis is based on a longer-term participant observation of the execution of the participatory budgeting in Helsinki 2018–2019. One of the researchers has conducted ethnographic fieldwork concentrating on the experiences of both participants and organisers of the process since its inception stage in 2017, paying special attention to the shifts in intensities between online and offline environments in the PB different stages. The qualitative data gathered through discussions, observation of different events and participation in a group developing one of the proposals has been supported by the observations of the other researchers, feedback from the participants – as face-to-face discussions, comments on the digital platform as well as comments on the various social media platforms. The authors are researchers in BIBU – Tackling Biases and Bubbles in Participation project that evaluates the Helsinki PB trial.

To start with, in the PB kick-off seminar held in May 2018, the online and offline participation was organised in a blended manner. It was possible to follow the seminar using the Helsinki Channel streaming service and to send comments real-time to a large screen that was centrally located on the stage. The screen was in active use and the topics expressed were frequently raised into the general discussion. However, the seminar was organised in a highly structured manner and some of the participants would have hoped to have the chance for more open-ended discussions.

An important way to facilitate synergies between online and offline activities was the establishment of the borough liaison positions (stadiluotsi, in Finnish). In May 2018, seven borough liaisons were hired by the City of Helsinki to facilitate citizen participation and to provide information about PB. Each of the seven districts of Helsinki (suurpiiri) was assigned their own borough liaison to enable smooth communication between citizens, the city administration, and other partners in the process. Borough liaisons became central actors with several roles in integrating online and offline activities when the local administration began to implement the PB trial.

Since May 2018, the borough liaisons have been very active in meeting citizens both on formal occasions (e.g. neighbourhood association meeting) and during informal face-to-face meetings in public libraries and other easily accessible spaces. A big part of the borough liaisons' time was used in helping the citizens use the OmaStadi platform as some of them were more willing to express their wishes verbally rather than filling in templates using the platform. The borough liaisons' role also extended to their capacity to reply to numerous emails and messages via social media platforms about PB. A significant part of their work took place on their Facebook profiles that were actively used to inform people about the ongoing process. The comment sections contained various questions about the conditions that PB ideas and suggestions have to meet as well as the timetable and the forthcoming events. Many of the people commenting had also met the borough liaisons face-to-face and used social media to continue discussions initiated in the meetings. This provided also a way for the followers to connect with one another while reacting to comments posted on the Facebook profiles. On the other hand, the number of followers of the borough liaisons' Facebook profiles has varied between 400 and 1000, suggesting that this form of digital communication has been a tool used very effectively but has a quite limited reach.

The ideation stage span from November until mid-December 2018. During the ideation stage of the PB, each of the borough liaisons hosted ideation events in their respective Helsinki district. These events provided personal support for crafting and brainstorming the ideas, opportunities to meet with neighbourhood associations and submit ideas to the OmaStadi platform. In addition, the City of Helsinki printed several brochures and posters to inform the citizens about PB stages and procedures, eligibility criteria, and next steps. In these face-to-face events, the emphasis was on including people who were not active in the online environments to the process. Borough liaisons provided IT support for citizens, specifically helped them sign in on the platform and complete the available template to submit an idea.

The offline aspect of the process was also enriched by a board game specifically designed to support the gathering of the new ideas. The game consists of a set of cards with various tasks and methods to support the ideation process. The logic behind employing the game was to both inform and encourage citizens to engage in a form of direct democracy they were not familiar with. The aim was to create a sociable atmosphere that would turn participants' attention into solving real problems affecting their communities, rather than concentrating on the complex bureaucracy and conditions for proposal acceptance. Borough liaisons organized several sessions that brought together hundreds of Helsinki residents from different backgrounds to sit down and go through the participatory process with its different dimensions over the course of one to two hours. The game was promoted enthusiastically as a new way to bring people together, provide fruitful encounters and extend the reach of participatory budgeting to people not familiar with it. However, some people who had already filed ideas found the structure of the game disruptive and would have rather wanted to discuss their ideas in a direct way. The game has also been "given away" to residents and communities so that they can play it on their own. As the game contains instruction for facilitation, it can be played both as coordinated by the borough liaisons as well as regular citizens with their friends, families, or communities. The OmaStadi platform made it possible to support ideas and comment on them but these features were used seldomly. The ideation phase relied on face-to-face events and discussions and the input of ideas on the OmaStadi platform.

After the ideation events with the borough liaisons and the game sessions were over, participants had filed 1274 ideas on the OmaStadi platform. Of these, 840 were selected by public officials to advance to the next stage as they have met the city's eligibility criteria (e.g. that fall under the municipal jurisdiction). The evaluation of ideas happened online on the OmaStadi platform, with each idea decisioned: either to advance it to the proposal stage or reject it. The rejected ideas received justifications for the decision, so citizens were informed about the specifics as to why their ideas were rejected.

The next phase consisted of PB proposal development (Omastadi raksat) and started in February 2019. Several workshops were organised, one in each municipal district hosted by the respective borough liaison. These workshops were attended by public officials from the city administration, who were invited to provide help to citizens to develop their ideas into proposals. The public officials were invited based on the themes present in the ideas submitted (e.g. parks and recreation, leisure services, youth services). The smooth functioning of these workshops was supported by grouping ideas under specific themes; each theme sat at a table. Based on our participant observations at the workshops, there were clear differences depending on the composition of the participants and the facilitation. At times, the vividness of face-to-face interactions during the workshops enabled detailed communication in a group setting and led to effective decision-making that still relied on equal participation. Ideas submitted on the OmaStadi platform were developed either individually or merged with ideas having similar foci and in collaboration with the public officials and fellow participants. Co-creation took a highly practical shape during the proposal development events through the multiple interactions of citizens with public officials, liaisons, and those who commented or supported the ideas online. A separate corner for IT support was set up for the workshops; they drew long queues and frequent mentions about the bugs in the platform and how it is constantly developed to suit the PB project better. These IT support functions were designed to help those who need IT guidance.

We have gathered the data outlined above during our fieldwork on the PB trial. Our methods include participant observation and documentation. Two of the three authors have participated as Helsinki residents in the proposal development workshop in their own borough, in addition to attending other workshops in other boroughs as external observers. In the ideation phase, one of the authors has attended the workshops as researcher conducting ethnographic participant observation as mentioned above. In total, we've attended over ten ideation and proposal development events. All of the ten events have been organized and run by the City of Helsinki. In addition to participant observation, another method employed has been that of a case study, specifically an embedded case study [16]. We have followed the entire development of the PB process (case) and studied its different stages and events (several units within the case to use Yin's [16] terminology). Thus, the authors have followed the PB process during a longer-term from understanding the context in which PB evolved to the very concrete co-creation actions in the proposal development stage.

3 Results and Discussion: Blending Online and Offline Co-creation Activities in Helsinki's PB Trial

This section structures our observations from the field about blending online-offline activities in the Helsinki PB to support co-creation activities and discusses their implications against the theoretical framing outlined in the beginning of the article.

The Helsinki PB process described in this article reviews Helsinki's first major PB trial. As a trial, the efforts to increase awareness and organize events, inform residents of the opportunity to participate, about the technicalities of the project have been extensive. In considering PB as a democratic innovation, the trial introduced new ways of soliciting ideas and co-creating them with residents as well as establishing ways to respond to citizens' ideas inside the city administration.

Following the PB process stages, particularly ideation and proposal development, online and offline activities blended concurrently. Each event sought to increase understanding of the PB process and lead to active participation on the OmaStadi platform. In the kick-off seminar, the questions sent via online tools supported and spurred the discussion present in the room. Ideas were formally submitted on the platform but the pre-stage - when citizens ideated what to submit - took sometimes place offline, for instance by playing the participation game. Ideas have been somewhat commented and supported on the OmaStadi platform, but discussions took mainly place offline in the events organized. In the development stage, the online-offline integration was most visible as citizens co-created their ideas with public officials after which they submitted their proposals on the OmaStadi platform. Further, the presence of IT support in the proposal development workshops facilitated capacity building for those less experienced with online tools. For certain demographics, the existence of IT support can be considered critical to their participation in PB. In contrast, idea selection - choosing ideas to be developed into proposals - took place entirely on the OmaStadi platform.

On an institutional level, creating roles that further the integration of online and offline activities and facilitate co-creation processes was vital to support citizens in the PB trial. Borough liaisons represented a new position created within the city administration to support the nascent PB ecosystem formed of citizens, public officials, non-governmental organizations, communities, and groups. Much of the liaison's work consists of fieldwork and answering citizen queries online about the PB. Similarly, they guide and support citizens to submit and develop their ideas. Essentially, they act as facilitators and intermediaries between the city administration and citizens.

In this article, the focus is on the early stages of the PB process which, we argue, are critical for co-creation. It sets out the ideas, opportunities, and proposals that citizens initiate and co-create with the other actors involved in PB. Our results show that online and offline activities are seamlessly integrated but not in equal proportions in the PB process. There are PB stages at which both online and offline activities are blended such as ideation and proposal development. We find that offline, face-to-face events and workshops are meant to support the input of ideas and proposals on the OmaStadi platforms. While [8] detail how features on the online platform takes inspiration from face-to-face meetings, the Helsinki PB shows how the two can be integrated concurrently. All the documentation on the PB proposals is formally submitted via the OmaStadi platform. The IT support by the borough liaisons integrates the online-offline activities. However, the selection of ideas took place online. To sum up, we find that face-to-face meetings support the use of the platform, making the PB process also facilitate IT capacity building in addition to the democratic inclusion. This lets us appreciate the benefits of blended activities for PB as proposed by [1, 12]. For this article, we have no quantitative data to detail the characteristics of the demographics who participated in PB; we recognize that this is a substantial limitation of our study. We intent to investigate the effect of the IT support provided for marginalized groups to develop the IT skills to be able to assess the digital equity of PB.

Following [6], we observe that in the PB trial in practice, co-creative engagements are unequally organised. As mentioned, ideation and proposal development heavily rely on co-creation activities. Whether it is the participation game that helps to ideate together or an idea a citizen had that received support and comments online and offline, the ideation stage opens the co-creation process. When ideas are decisioned, this is mainly the duty of public officials in city departments. Proposal development, on the other hand, makes co-creation between idea proponents and public officials an essential component to enrich citizens' proposals. The results highlight how co-creation developed in the specific instance of the Helsinki PB stages, contributing to a deeper understanding of the variation, national context, and different phases of the process [17].

"Participatory budgeting is not [...] a time-saving institution. It is resource intensive. Its civic appeal lies precisely in the deliberative process and the information ecosystem it creates" notes Hollie Gilman [10: 3]. Indeed appreciating the online and offline activities in PB [1, 12] on the one hand, and "transform[ing] the entire perception of the public sector" through co-creation [6: 4] on the other hand, requires particular attention to detail in facilitating social innovations, ideals of democratic governance, including transparency and inclusion.

Given that the PB case presented in this article is a trial, it has required considerable effort to create awareness about the opportunity it represents for citizens. Getting the PB process - like any participatory method - off the ground necessitates effort to get acquainted with the PB (for citizens) as well as managing the process (within the city administration and in terms of stakeholder management). The next PB round is expected to build and expand on the lessons learned in this trial. We anticipate that citizens' awareness will increase with each PB round and the efforts will shift towards other stages. As the PB trial progresses, one area of future research we will develop will be to determine who participated, assessing whether offline and online participants were the same and the effect of the alternating online-offline activities had on different demographic groups during the PB trial.

4   Conclusions

Participatory budgeting facilitates structures that enable citizens to propose ideas, develop them into proposals together with public servants, gain support and vote on proposals they consider important for their communities. Lately, dedicated technologies have sustained participatory budgeting efforts, such as the Decidim platform. This article has reviewed the case of the Helsinki participatory budgeting trial, illustrating how online-offline activities have supported co-creation activities in the Helsinki. We found that online and offline activities are integrated seamlessly during the early stages of the process and that co-creation activities tend to aggregate in the ideation and proposal development phases that coincide with face-to-face events. Offline activities support the creation and development of formal submissions on the OmaStadi platform. Central to supporting these activities are borough liaisons, who support the PB process online and offline.

The results of this analysis will contribute to a better understanding of "deliberative systems" [18] and participatory ecosystems more generally. As some studies have suggested [19], the field of public participation has recently encountered a shift from a focus on individual participatory events to a focus on more systemic and institutional considerations. Core issues are how to connect formal institutions with informal networks and civil society, in a meaningful way, thus engaging different discourses with each other. As our analysis has suggested, adding new types of intermediaries, such as borough liaisons, can help in such development, by using participatory technologies combined with direct communication with the citizens involved.

Yet another important contribution of this line of research is gaining more detailed understanding of the factors contributing to more inclusive and equal strategies in designing and implementing participatory processes. Previous studies have paid attention on factors such as framing of the issues, marketing of the events, differences in citizen recruitment strategies and socio-demographic variables [see e.g. 11, 20]. This study has raised the issue that the right balance between online-offline participation can also contribute to better involvement strategies. Our limited data did not allow drawing exact conclusions on this matter, but we observe that future studies should pay more close attention on this aspect of participatory democracy innovations.

Acknowledgements. This study has received funding from the Strategic Research Council at the Academy of Finland (consortium decision number 312710, BIBU-Tackling Biases and Bubbles in Participation, sub-project number 312796). The authors would like to thank the three anonymous reviewers for their comments, that have greatly developed this study.

References

1. Gilman, H.: Participatory Budgeting and Civic Tech: The Revival of Citizen Engagement. Georgetown University Press, Washington DC (2016)
2. Godwin, M.: Studying participatory budgeting: democratic innovation or budgeting tool? State Local Gov. Rev. **50**, 132–144 (2018). https://doi.org/10.1177/0160323X18784333
3. Schuler, D.: A hacking atlas: holistic hacking in the urban theater. In: De Lange, M., de Waal, M. (eds.) The Hackable City. Digital Media and Collaborative City-Making in the Network Society, pp. 261–282. Springer, Singapore (2019). https://doi.org/10.1007/978-981-13-2694-3
4. Cabannes, Y., Lipietz, B.: Revisiting the democratic promise of participatory budgeting in light of competing political, good governance and technocratic logics. Environ. Urban. **30**, 67–84 (2018). https://doi.org/10.1177/0956247817746279
5. Sintomer, Y., Röcke, A., Herzberg, C.: Participatory Budgeting in Europe: Democracy and Public Governance. Routledge, New York (2016)
6. Torfing, J., Sørensen, E., Røiseland, A.: Transforming the public sector into an arena for co-creation: barriers, drivers, benefits, and ways forward. Adm. Soc. **51**, 1–31 (2016). https://doi.org/10.1177/0095399716680057
7. Liu, H.K.: Crowdsourcing government: lessons from multiple disciplines. Public Adm. Rev. **77**, 656–667 (2017). https://doi.org/10.1111/puar.12808
8. Holston, J., Issarny, V., Parra, C.: Engineering software assemblies for participatory democracy: the participatory budgeting use case. In: ACM IEEE International Conference on Software Engineering Companion, pp. 573–582 (2016). https://doi.org/10.1145/2889160.2889221
9. Firmstone, J., Coleman, S.: Public engagement in local government: the voice and influence of citizens in online communicative spaces. Inf. Commun. Soc. **18**, 680–695 (2015). https://doi.org/10.1080/1369118X.2014.986180
10. Gilman, H.: Democracy Reinvented: Participatory Budgeting and Civic Innovation in America. Brookings Institution Press, Washington, DC (2016). (with Ash Center for Democratic Governance and Innovation, Harvard)
11. Pina, V., Torres, L., Royo, S.: Comparing online with offline citizen engagement for climate change: findings from Austria, Germany and Spain. Gov. Inf. Q. **34**, 26–36 (2017). https://doi.org/10.1016/j.giq.2016.08.009
12. Stortone, S., De Cindio, F.: Hybrid participatory budgeting: local democratic practices in the digital era. In: Foth, M., Brynskov, M., Ojala, T. (eds.) Citizen's Right to the Digital City, pp. 177–197. Springer, Singapore (2015). https://doi.org/10.1007/978-981-287-919-6_10
13. Decidim platform. https://decidim.org/. Accessed 16 Mar 2019
14. Helsinki participatory model. https://www.hel.fi/static/liitteet/kanslia/asukasyhteistyo/osalli suusmalli-yleisesitys-2018.pdf. Accessed 16 Mar 2019
15. OmaStadi platform. https://omastadi.hel.fi/. Accessed 16 Mar 2019
16. Yin, R.K.: Case Study Research: Design and Methods, 5th edn. Sage, Thousand Oaks (2013)

17. Nabatchi, T., Steen, T., Sicilia, M., Brand, D.: Understanding the diversity of coproduction: introduction to the IJPA special issue. Int. J. Public Adm. **39**, 1001–1005 (2016). https://doi.org/10.1080/01900692.2016.1177836
18. Dryzek, J.S., Niemeyer, S.: Deliberative democracy and climate governance. Nat. Hum. Behav. **3**, 411–413 (2019). https://doi.org/10.1038/s41562-019-0591-9
19. Rask, M., Worthington, R.: Communicating about biodiversity, public engagement, and climate change. In: Oxford Research Encyclopedia of Climate Science. Oxford University Press, Oxford (2017). https://doi.org/10.1093/acrefore/9780190228620.013.420
20. Goldschmidt, R., Tomblin, D., Rask, M.: The role of gender in global citizen deliberation. In: Rask, M., Worthington, R. (eds.) Governing Biodiversity Through Democratic Deliberation, pp. 130–151. Routledge, London and New York (2015)

'Trendy' Cities: Exploring the Adoption of Different Types of Social Media by Portuguese Municipalities

Tiago Silva[1] ⓘ, António Tavares[2] ⓘ, and Mariana Lameiras[3](✉) ⓘ

[1] Institute of Social Sciences, University of Lisbon (ICS-ULisboa),
Lisbon, Portugal
Tiago.Silva@eui.eu
[2] United Nations University Operating Unit on Policy-Driven Electronic
Governance (UNU-EGOV), Research Center in Political Science,
University of Minho, Braga, Portugal
atavares@eeg.uminho.pt
[3] United Nations University Operating Unit on Policy-Driven Electronic
Governance (UNU-EGOV), Communication and Society Research Center
(CSRC), University of Minho, Braga, Portugal
lameiras@unu.edu

Abstract. What are the determinants of social media adoption by local government? This ongoing research provides a tentative answer to this question by analysing the 308 municipalities in Portugal. Extending previous analyses of Facebook and/or Twitter usage levels, we examine why local governments adopt a particular social media platform. More concretely, we explore, with statistical analyses, the determinants of the adoption of different types of social media. We investigate the adoption of three extremely popular social media (i.e. Facebook, Twitter and YouTube) as well as possible alternatives to those, more popular, applications. Since these platforms have distinct natures and can serve diverse purposes, we examine to what extent aspects such as local government's commitment to transparency and participation, administrative capacity, media landscape, and socio-demographic and economic factors can explain the adoption of certain social media platforms. The results show that, indeed, demographic characteristics and administrative capacity are important factors for the adoption of less popular social media. Surprisingly, we also observe a geographical difference in municipalities' social media adoption, with the south, in this regard, being 'trendier', or more innovative, than the north.

Keywords: Local government · Social media · Transparency · E-Participation

1 Introduction and Short Literature Review

Recently, much has been written in academia about social media. Undoubtedly, these inexpensive and user-friendly online platforms became extremely popular and widely used around the world. With billions of users worldwide, we live in a post mass media society where a large part of the population relies on those online applications to get

© IFIP International Federation for Information Processing 2019
Published by Springer Nature Switzerland AG 2019
P. Panagiotopoulos et al. (Eds.): ePart 2019, LNCS 11686, pp. 26–34, 2019.
https://doi.org/10.1007/978-3-030-27397-2_3

information [1]. Naturally, the popularity of social media has also captured the attention of public administration and different levels of government.

By allowing their users to generate and share original content within very large, and relatively diverse, networks, social media have opened the door to real-time interaction between public sector officials and citizens [2]. Understandably, this has brought some expectations to improve public administration, different levels and sectors of government and, more broadly, democracy as well. Amid reports of a steady increase, in the last decades, of citizens' discontent with democratic institutions [3, 4], it seems that social media can play an important role in the future of our societies by promoting, together with other ICTs, a culture of receptiveness and transparency in public organizations and political institutions [5]. Indeed, under certain conditions, the Internet and social media can contribute positively to political participation [6], even though, despite this recognized capacity, they can as well lead to the exact opposite effect [7]. In the end, this perceived potential of social media to mitigate important challenges in established democracies make the study of the adoption and usage of those platforms by political and public organizations extremely relevant. In this paper we focus on social media use by local government.

Regardless of the reasons behind their adoption and use (i.e. either simply to inform or to promote citizens' interaction, participation and collaboration), a large number of local governments are nowadays incorporating social media in their communication repertoire [8]. The study of local government use of social media has been mainly focusing on frequency of use (e.g. post count) and levels of citizen's engagement with the messages [9]. Much less attention has been paid to (a) what are the types of social media adopted by the municipalities and (b) the communication strategies of the municipalities for those platforms. This paper addresses precisely those two untapped aspects of social media use by local governments, offering an empirical contribution to the former and providing an initial discussion and hypotheses for the latter.

There are two fundamental assumptions, or social media aspects, guiding this study. The first one is that there is a great amount of uncertainty in both using and adopting those platforms. Regarding their use, differently from mainstream media, the reach and impact of the content generated on social media is extremely uncertain. As Castells [10] nicely puts it, communication on social media is like casting a message in a bottle into the ocean. Any message can either go viral or unnoticed in the massive ocean of information called cyberspace. In other words, institutions cannot fully control the visibility and impact of their online communication. The uncertainty in the adoption of social media concerns the fact that institutions have an extremely vast and growing catalogue to 'choose' from. It is difficult to foresee which applications will become popular and persevere and which ones will abruptly end. For this reason, institutions must choose carefully those applications, especially since "being active" is a key requirement for their success [11].

The second important aspect of social media is that those online applications can be quite distinct. In fact, the only common aspect shared by all of them is the fact that, differently from Internet forums, they are structured or built around people rather than topics [12]. However, they can be public, semi-private or private, and they differ regarding the type of content that they allow its users to generate and share. Depending on the type of content allowed on those platforms, the costs of adopting a particular social media will vary as well (i.e. sharing original text/photo is easier/cheaper than sharing original video). As a consequence, not only the users of those platforms vary considerably, in terms of volume and characteristics, but also, partially as a consequence of that, social media can be used in different ways and for different purposes. It is normal for institutional actors to give different uses to different social media [13].

Overall, besides focusing on usage levels, it is important to take a step back and understand why municipalities adopt a particular type of social media. While there are relevant benefits from using them, the risks associated with their use are equally important. The goal of this paper is precisely to explore what factors explain the adoption of a particular social media by the Portuguese local governments.

2 Research Question, Hypotheses and Methodology

This paper's research question is: What are the determinants of social media adoption by the Portuguese local governments? Even though our main research hypotheses derive from the literature, this study, at this stage, has a strong exploratory component. We investigate this research question by looking at three of the most internationally popular social media: Facebook, Twitter and YouTube. Our three dependent variables are dichotomous measures for whether a municipality has a Facebook, Twitter, and YouTube account (1 = Yes). Additionally, a fourth dependent variable is included to assess the presence of municipalities in alternative social media platforms besides those three main ones (e.g. Flickr, Google+, etc.) (1 = Yes). All variables refer to 2016.

Concerning our research hypotheses and independent variables, the use of social media by different organizations is often associated with efforts to increase both transparency and citizens' participation and collaboration with those organizations, since it allows dialogic communication [14]. Indeed, studies have found a positive relationship between social media usage levels and the municipalities' commitment to transparency [8, 9]. We therefore expect those two motivations to be associated with the adoption of different social media. More concretely, we expect that:

(H1) Municipalities with higher commitment to participation are more likely to be present on social media.
(H2) Municipalities with higher commitment to transparency are more likely to be present on social media.

In this study we have two variables measuring the municipalities' commitment to participation and transparency. The former is measured by a dummy variable called "Participation" coded "1" if the municipality has been conducting participatory budgeting initiatives and "0" otherwise. Commitment to local government transparency is measured with an index, ranging from 0 to 100, based on an assessment of the information provided in municipalities' websites [15].

Even though creating a social media account is an easy and, usually, costless process, being active (and original) on them, which is a crucial aspect for the success of the online communication of any organization, is not as easy or straightforward. An effective use of social media requires the allocation of important resources. In fact, lack of resources can be a factor hindering local governments' use of those platforms [16, 17]. This factor is particularly important in the case of less popular social media, with higher cost/benefit, and the ones that only allow more elaborated/costly content (e.g. YouTube). Therefore, we expect that:

(H3) Municipalities with higher administrative/economic capacity are more likely to adopt social media, particularly the less popular or costlier ones.

Administrative capacity is measured with two different variables. The first one is the number of local government employees. The second is the proportion of own revenues raised by the municipalities.

Two other aspects examined in this study are the political setting and the media landscape of the Portuguese municipalities. Concerning the first one, we expect political participation and political competition to have an effect on municipalities' adoption of social media. Citizens' use of social media and political behavior should be positively correlated [18] and political competition should also affect positively governments' commitment to transparency and disclosure of information [19–21]. For this reason, we expect that:

(H4) The higher the level of political participation and political competitiveness, the more likely municipalities will be to adopt different social media platforms.

Political participation is measured by the average turnout in the last three local elections. Similarly, political competitiveness is the average margin of victory (i.e. the difference, in percentage points, between the two first candidates/parties) in the last three mayoral elections. We use an average of three elections in order to capture long-lasting trends of these two variables.

Regarding media landscape, we employ the number of local radios and newspapers in the municipality. The goal is to explore a possible relationship between the local media environment and the use of social media. We expect that local governments might rely more on different social media when the number of local media outlets is lower.

Finally, we include a set of control variables in the estimations: population size, level of education, number of parishes, proportion of foreign population, purchase power and latitude.

3 Results

Concerning the adoption of different social media by the Portuguese municipalities, our analysis shows that Facebook is, by far, the most popular social media platform. As displayed in Table 1, 85% of all Portuguese municipalities had, in 2016, an official Facebook account. The second most popular Social Networking Site (SNS) was YouTube. More than half of the Portuguese municipalities had an account in this platform. With respect to Twitter, only 36% of the municipalities used this platform. Finally, around 33% of the 308 Portuguese municipalities had accounts in some other social media applications that were not one of the three majors (e.g. Google+, Flickr).

Table 1. Descriptive statistics of the variables.

	Mean	Sd	Min	Max
Facebook	0.851	0.357	0	1
Twitter	0.357	0.480	0	1
YouTube	0.523	0.500	0	1
Other Social Networking Sites (SNS)	0.331	0.471	0	1
Participation	0.338	0.474	0	1
Transparency	44.30	17.21	0.82	94.23
#Employees	385.0	580.7	27	7417
Own revenues	39.01	18.33	2.31	90.21
Political participation	62.86	6.39	44.86	79.13
Political competition	27.85	7.77	10.99	49.16
Latitude	39.60	1.86	32.65	42.11
#Parishes	10.04	8.51	1	61
Population (log)	9.70	1.14	6.11	13.21
Education	9.944	4.554	2.87	33.55
Foreign Pop.	2.677	2.829	0.31	21.63
Purchase Power	80.55	18.15	56.54	207.9
Local Media	3.640	5.019	0	49

The results of the logistic regression analyses are presented in Table 2. Odds ratios (OR) and robust standard errors (in parentheses) are reported. OR higher than one indicate a positive relationship between the variables. Contrarily, OR lower than 1 imply a negative relationship between variables. The only difference between the four models is the dependent variable.

The first model investigates the adoption of Facebook. Since a large number of municipalities have adopted this platform, nothing very relevant can be taken or interpreted from these results. The only variable that is statistically significant is Latitude (with an OR lower than 1), which measures the geographical location of the municipality in the country (more north or south). The results suggest that municipalities from the north are less likely than the ones in the south to have a Facebook account. Overall, we can just say that Facebook is widely popular among Portuguese municipalities.

The results become far more interesting when we look at the other, less popular, social media Sites. In the case of Twitter, five variables display statistical significance. Again, municipalities from the south are more likely to use Twitter. Indeed, this was a consistent finding across all dependent variables, suggesting that municipalities from the north of Portugal are less likely to adopt social media compared to their southern counterparts. In addition to that, the results show that municipalities more committed to participation initiatives (i.e. with participatory budgeting) are almost twice as likely as the others to have a Twitter account. Besides that, municipalities with a higher number of parishes (sub-municipal governments/districts), with more economic resources and more employees are also more likely to be present on Twitter. Overall, our analysis shows that Twitter is not a popular platform among Portuguese local governments and that its adoption is positively associated with the municipalities' resources and commitment to engage with the citizens. However, it is also possible that the use of Twitter is not a direct consequence of municipalities wanting to engage citizens but rather a consequence of their efforts to get more visibility to specific e-participation initiatives.

Table 2. Logistic regression analysis of the determinants of social media adoption by the 308 Portuguese Municipalities.

	(1) Facebook	(2) Twitter	(3) YouTube	(4) Alternative SNS
Participation	1.000 (0.381)	1.970** (0.549)	1.087 (0.301)	1.719* (0.491)
Transp.	1.016 (0.0106)	1.010 (0.00808)	1.006 (0.00785)	1.000 (0.00855)
Parishes	1.031 (0.0267)	1.062*** (0.0244)	1.071** (0.0306)	1.043* (0.0248)
Pop. (log)	1.168 (0.448)	0.639 (0.206)	0.340*** (0.111)	0.556* (0.178)
Education	1.000 (0.0835)	0.950 (0.0625)	0.979 (0.0668)	0.969 (0.0625)
Foreign Pop.	0.908 (0.0716)	0.961 (0.0653)	0.975 (0.0715)	0.849** (0.0574)
Purchase P.	1.013 (0.0227)	0.991 (0.0173)	1.004 (0.0175)	1.004 (0.0166)
Local Media	0.965 (0.0484)	0.972 (0.0720)	0.981 (0.0453)	0.900** (0.0470)
Employees	1.000 (0.000830)	1.001** (0.000605)	1.003*** (0.00106)	1.002*** (0.000606)
Revenues R.	1.010 (0.0193)	1.042** (0.0182)	1.040** (0.0177)	1.044*** (0.0165)
Turnout	0.993 (0.0371)	1.008 (0.0302)	0.978 (0.0283)	0.976 (0.0289)
Margin of V	1.030 (0.0252)	1.001 (0.0200)	1.011 (0.0188)	1.006 (0.0206)
Latitude	0.724*** (0.0886)	0.829** (0.0705)	0.838** (0.0688)	0.785*** (0.0636)
Constant	48,883 (330,488)	5,555* (28,142)	3.629e+06*** (1.892e+07)	888,589*** (4.545e+06)
Obs.	308	308	308	308
Pseudo R2	0.0844	0.103	0.121	0.105

The results for YouTube are similar to the ones we found for Twitter. There are only two exceptions. The first one is that the difference in "Participation" is not statistically significant. The second one is that population size becomes statistically significant with a negative coefficient. This means that municipalities with larger populations are less likely to adopt YouTube. Overall, these results further confirm that, when it comes to the adoption of social media, human and financial resources are important for municipalities to venture on alternatives to Facebook. Indeed, we can say that having less resources hinders local governments from being present on less popular social media.

Finally, when it comes to alternative social media, we also get very interesting results. The first one is that "Participation" is significant. The municipalities with Participatory Budgeting initiatives are about 70% more likely to have an account in one alternative (less popular) social media. Again, it might be the case that rather than using them to interact with citizens, municipalities are simply trying to expand their online communication channels to give more visibility to those initiatives.

The municipalities' resources are an important factor to explain presence in alternative SNS. The number of parishes, population size, the percentage of foreigners and latitude are also statistically significant. In the case of population, foreign population and latitude, their OR is lower than 1, meaning that the relationship between the variables is negative. However, what is perhaps more interesting in this last model is the statistically significant and negative relationship between local media and the adoption of alternative social media. To put it in other words, municipalities with a higher number of local radio stations and newspapers are less likely to adopt alternative (less popular) social media. This suggests that perhaps Portuguese local governments rely on social media to circumvent some limitations (or lack of traditional alternatives) to inform their citizens.

4 Conclusion

There are important limitations in this paper due to the fact that it is an ongoing research. In specific, the nature of our dependent variables does not allow us to explore short-term factors such as the characteristics of mayors and executives and the institutional configuration of communication departments inside municipalities. These are factors that indubitably might play an important role in the adoption of different social media and that allow an in-depth study of the determinants of social media adoption by Portuguese local governments. Therefore, we exclusively focus on long-term, less mutable, variables. Nevertheless, our study revealed important aspects regarding the adoption of those platforms by local government and provides grounded clues for further research and methodology.

Perhaps the most important, or at least consistent, finding of this study was that resources and local government capacity matter. And they seem to matter a lot. That was the only hypothesis (H3) that the quantitative analysis fully confirmed. We knew already, from previous studies, that resources matter for usage levels (i.e. municipalities with more resources are more active on social media [9]). Now we also know that these are important factors for the adoption of less popular social media. Contrarily, political aspects (turnout and competition) (H4) do not seem to affect the adoption of those platforms. Overall, this study suggests that Portuguese municipalities are indeed aware of the risks involved in adopting social media. They are more likely to adopt more alternative platforms when they have resources to guarantee their successful use (i.e. being active on them).

We also found that while commitment to transparency does not have any impact on social media adoption, municipalities that have participatory budgeting initiatives are more likely to have accounts on alternative, less popular platforms. We can, however, interpret this result in two different ways. It can indeed be that these alternative SNS are more suitable to engage citizens, since there is an understanding that Twitter is more suitable for sharing ideas while Facebook is used for leisure or networking. However, it can also be that these municipalities are simply using a larger variety of online applications to promote their participatory budgeting initiatives. Further analyses must be conducted to better investigate these two hypotheses. This is, indeed, the next step of this project that aims, with a multi-method approach, to better understand the use of social media by local government.

One final aspect worth mentioning is that we found that municipalities from the north of Portugal tend to be more conservative when it comes to social media adoption, a difference observed even for the most popular application - Facebook. This is interesting since the north is also more conservative when it comes to local politics and the importance of religion. When it comes to the adoption of new communication channels, we can say that southern municipalities seem to be trendier than their counterparts in the north.

Acknowledgments. This paper is a result of the project "SmartEGOV: Harnessing EGOV for Smart Governance (Foundations, methods, Tools)/NORTE-01-0145-FEDER-000037", supported by Norte Portugal Regional Operational Programme (NORTE 2020), under the POR-TUGAL 2020 Partnership Agreement, through the European Regional Development Fund (EFDR). António Tavares acknowledges the financial support of the Portuguese Foundation for Science and Technology and the Portuguese Ministry of Education and Science through national funds [Grant No. UID/CPO/0758/2019].

References

1. Gottfried, J., Shearer, E.: News Use Across social medial Platforms 2016. Pew Research Center (2018)
2. Rybalko, S., Seltzer, T.: Dialogic communication in 140 characters or less: how fortune 500 companies engage stakeholders using Twitter. Public Relat. Rev. **36**(4), 336–341 (2010)
3. Dalton, R.J.: Citizen Politics: Public Opinion and Political Parties in Advanced Industrial Democracies. Chatham House Press, New York (2002)
4. Flickinger, R.S., Studlar, D.T.: The disappearing voters? Exploring declining turnout in Western European elections. West Eur. Polit. **15**(2), 1–16 (1992)
5. Bertot, J.C., Jaeger, P.T., Grimes, J.M.: Using ICTs to create a culture of transparency: e-government and social media as openness and anti-corruption tools for societies. Gov. Inf. Q. **27**(3), 264–271 (2010)
6. Bakker, T.P., De Vreese, C.H.: Good news for the future? Young people, Internet use, and political participation. Commun. Res. **38**(4), 451–470 (2011)
7. Kent, M.L.: Using social media dialogically: public relations role in reviving democracy. Public Relat. Rev. **39**(4), 337–345 (2013)

8. Bonsón, E., Torres, L., Royo, S., Flores, F.: Local e-government 2.0: social media and corporate transparency in municipalities. Gov. Inf. Q. **29**(2), 123–132 (2012)
9. Lameiras, M., Silva, T., Tavares, A.: An empirical analysis of social media usage by local governments in Portugal. In: Proceedings of the 11th International Conference on Theory and Practice of Electronic Governance, pp. 257–268. ACM (2018)
10. Castells, M.: Communication Power. OUP, Oxford (2013)
11. Kaplan, A.M., Haenlein, M.: Users of the world, unite! The challenges and opportunities of social media. Bus. Horiz. **53**(1), 59–68 (2010)
12. Boyd, D.M., Ellison, N.B.: Social network sites: definition, history, and scholarship. J. Comput.-mediated Commun. **13**(1), 210–230 (2007)
13. Morini, M.: Twitter for politics and Facebook for Leisure? The social media behaviour of Italian Politicians. Malaysian J. Media Stud. **17**(1), 58–69 (2015)
14. Linders, D.: From e-government to we-government: defining a typology for citizen coproduction in the age of social media. Gov. Inf. Q. **29**(4), 446–454 (2012)
15. da Cruz, N.F., Tavares, A.F., Marques, R.C., Jorge, S., de Sousa, L.: Measuring local government transparency. Public Manag. Rev. **18**(6), 866–893 (2016)
16. Omar, K., Stockdale, R., Scheepers, H.: Social media use in local government: an Australian perspective. Int. J. Public Adm. **37**(10), 666–675 (2014)
17. Moon, M.J.: The evolution of e-government among municipalities: rhetoric or reality? Public Adm. Rev. **62**(4), 424–433 (2002)
18. Gil de Zúñiga, H., Jung, N., Valenzuela, S.: Social media use for news and individuals' social capital, civic engagement and political participation. J. Comput. Commun. **17**(3), 319–336 (2012)
19. Tavares, A.F., da Cruz, N.F.: Explaining the transparency of local government websites through a political market framework. Gov. Inf. Q. Forthcom. 1–13 (2017)
20. Gandía, J.L., Archidona, M.C.: Determinants of web site information by Spanish city councils. Online Inf. Rev. **32**(1), 35–57 (2008)
21. García, A.C., García-García, J.: Determinants of online reporting of accounting information by Spanish local government authorities. Local Gov. Stud. **36**(5), 679–695 (2010)

Acceptance of Tools for Electronic Citizen Participation

Michael Sachs[1(✉)] and Judith Schossböck[1,2(✉)]

[1] Danube University Krems, Dr. Karl Dorrek-Str. 30, 3500 Krems, Austria
{michael.sachs, judith.schossboeck}@donau-uni.ac.at
[2] City University of Hong Kong, Tat Chee Avenue, Kowloon, Hong Kong SAR
jschossbo2-c@my.cityu.edu.hk

Abstract. In order to motivate diverse user groups to participate in e-participation, platform designers are keen to offer attractive communication formats in combination with modern tools and suitable forms of online identification. This does not come without difficulties, as individual users prefer different solutions. Research on tools and electronic identification in this context has investigated the appropriateness of different e-IDs for different stages of e-participation. In this respect, this paper offers three contributions to questions of technology application and acceptance in e-participation: Firstly, it showcases two scenarios from a platform simulation on different levels of e-participation. Secondly, the authors present results on the acceptance of these scenarios and tools based on questionnaires and usability tests. Thirdly, viewpoints from interviews with key stakeholders for e-participation in governance and politics are included. Results shall be useful for the future design and implementation of e-participation platforms.

Keywords: E-Participation · Decision-making · Identification · Trust · Usability

1 Introduction

E-participation is an interdisciplinary research area dealing with the electronic support of all public activities that enable citizens to participate in processes relevant for society [1]. This often comes with demands to introduce new participation facilities into the traditional processes of decision-making [2]. Tools for citizen decision-making must attract a variety of users with different preferences, literacies and demands for content and processes, especially when it comes to inclusion [3]. Some stress the importance of institutional context and careful design for e-participation performance [4].

Concepts of e-participation, reflecting either the way of participation (top-down or bottom-up), the legal foundation (formal or informal), the goals of a measure or the intensity of e-participation in tiers [5, 6]. In this paper, we draw on structured concepts of citizen involvement and decision-making, where each level of participation increases citizen power or the intensity of participation. In line with the idea of the meta-analytical study of Al-Dalou' and Abu-Shanab [7] that the most comprehensive model is a five levels schema, a 5-level concept of e-participation levels was chosen in the

© IFIP International Federation for Information Processing 2019
Published by Springer Nature Switzerland AG 2019
P. Panagiotopoulos et al. (Eds.): ePart 2019, LNCS 11686, pp. 35–46, 2019.
https://doi.org/10.1007/978-3-030-27397-2_4

context of this paper: (1) Information, (2) consultation, (3) cooperation, (4) co-decision, and (5) decision [5].

Previous research of the authors study group has utilized this classification for a model of tool assessment, specifically for investigating which e-ID is appropriate on which particular level of e-participation, with special regard to voting and rating mechanisms, participation threshold and security [5, 8]. This paper focuses on the acceptance of users and potential stakeholders when it comes to choosing appropriate means of identification (e-IDs) for authentication in different e-participation levels. The authors assess potential areas of application from a stakeholder perspective and the acceptance of tools from users' points of views (micro-level or project perspective, see the evaluation framework below).

For that purpose, an e-participation platform demonstrator-software was developed in a project for assessing acceptance and demand of modern e-participation tools in the Austrian context. While we can draw conclusions from the project in the sense of users' and stakeholders' expectations, we are not accessing socio-technical perspectives in the sense of public take up or the greater democratic perspective (macro level in the sense of real-life application). In reference to the domain model of e-participation evaluation [9] and the four layers of this framework, our analysis focuses on participation areas and processes, actors as well as tools and technologies more than the democratic context. We also exclude the socio-economic conditions beyond stakeholder opinion or sustainability of e-participation processes [10] due to the scope of the project. However, we will glimpse at the macro level in the sense of its political situatedness and context. While the project is not tied to a specific planned initiative of citizen involvement, an assessment of acceptance lays the foundations for the implementation of e-participation projects in the future.

2 Project "E-Partizipation"

The Austrian government program of the 2017-elected federal conservative-right government declares in its preamble that citizen participation in political processes shall be increased through the expansion of direct democratic opportunities. Participation shall be improved at the parliamentary level and in the legislative procedures. In addition, direct democratic processes such as popular petitions and consultative referenda are promoted in the government program. However, a single platform comprising various e-participation opportunities and activities for a broader target group is missing.

In general, some efforts towards more citizen decision-making in Austria have not been without controversy in the past. The 2009 e-voting for representation in the Austrian students body [11] was met with criticism regarding its implementation [12] and led to a numerous appeals and a final repeal by the Austrian high court. Given this background, an assessment of the acceptance of e-participation solutions is indicated if Austria wants to foster citizen decision-making within e-participation, and affirm citizens' trust in digital solutions.

The Austrian Research Promotion Agency (FFG) funded the project "E-Partizipation - Authentifizierung bei demokratischer Online-Beteiligung"[1] to research means of online participation with use of different authentication and identification methods. The 2 years project ended in Autumn 2016. Its goal was the development of a flexible and modular platform demonstrator-software that uses several means of authentication in the context of citizen e-participation, including the existing state e-ID solution in Austria. The platform enabled an adaptive set up of various e-participation processes. The consortium consisted of actors from public administration, academia and industry:

- Austrian Institute of Technology as leader of the consortium,
- Federal Ministry of Internal Affairs, as public agency responsible for election processes,
- Danube University Krems, Centre for E-Governance,
- University of Vienna, Legal Informatics,
- Austrian State Printing House, and
- Rubicon IT GmbH.

2.1   Applied Evaluation Framework and Research Questions

Scholars have offered a variety of evaluation methodologies for citizen participation, with different criteria for project specific factors [4, 13–15]. However, a too general evaluation framework would also miss the goal of accessing context and actor specific aspects [16]. Starting from the idea of a systematic analysis using defined criteria, [17] we followed an evaluation design recommended in the literature. Our starting point were the categories for e-participation evaluation as suggested by Macintosh and Whyte [18] with adaptations towards project goals and the national context. Building on the experiences from other evaluations, [19] we used the following analytical dimensions:

- Political dimension: attractiveness of the selected cases for users and stakeholders; relevance of the platform (for real-life application); strengthening of e-participation (motivation).
- Technical dimension: fulfillment of technical requirements; processes and functionality; security aspects.
- Socio-technical dimension: acceptance of the selected solutions; e-ID variants; trust in the platform; sustainability.
- Legal dimension: data security compliance; trust of users in data security; protection and privacy.
- Methodological dimension: Practicability of the model for practitioners; suitability of the tool for the specific areas of application.

Based on the evaluation of the project within that framework, we formulate the following research question for this paper: How do users and stakeholders trust

---
[1] The project "E-Partizipation" was funded by the Austrian security research programme KIRAS of the Federal Ministry for Transport, Innovation and Technology (bmvit).

e-participation tools with view to platform specifics and authentication providers? How can these become more attractive to use?

In this paper, we mainly present the results of the user and stakeholder perspective based on the testing simulations with 33 test users as well as the 10 qualitative interviews with stakeholders in governance and public administration (6 interviewees) and politics (4 interviewees stratified by political parties).

2.2 Research and Development Design

The research design used in the project combined qualitative and quantitative methods for the development of the demonstrator platform consisting of a literature review, an internal assessment workshop (within the project consortium), expert interviews, a workshop and questionnaire within the scientific community. The project consortium provided continuous technical evaluation, internal testing and legal feedback throughout the development and scenario set-up period. The demonstrator of the platform was evaluated with a testing simulation, subsequent questionnaires and plenum discussions with user groups. In addition to user testing, stakeholder interviews were conducted. The following Fig. 1 shows the workflow of the entire project starting in autumn 2014.

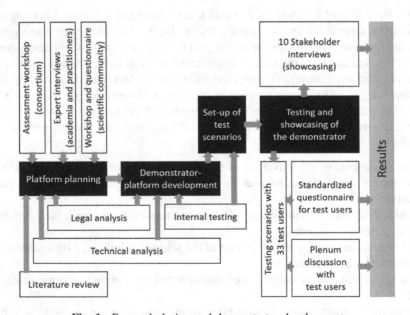

Fig. 1. Research design and demonstrator development

Testing scenarios were conducted by using the demonstrator-software, tested on the 13th and 15th of June, 2016. This was based on usability tests in a lab with 33 participants in two testing groups at university facilities. In addition, feedback was received during the testing sessions via standardized questionnaires and qualitative plenum discussions following the simulations.

2.3   Testing Scenarios with Users

User Test Groups. In order to assure comparability of results, the two user test groups did not differ with regards to the testing scenarios presented. While the results of the questionnaires are not comparable to the representability required for surveys and follow a predominantly qualitative setup, we still tried to stratify along demographic characteristics, as it is common in user-testing or usability-testing, in order to simulate a realistic mix of potential users. Furthermore, studies have shown that several important aspects of our study (like privacy or data security) can be influenced by demographic features like gender or age. Privacy can be defined as one's ability to control the release of personally identifiable data in the context of institutional practices, and the level of privacy protection can differ by gender [20]. Gender is a factor in understanding privacy and disclosure practices [21]. Research on social network sites also found associations between gender and disclosure in young adults [22]. Also age and education can relate to how users evaluate aspects of information privacy [23]. User test groups were selected as effectively as possible according to the demographic criteria age, gender and educational level. Further variables (f.i. self-assessment regarding tech-savviness) were included in the questionnaire.

Participants received as compensation € 15 gift vouchers. People were contacted on the basis of a call within the premises of the University of Vienna, leaflets, posters, Facebook groups, within the networks of consortium members and private networks of project workers. Citizenship was not mandatory for participation, but sufficient command of German was a necessary criterion. Registration for the two test events was done online and people had to provide age, education and gender for the composition of the test groups. The final composition of the testing groups was:

- *Age.* 16–24: 16 persons, 25–44: 13 persons, 45–99: 5 persons.
- *Gender.* Female: 15 persons, male: 18 persons, gender-diverse: 1 person.
- *Education.* Compulsory school: 9 persons, Higher School certificate (Matura): 17 persons, university/college: 8 persons.

Additional assessment of user groups showed that participants used the internet on average for 2.8 hours per day professionally, and 3.4 hours per day privately. Regarding mobile usage participants used the internet on average for 2.8 hours per day. The majority of our participants used social media daily. Regarding political activity, about half of participants saw themselves as politically active, however, only a few were politically very active. A bare majority was not very or not politically active. Participants use the internet predominantly for information retrieval purposes (election program or politicians), less so for expressing their political opinion or for discussion. Around a fifth of our participants used the internet for polling or voting. It must be pointed out that we received 34 questionnaire responses despite 33 participants, and this error could not be definitely solved in the analysis thereafter.

Test Scenarios. The testing was conducted in a PC lab, where two testing scenarios were simulated under the guidance of a moderator. While the platform was modular and adaptive, two testing scenarios had to be selected, that were realistic in the Austrian context. Due to project goals, each scenario needed a voting phase, hence the scenarios had to include the e-participation level of co-decision-making or decision-making. In the testing procedures specific aspects could be tested within the timeframe of 1 h and 15 min (10 min. introduction, 10 min. scenario 1, 25 min. scenario 2, 10 min. questionnaire, 20 min. feedback in a plenum discussion). The testing procedures were pretested with associates of the consortium that were not directly involved in the development of these procedures.

Scenario 1 simulates the election of a works council by employees in a company. Two electable lists provide information about their agendas and candidates can be selected (Table 1).

Table 1. Test scenario 1.

Phase 1	Participants read information about the electable lists, the list's candidates and the voting process
Level of participation	Information
Authentication	Username and password (as member of the company)
Duration	5 min
Phase 2	Users vote for their preferred candidate
Level of participation	Decision-making
Authentication	Username and password (as member of the company)
Duration	3 min

Scenario 2 simulates urban planning in a future construction site in Vienna. A part of the new space is to become a public place, and citizens are invited to suggest ideas for a plaza design or similar. The submitted ideas are preselected by the hosts of the participatory process, turned into concepts of urban design, and then discussed and evaluated by the users. Finally, users can select one of final concepts to be presented to the jury that will decide on the development of the public space (Table 2).

Table 2. Test scenario 2.

Phase 1	User inform themselves about the urban planning project and can submit ideas. After handing in their idea, a pop-up window appears displaying "thank-you". Users do not see other submitted ideas
Level of participation	Consultation
Authentication	Not required
Duration	8 min

(continued)

Table 2. (*continued*)

Phase 2	Four previously prepared concepts for the plaza are presented. Participants can comment, discuss, and rate "like" and "dislike". Ratings are visible for all participants
Level of participation	Consultation
Authentication	Social IDs[a], mobile electronic citizen card[b], or identities register number (the latter was simulated via the social security number)
Duration	12 min
Phase 3	Two concepts from phase 2 with the most "likes" are put to a vote
Level of participation	Co-decision making
Authentication	Mobile electronic citizen card, or identities register number (simulated via the social security number).
Duration	5 min.

[a]Steam, WordPress, PayPal, LinkedIn, GitHub, Flickr, Dropbox, BattleNet, Instagram, Twitter, Facebook, Google, Windows Live.
[b]State issued e-ID or electronic signature (Bürgerkarte or Handy-Signature).

After the simulation, participants in both groups had to fill in a standardized questionnaire. Thereafter they were invited to a moderated qualitative feedback discussion on the basis of semi-structured guidelines. Moderators guided the 20 min long discussion via prompting questions, and the discussion was generally fluent and active among participants. The goal of the plenary discussion was to test the acceptance of e-participation solutions. Moderators observed the users during the discussion and took notes of nonverbal clues of approval or disapproval. The discussion was held structured along the political, socio-technical and legal dimensions and criteria.

2.4 Stakeholder Interviews

To access the stakeholder perspective, interview partners were selected by key-informant sampling [24] and comprised 6 representatives from governance and public administration, including one representative from the data protection authority, and 4 persons from parliamentary political parties. They were selected according to whether they could potentially employ such a platform, and asked whether and how they could imagine its real-life implementation. The data protection authority was asked specifically about aspects of data protection relevant for the implementation of such a platform.

Stakeholders from public administration were selected according to the levels of administration: city, regional and country level were all represented. They were contacted per email, invited to the interview per telephone, and interviewed mostly in their offices. While some interviewees in the stakeholder categories were responsible for citizen participation, others were responsible for elections (thus representing one specific level of e-participation). The interview partners were selected from the following institutions and departments: the Federal Ministry of the Interior (Department III/6), the Federal State Government of Lower Austria (Department for citizenship and elections), the Josefstadt district, the City of Krems (2 interviewees) and the Federal Ministry for Women, Families & Youth (BMFJ). The stakeholders from the domain politics were selected to represent all political parties of the National Council (parties selected their representative after invitation). All parties, except from one party, were available for an interview.

The stakeholder interviews were conducted between the end of April and mid-June 2016. On average, the interviews lasted 45 min each. The interviewer followed semi-structured interview guidelines [25] and a receptive interviewing strategy. [26] They were recorded, thematically coded [27] along the evaluation dimensions, and interpreted via a summary analysis, using paraphrasing methods. At the beginning, the stakeholders were shown the platform from both a user and admin perspective by showcasing the two scenarios with a live presentation. Two times the live demonstration did not work, so the presenter retreated to a PowerPoint-Presentation to show the demonstrator as it would look in the live scenario.

3   Results

According to user feedback, the tested platform was suitable for use in the defined areas of applications. Both users and political stakeholders found the location- and time-independent aspects of e-participation appealing as well the transparency of the processes.

3.1   Technology Application

Multi-ID Design Principle. Regarding the socio-technical evaluation dimension, user feedback after the test run showed that the option to use various e-IDs was considered as especially user-friendly. Users expect secure, mobile and barrier-free technical solutions, and an adaptive design is advised to meet the diversity of user requirements.

Transparent Operations and Usage Statistics. Criticism was related to the desire for more information about certain operations and processes on the platform, e.g. how comments and likes influence the ranking of results. While such questions were mostly explained by the moderator during user testing, the use of corresponding information tools (for example a video explaining the ranking and selection processes, or a F.A.Q.) is by all means recommended for such a platform. Users did not see relevant benefits in the transparent presentation of usage statistics of the e-participation phases. This led to some irritation especially in the voting phase, even though the actual voting results were only displayed after the voting phase was closed. It is thus advisable to proactively and clearly communicate information relating data processing, security and data protection (identification and authentication issues), especially when it comes to voting procedures in e-participation, such as the example of work council elections [28].

Perceived Risk of Manipulation. Users generally rate the perceived risk of manipulation of results as high. A cooperation of public body with NGOs as controlling body seemed to be the most trustworthy solution for operators of e-participation platforms. Security concerns were not only related to the operators, but also to hacker attacks. Thus, transparent and pro-active communication regarding the prevention of manipulation can enhance trust.

3.2   Trust in the Proposed Solutions (e-IDs)

Clear Identification Methods for Sensitive Processes. If an e-participation platform as the one presented was to be used by political parties for deliberation, they want to get an accurate picture of the participating population, hence clear identification methods are important. To the parties, the more sensitive the process is (e.g. in terms of financial impact or legal implications), the more desirable background information of participants becomes for analysis. In addition, some parties have already internally used electronic tools for voting, opinion forming or project development. While parties want to know background data of the users for analysis, anonymity on the platform remains very relevant to users, but opinions on the use of real names are indifferent.

Acceptance of e-IDs and Strengthening the Attractiveness of the Electronic Citizen Card. The integration of the electronic citizen card into e-participation is likely to promote the dissemination or increased use of citizen e-IDs according to user feedback. Identification with an e-ID issued by the state provides a sense of security and adds to the trustworthiness of the platform. Yet, only a few people actually used their electronic citizen card (possibly because only a few users had one) in the simulation and the majority used their social security number for authentication. Nonetheless, no participant refused the demand for unique personal identification in the final stage of the testing simulation scenario 2. The use of unique e-IDs increases trust in the results. Social IDs are a first low-threshold entry into e-participation, although users critically evaluated the application of such IDs in e-participation platforms operated by the state and in terms of data protection. At the same time, the use of existing electronic identities seems preferable to the ability to create a new e-ID for yet another platform. Users mainly used their Facebook and Google IDs, some used LinkeIn and Windows Live, but other social IDs were not used. The users rated various options of authentication options on the platform positively. While it is thus recommended to offer a flexible design with different identification options on the different levels of e-participation, platform providers should be aware that in the context of e-participation, users predominantly hold a critical stance towards social IDs they know from other (non-state) contexts.

Reservations Towards Private Platform Providers. Users expressed general low confidence in all platform operators, but even more negative concern towards private enterprises as platform hosts. The usage of personal data that would be collected and saved by platform providers was emphasized, despite the demonstrator-software of the project using only the required data in a secure way. In particular users were insecure regarding the options of the e-participation platform provider to access the collected data, also from a technical point of view, as users had to accept that the platform exchanges data with their e-ID. These confirmation messages often ask for more data than is actually used by the demonstrator-software.

Practicality of the e-IDs-Model for Practitioners. Feedback from stakeholders has confirmed the basic principle of the multi-ID approach, in particular with regard to the use of high-quality e-IDs for high-level e-participation processes such as the level of collaboration or co-decision making. At lower levels of e-participation, diverse options of identification are perceived as positive. As the e-participation procedures have to be designed according to the needs of the target group, in relation to the respective topics and expected outcomes, generalization for the whole field of e-participation, with many variations and contexts, is always problematic.

Regulatory Issues. The platform was tested before the implementation of the General Data Protection Regulation in the European Union, but users were already very well aware of needs for data protection and regulations. There was a clear differentiation between the e-ID provider and the host of the e-participation platform and both need to gain the users trust. The development of the platform was closely monitored by legal advisors within the consortium for legal compliance, and it was also crucial to follow the regulations of voting processes, such as the option to cast a blank vote.

4   Conclusion and Discussion

Research emphasizes that the utilization of ICT does not lead to more participation per se, and that certain measures of inclusion need to be undertaken if that should be the case [29]. However, e-participation can theoretically serve as legitimizing mechanism of democracy if it affords a way of empowerment for citizens [30]. When it comes to sensitive information and different views on privacy and new tools like social identification methods (social IDs), these often sensitive subjects might clash with otherwise well-meant intentions. This study showed that there might be a demand for official sites for participation purposes, as the user feedback in this project has also shown with regard to online authentication and data protection, that platforms hosted by states or NGOs still enjoy greater trust than private platform providers do. Transferring political discussions from semi-public spaces such as social media to official platforms could increase the chances to bring people out of the "echo chambers" of one-sided information, [31] and potentially foster a more direct and open discussion culture, in which several sides actively participate. Accompanying direct democratic processes with digital tools has the potential to reach decisions that are more satisfying. If citizens are provided platforms that meet their needs and enable them to control the ways of their participation, purposefully built digital platforms could support the transparency of the opinion making process, the accountability of the democratic participation and the overall acceptance of the outcomes [30].

The limitations of our methodology lie in the inability to evaluate the impact perspective, as our results are based on a demonstrator-software and not an e-participation project in the field. Thus, a replication of the method in an open phase would be desirable. Further limitations can be seen with view to the creation of trust in modern technological solutions: It is to be expected, that mobile devices will enjoy more trust from people in the future. Thus, future assessments of e-participation solutions should by all means include such dimensions. In our study, participants were not in agreement regarding mobile access: While some took such an option for granted, for others it was not high priority. But overall, users will surely expect mobile, secure and accessible solutions in the future.

References

1. Schoßböck, J., Rinnerbauer, B., Parycek, P.: Digitale Bürgerbeteiligung und Elektronische Demokratie. In: Leitner, M. (ed.) Digitale Bürgerbeteiligung, pp. 11–40. Springer, Wiesbaden (2018). https://doi.org/10.1007/978-3-658-21621-4_2
2. Scherer, S., Wimmer, M.A.: E-participation and enterprise architecture frameworks: an analysis. Inf. Polity 17(2), 147–161 (2012)
3. Schoßböck, J., Terbu, O., Sachs, M., et al.: Inclusion and privacy in E-participation platform design. In: Scholl, H.J., et al. (eds.) Innovation and the Public Sector. Electronic Government and Electronic Participation, vol. 23, pp. 51–58. IOS Press (2016)
4. Chugunov, A.V., Kabanov, Y.: Evaluating e-participation institutional design. A pilot study of regional platforms in Russia. In: Edelmann, N., Parycek, P., Misuraca, G., Panagiotopoulos, P., Charalabidis, Y., Virkar, S. (eds.) ePart 2018. LNCS, vol. 11021, pp. 13–25. Springer, Cham (2018). https://doi.org/10.1007/978-3-319-98578-7_2
5. Schossböck, J., Rinnerbauer, B., Sachs, M., Wenda, G., Parycek, P.: Identification in e-participation: a multi-dimensional model. Int. J. Electron. Gov. 8(4), 335–355 (2016)
6. Phang, D., Kankanhalli, A.: A framework of ICT exploitation for e-participation initiatives. Commun. ACM 51(12), 128–132 (2008)
7. Al-Dalou', R., Abu-Shanab, E.: E-participation levels and technologies. In: 6th International Conference on Information Technology, pp. 325–331 (2013)
8. Parcyek, P., Schossboeck, J., Rinnerbauer, B.: Identification in e-participation: between quality of identification data and participation threshold. In: Tambouris, E., et al. (eds.) ePart 2015. LNCS, vol. 9249, pp. 108–119. Springer, Cham (2015). https://doi.org/10.1007/978-3-319-22500-5_9
9. Kalampokis, E., Tambouris, E., Tarabanis, K.: A domain model for e-participation. In: Mellouk, A., et al. (eds.) Proceedings of the 2008 Third International Conference on Internet and Web Applications and Services, pp. 25–30. IEEE (2008)
10. Islam, M.S.: Towards a sustainable e-Participation implementation model. Eur. J. ePractice 5, 1–12 (2008)
11. Krimmer, R., Ehringfeld, A., Traxl, M.: The use of E-voting in the Austrian federation of students elections 2009. In: Krimmer, R., Grimm, R. (eds.) Proceedings of the 4th International Conference on Electronic Voting 2010, Köln Druck, Bonn, pp. 33–44 (2010)
12. Goby, B., Weichsel, H.: Das E-Voting-Erkenntnis des VfGH: gesetzwidrige Ausgestaltung der ÖH-Wahlordnung. Zeitschrift Für Hochschulrecht 11, 118–125 (2012)
13. Kubicek, H., Lippa, B., Koop, A.: Erfolgreich beteiligt? Nutzen und Erfolgsfaktoren internetgestützter Bürgerbeteiligung – eine empirische Analyse von 12 Fallbeispielen. Verlag Bertelsmann Stiftung, Gütersloh (2011)
14. Loukis, E.: Evaluating eParticipation projects and lessons learnt. In: Charalabidis, Y., Koussouris, S. (eds.) Empowering Open and Collaborative Governance, pp. 95–115. Springer, Heidelberg (2012). https://doi.org/10.1007/978-3-642-27219-6_6

15. Téran, L., Drobnjak, A.: An evaluation framework for eParticipation: the VAAs case study. Int. J. Soc. Behav. Educ. Econ. Manag. Eng. **7**(1), 77–85 (2013)
16. Kubicek, H., Aichholzer, G.: Closing the evaluation gap in e-participation research and practice. In: Aichholzer, G., Kubicek, H., Torres, L. (eds.) Evaluating e-Participation. PAIT, vol. 19, pp. 11–45. Springer, Cham (2016). https://doi.org/10.1007/978-3-319-25403-6_2
17. Aichholzer, G., Westholm, H.: Evaluating e-participation projects: practical examples and outline of an evaluation framework. Eur. J. ePractice **7**, 1–18 (2008)
18. Macintosh, A., Whyte, A.: Towards an evaluation framework for e-participation. Transforming Gov.: People Process Policy **2**(1), 16–30 (2008)
19. Parycek, P., Sachs, M., Sedy, F., Schossböck, J.: Evaluation of an E-participation project: lessons learned and success factors from a cross-cultural perspective. In: Tambouris, E., Macintosh, A., Bannister, F. (eds.) ePart 2014. LNCS, vol. 8654, pp. 128–140. Springer, Heidelberg (2014). https://doi.org/10.1007/978-3-662-44914-1_11
20. Park, Y.J.: Do men and women differ in privacy? Gendered privacy and (in)equality in the Internet. Comput. Hum. Behav. **50**, 252–258 (2015)
21. Litt, E.: Understanding social network site users' privacy tool use. Comput. Hum. Behav. **29**, 1649–1656 (2013)
22. Hoy, M.G., Milne, G.: Gender differences in privacy-related measures for young adult Facebook users. J. Interact. Advertising **10**(2), 28–45 (2010)
23. Zukowski, T., Brown, I.: Examining the influence of demographic factors on internet users' information privacy concerns. In: Proceedings of the 2007 Annual Research Conference of the South African Institute of Computer Scientists and Information Technologists on IT Research in Developing Countries, pp. 197–204. ACM (2007)
24. Young, J.C., Rose, D.C., Mumby, H.S., et al.: A methodological guide to using and reporting on interviews in conservation science research. Methods Ecol. Evol. **9**(1), 10–19 (2018)
25. DiCicco-Bloom, B., Crabtree, B.F.: The qualitative research interview. Med. Educ. **40**(4), 314–321 (2006)
26. Wengraf, T.: Qualitative Research Interviewing: Biographical Narrative and Semi-structured Methods. Sage, London (2001)
27. Kluge, S.: Empirically grounded construction of types and typologies in qualitative social research. forum qualitative sozialforschung/Forum. Qual. Soc. Res. **1**(1) (2000). Art. 14
28. Parycek, P., Sachs, M., Virkar, S., Krimmer, R.: Voting in e-participation: a set of requirements to support accountability and trust by electoral committees. In: Krimmer, R., Volkamer, M., Braun Binder, N., Kersting, N., Pereira, O., Schürmann, C. (eds.) E-Vote-ID 2017. LNCS, vol. 10615, pp. 42–56. Springer, Cham (2017). https://doi.org/10.1007/978-3-319-68687-5_3
29. van Dijk, J.A.G.M.: One Europe, Digitally Divided. Routledge, Oxford and New York (2010)
30. Parycek, P., Rinnerbauer, B., Schossboeck, J.: Democracy in the digital age: digital agora or dystopia. Int. J. Electron. Gov. **9**(3/4), 185–209 (2017)
31. Del Vicario, M., Bessi, A., Zollo, F., et al.: The spreading of misinformation online. PNAS **113**(3), 554–559 (2016)

Digital Transformations

New Wine in Old Bottles: Chatbots in Government

Exploring the Transformative Impact of Chatbots in Public Service Delivery

Colin van Noordt[2]([✉]) and Gianluca Misuraca[1]

[1] Joint Research Centre Seville, Seville, Spain
gianluca.misuraca@ec.europa.eu
[2] PIONEER, Public Governance Institute, KU Leuven, Leuven, Belgium
colin@vannoordt.nl

Abstract. Advances in Artificial Intelligence technologies have revived the interest in Chatbots in both the private and the public sector. Chatbots could improve public service delivery by being able to answer frequently asked questions and conduct transactions, relieving staff from mundane tasks. However, previous e-Government research shows that the adoption of newer technologies does not always mean public services get improved. It is therefore of interest to research to which degree newer, advanced technologies such as Chatbots are able to improve, change and restructure public service delivery. This paper gives an exploratory insight using desktop research into three Chatbots currently used in the public administrations of Latvia, Vienna and Bonn. The findings suggest that minor organisational changes are accompanied with the introduction of Chatbot-technology in public administrations, but question whether Chatbots are able to transform traditional services to digital, integrated public service transactions.

Keywords: Digital transformation · E-Government · Artificial Intelligence · Chatbot

1 Introduction

There has been a big interest in the possible gains of using Information and Communication Technologies (ICT) for the delivery of public services to citizens. Already during the 1990s, there was a strong belief that information technology services are able to create a new, better functioning government of the future [1]. Government operations would be able to become more efficient, of higher quality and also more accessible to the public.

C. van Noordt—Public Sector Innovation & eGovernance. This is a joint-master degree from the KU Leuven, WWU Münster and the Tallinn Technological University.

© IFIP International Federation for Information Processing 2019
Published by Springer Nature Switzerland AG 2019
P. Panagiotopoulos et al. (Eds.): ePart 2019, LNCS 11686, pp. 49–59, 2019.
https://doi.org/10.1007/978-3-030-27397-2_5

The internet is always available 24 h every day, so citizens would be able to avoid the slow and hierarchical structures of traditional government. They would not have to rely on the opening times of the government anymore since the Internet allows citizens to find information themselves online and is able to deliver services through the web [1, 2].

Lately, another technology has captured the attention of the field. Coming from the realm of Artificial Intelligence, advances in Natural Language Processing-technologies have revived the potential of Chatbots [3]. Early Chatbots were limited in their functionalities as they were only able to respond to simple queries. Recent advances in Artificial Intelligence technologies, in particular the ability for machines to understand the context of languages better, made it possible for Chatbots to tackle more complex tasks and host more human-like conversations [3]. The optimism for this technology is great; it has already been predicted by Gartner that by 2020, the average person will have more conversations with Chatbots than with their own spouse [4].

In this paper, three cases of Chatbot used in European public administrations are described and briefly discussed on their transformative potential and integrated service delivery. As these Chatbots are frequently mentioned and have won numerous awards, they could be an indicator of how the future of Chatbots in the European public sector might look like in the upcoming years. The main aim of this research is therefore to answer *"Which organizational changes occur within public service delivery due to the introduction of Chatbot-technologies?"*. By analysing the transformative impact of three cases, a greater understanding could be achieved on the impact of Chatbots within the public sector. In order to answer the research question, this paper follows a multiple case study design to identify which kind of changes the Chatbot technology introduced. By analysing three well-known cases of Chatbots technologies, the findings could be more robust and generalizable rather than relying on one single case study [5]. The data collection had been done by document based desktop research. While this enables research from a distance, it does limit the correct interpretation of documents found online and restricts the researcher from gaining additional information not found on websites by for example conducting interviews [6].

2   The Promise of e-Government

An ICT-driven government is argued to be more responsive to citizen-needs, more democratic, transparent and efficient than a traditional government [2]. Early e-Government documents have showed that there was a great wish that technologies would enable a more joined up government apparatus, where different sectors of the government work together across organisational barriers to tackle public problems in an integrated approach, rather than different public organisations working isolated from each other [2, 7]. Government-wide information structures would allow different departments to work together in a more quicker and efficient way as ICT would ease the communication across organisational barriers [8].

The ICT-reformed public services would then improve government-citizen relations, reducing democratic gaps and other disappointments experienced by citizens [9]. For digital public service delivery, it was expected that there would be continuous progress from information provision online to one and two-way communication between citizens and the public organisation, transactional services and lastly cross-agency integrative e-services with more citizen engagement [10].

However, many of the proclaimed benefits of e-government have not been realized [11]. Despite many investments and projects to realize new innovative forms of governance and government service delivery, no substantial gains have been made in the e-government field. While there are many government services now available online, there is a significant mismatch within the supply and the demand for these online services [11]. The techno-deterministic premise that ICT-introduction within the public sector would eventually lead to significant reforms within public organisations did not come by as expected [9]. In fact, most government agencies did not change their organizational practices towards more citizen-oriented public services if they adopted ICT as there is still a lack of integration between different public organisations [2]. When public organisations actually do provide public services online, it is frequently only possible to gain information from the website rather than being able to conduct interactions or transactions with the public organisation [1, 12]. It has been argued that this strong focus on information provision exists because it is seen as "low-hanging fruit"; implementing transactional digital services would require much more resources and effort [12].

The promise of fully integrated public service delivery, without the need to go to multiple organisations, is usually not implemented [13]. This lack of integration among different public organisations was one of the challenges e-Government was supposed to solve, but rather, it is one of the greatest challenges which hinder the potential of e-Government [2]. IT-adoption in governments rather supports current organisational practices and power rather than changing the processes towards citizen's needs [14].

The introduction of eGovernment-technologies has been argued to enable changes of different magnitudes within public administrations: at the workplace level, organisational level and inter-organisational level [15]. Firstly, technology allows for small, incremental changes by automating existing processes and thereby improving the efficiency of government operations. Secondly, ICT could allow more general organizational changes to support the introduction of newer technologies. These changes are small adaptions and internal changes, commonly referred to as first-order changes [16]. Technology introductions in the public sector frequently bring about these kinds of changes [15]. Thirdly, ICT could also enable transformative or even disruptive changes by enabling new mechanisms for public service delivery or policymaking, but limited empirical examples of these changes exist. Lastly, there could be more radical changes which change the governance systems or radically transform policy-making mechanisms [16]. These second-order changes are much more substantial as they radically alter traditional practices, but are more difficult to organize, especially in the public sector [15].

3   The Revival of Chatbots

Chatbots, shorter for conversational agents, are computer programmes which are able to detect and understand language, through text or through speech, and have the ability to communicate back [3]. Simply put, Chatbots are computer programs which are able to recognise the input from a user using pattern matching technologies, access information and reply with the information found in the knowledge database [17]. Conversational agents are not really a new technology; the first Chatbot was already programmed in 1966 in order to discover if humans would be able to find out if they would be talking to a person or a machine [18]. However, the potential for Chatbots is now taken much more seriously due to advances in AI-technologies and changing communication patterns. A lot of our daily communication occurs through messaging apps and we have grown quite comfortable with communicating with them; this makes the introduction of Chatbots quite frictionless [19]. Currently, there are already numerous applications of Chatbots used by the private sector, with the most well-known being the virtual assistants of our mobile phones: Siri, Alexa and Google. Chatbots are starting to appear into numerous other business sectors in order for people to obtain information or to complete interactions without the need for humans [3]. Common usages of Chatbots are as customer service assistants, making reservations, paying bills and allowing customers to buy products or services online [20].

The public sector has also been looking into the usage of Chatbots to improve public service delivery. The main proclaimed benefits of Chatbots are that they allow organisations to reduce their administrative burden and enhance communication with citizens [3]. In addition, Chatbots would enable people to overcome information overload; rather than having to find information themselves, the Chatbot will help them to find what they need [21]. Early use cases of Chatbots within public organisations focus on answering citizen's questions or complaints through customer support, searching documents, routing citizens to the correct office, translations or drafting documents [22]. Most Chatbots are well suited to help citizens navigate through websites with lots of information, answer simple questions or conduct transactions.

This removes the need for humans to answer the same kinds of questions over and over again, allowing human operators to spend more time on complex cases [23, 24]. Others even see the potential of Chatbots to radically improve the citizen experience, improve citizen engagement and enabling new forms of decision-making with the help of citizen's interactions with Chatbots. Chatbots could be used to conduct surveys and gain feedback on public services in a more useful way as the Chatbot would be able to ask follow-up questions [25, 26]. There is certainly a potential value for government organisations to embrace Chatbots, but based on the history of e-Government progress, there is a strong need to gather empirical evidence from its effects.

4   Current Chatbots in Government Service Delivery

4.1   UNA in Latvia

In 2018, the Register of Enterprises of Latvia introduced the Chatbot UNA to answer frequently asked questions regarding the process of enterprise registration. The name UNA has a symbolic meaning as it stands for the Future Support of Entrepreneurs in the Latvian language. This way, UNA acts as an indicator for the future of the Latvian public administration; Chatbots are available 24/7 and thus able to make communication between citizens and the state accessible and friendly [27]. UNA is available on both the website of the Register of Enterprises as well as on the Facebook page as part of the Facebook messenger application [28]. UNA is able to answer frequently asked questions about the registration of their businesses as well as the liquidation, merchants, companies and organizations. If citizens already have an application in progress, they are also able to ask about the progress of their documents. At the moment, UNA only works in the Latvian language [27].

The Chatbot has been developed because the organization had to respond to a lot of calls and emails, which were more or less the same each time. The high numbers of organizational resources spent to answering the same kinds of questions could easily be lessened by using Artificial Intelligence, especially Natural Language Processing techniques [29]. A Latvian company, Tilde, specializing in Artificial Intelligence technologies cooperated in the development of UNA. The usage of the conversational agent has been argued to be highly successful and has been nominated for numerous awards such as the OECD's Public Excellence, World Summit Awards and others [30, 31]. According to the first performance indicators, 44% of the questions asked on UNA are considered to be general of nature and easily taken care of by the Chatbot.

Other non-standard issues are still handled by the support staff, but now they have more time to focus on more complex tasks [30]. While there are plans for UMA to perform the registration of legal subjects and legal facts in the future, currently, the Chatbot is only available to provide information to commonly asked questions. Citizens are still required to collect and fill in numerous documents, sign and stamp, send the filled in documents to the Register and pay the fees using the traditional processes [32].

Another element worth considering is that UMA is not designed to assist citizens with the whole process of starting a business, but solely answers questions about the process of registering the Enterprise as this is the task of the Register of Enterprises of Latvia. Arguably, there are numerous other services which new business owners have to conduct such as applying for licenses, permits, getting a business bank account, buying property, paying taxes and others which UMA is not able to answer questions about.[1]

4.2 WienBot in Vienna

In 2017, the Chatbot WienBot was launched in Vienna. This conversational bot has been designed to provide answers to frequently asked questions people have. The City of Vienna discovered that there are thousands of searches every month on the municipal website in order to gain more information about the online services available in the city. WienBot improves this process by enabling citizens to find information "quickly, smart and on-the-go" [33]. Rather than having to search for the correct page on the municipal website, citizens are able to ask the WienBot which will provide an immediate answer. The amount of information WienBot provides is very broad and

---

[1] Starting a business is considered a "life event", whereby numerous processes from different (public) organizations have to be followed by a citizen. See also the Quality of Public Administration Toolbox from the European Commission about why redesigning digital services based on these events has many benefits to citizens.

diverse as the website of the municipality has many different online services [33]. At the moment, WienBot is able to provide answers to around 350 different topics and services of the city. WienBot works solely in the German language, but is also able to reply in the local dialect [34].

The WienBot has been developed in order to make the information about the different services the City of Vienna provides more easy and understandable. It follows the current trend that much more information about the municipal services is looked up on the smartphone. However, rather than having the citizen to look up the information themselves, the Chatbot will give a quick answer to any question someone might have [33].

Citizens will still be able to find additional information on the websites, but for quick information, WienBot should be sufficient. Especially information about the availability of public parking spaces in the city is mentioned as a well-desired functionality of WienBot [33]. The City of Vienna was responsible for the development of the application themselves. It won the World Summit Award in 2017 for the best Government & Citizen Engagement application [35].

Even though there are a large number of topics WienBot is able to answer, the Chatbot is solely aimed at information provision for already existing governmental information. It is not possible to transact any governmental services through the Chatbot. Instead, citizens will get a link with more information about where to go to in order to obtain certain government services [33]. While the WienBot is arguably very useful to gain information, there is no possibility to avoid going to the office by conducting transactions online through the Chatbot. It is unclear if there are future plans in order to incorporate the future of transactions through the applications. For example, if a person tells the WienBot that he has lost an item; it will provide him or her with a link to the relevant pages of the lost property office (Fundamt) rather than allowing citizens to use the services through the Chatbot [33].

The transformative potential for the WienBot is hereby severely reduced as citizens would still be required to go through the traditional public services in order to gain what they need, rather than being able to ask WienBot to conduct these transactions for them.

4.3 GovBot/Botty Bonn in Bonn

In the City of Bonn, Germany, the GovBot [36] has been implemented in order to assist citizens with their administrative services. Citizens are able to ask for application forms, opening hours or are able to book an appointment through an interactive process with the Chatbot [37]. The City of Bonn didn't develop the Chatbot themselves but are using the GovBot developed by the software companies Publicplan and Materna. They developed a Chatbot which has been specifically designed for usage in the (German) public administration. Currently, the GovBot technology is used in the search engine of the administration of North-Rhein Westphalia, the City of Bonn and in the City of Krefeld [38]. Citizens are able to access the Chatbot on a specialized website.

GovBot is a Chatbot based on machine learning and an integrated knowledge base of administrative knowledge. The main aim of GovBot is to relieve the administrative staff within the public administration with labour-intensive and recurrent tasks of handling the same kind of citizen requests. Rather than having citizens ask the civil service themselves with questions, they are able to gain the same answers immediately through the use of the GovBot [37, 39].

In addition, the GovBot is able to assist citizens with administrative processes by helping citizens fill in administrative forms. Citizens are then able to come prepared to their appointment with the documents filled in correctly, such as the application of a license plate [40]. Currently, the Chatbot is still in a testing phase and will be added with more information in the future [37].

Even though the Chatbot is still in a testing phase, the main aim of the GovBot is to facilitate better information provision to citizens about general affairs or current administrative procedures. As of now, it seemed not to be possible to conduct any transactions or government services through the Chatbot rather than scheduling an appointment at the office. There is much to praise about assisting citizens with difficult forms and the GovBot definitely could play a big role in this. However, there is no actual change on existing administrative processes with the introduction of the Chatbot; citizens still need to make an appointment at the civil service after filling in the forms and go through the standard procedure, rather than being able to finish the transaction through the GovBot.

5 Discussion and Conclusions

This brief exploratory insight suggests that current Chatbots which have been implemented within the European public sector certainty provide a certain value for the citizens. All three Chatbots aim to improve the communication between citizens and the administrative bodies by providing easy answers to often asked questions. Citizens are able to find the information they are looking for in a quick and reliable way without the need to navigate the governmental websites themselves or contact the customer service, enabling staff to spend their time on other tasks (Table 1).

Table 1. Overview of Chatbots in government

Chatbot value	UNA	WienBot	GovBot
Information provision	Yes	Yes	Yes
Transactional services	Planned	No	No
Integrated information	No	No	No
Organisational changes	First order changes by having staff focus on more complex tasks	None identified	None identified

Even with the introduction of advanced technologies, there is a significant focus on information provision towards citizens, rather than using them to provide better government services to citizens. Instead of using Chatbots in such a way that citizens don't even need to come to the administrative office, citizens are still required to follow the traditional procedures, although this time empowered by the knowledge provided by the Chatbot. It would be truly a change if citizens would be able to send the documents online as well or conduct the whole process through the Chatbot. There seems to be awareness that transactions provide more value towards citizens. The developers from UNA in Latvia aim to facilitate transactions in the future through the Chatbot, but at the moment this is not yet the case.

There are technologies in place to facilitate these transactions; most countries have some form of e-ID system in place already which citizens could use to identify themselves with. An online payment system or e-Signature system would make it possible for citizens to conduct their government transactions fully digital. However, this does require that the actual administrative procedures should be replaced, a task which is significantly more challenging to accomplish.

Just like the lack of transactions, the e-Government literature frequently mentions that the lack of an integrative approach with joined-up public services hinders the potential of e-Government services. All of the mentioned Chatbots seemed to be fully based on the knowledge from the developing organization and don't take into account the knowledge from other, relevant public organizations. This is unfortunate as citizens frequently have to contact different public institutions when they are in need of public services.

The aim of this paper was to explore whether the introduction of Chatbot-technology within the public sector woul be accompanied with transformational changes. However, based on these early findings, we suggest that only first-order occur: namely the automation of current activities and some (minor) organizational changes to facilitate or as an effect to its introduction. Civil servants would be able to devote more time towards more complex cases when many questions get answered by the Chatbots, but the actual nature of their work doesn't seem to change at all.

They are still conducting the same processes as before, even when some of these tasks could be done by different technologies too.

Our findings do not suggest that any second-order changes happened due to the introduction of Chatbots. Public service delivery has not been radically changed, nor was there any mentioning of changes in the governance system, citizen engagement or reforms of the policy-making processes due to the implementation of the Chatbot.

If these practices are left unchanged, more institutions might implement Chatbots in order to improve their information provision towards their citizens. While this goal is very noble and paved with good intentions, there is a serious chance that these Chatbots are going to reflect the current fragmented landscape of governance. Instead of the current practice that citizens have to find the information they need from 10 different government websites, they will have to "talk" with 10 different Chatbots because the knowledge bases of the Chatbots are not integrated. Each of the Chatbots will only be able to answer the citizens the questions they have that correspond to the activities of the organization, rather than giving citizens a full, integrative respond that will cover the whole journey they will take.

If there is no sufficient amount of data sharing between public organizations, citizens will still be required to provide the same kind of information multiple times. Filling in the same kind of information on a government form is, with or without a

Chatbot, a tedious and annoying task for all. Just having a Chatbot is not going to make this procedure any more value adding. If the public sector truly wants to gain maximum benefits from emerging technologies, such as Chatbots, it will require massive public reform, a change in administrative culture and a strong reflection on the current organizational practices. Rather than having technology help understand citizens with the current administrative procedures, there should be questions raised if certain administrative procedures could be made easier or removed at all!

There is much more research needed to make more valid conclusions as this paper so far briefly scanned a couple of Chatbot implementations within the public sector. The field is still rapidly evolving and the reflections given here might quickly become invalid if multiple public organisations realise the potential which digital transformation could provide them. Furthermore, the lack of interviews limits the scope of changes which might have been introduced with the Chatbot technology. Possibly, certain organisational changes did occur but were not mentioned online. This restricts the current conclusion but should be seen as an invitation to conduct further research on these cases. Artificial Intelligence technologies such as Chatbots are an intriguing set of new technologies, likely to leave a big impact on our society in the near-future. However, it is advisable to take the transformative discourse of these technologies with a pinch of salt. A true understanding of the impact these technologies will bring the public sector requires a clear and realistic view on how they get adopted and used in practice, by institutions and by citizens.

Disclaimer. The views expressed in this article are purely those of the authors and may not be regarded as stating the official position of the European Commission they are affiliated to.

Acknowledgment. This article was made during the period of Colin van Noordt as Visiting Researcher to the European Commission's JRC-Seville as part of his PIONEER-Master.

References

1. Torres, L., Pina, V., Royo, S.: E-government and the transformation of public administrations in EU countries: beyond NPM or just a second wave of reforms? Online Inf. Rev. **29**, 531–553 (2005)
2. Bekkers, V., Homburg, V.: The myths of e-government: looking beyond the assumptions of a new and better government. Inf. Soc. **23**, 373–382 (2007)
3. Androutsopoulou, A., Karacapilidis, N., Loukis, E., Charalabidis, Y.: Transforming the communication between citizens and government through ai-guided chatbots. Gov. Inf. Q. **36**, 358–367 (2019)
4. Levy, H.P.: Gartner Predicts a Virtual World of Exponential Change. https://www.gartner.com/smarterwithgartner/gartner-predicts-a-virtual-world-of-exponential-change/
5. Yin, R.K.: Case Study Research and Applications. Design and Methods (2018)
6. Bryman, A.: Social Research Methods. Oxford University Press, Oxford (2016)
7. Dunleavy, P., Margetts, H., Bastow, S., Tinkler, J.: New public management is dead—long live digital-era governance. J. Public Adm. Res. Theory **16**, 467–494 (2006)
8. Lips, M.: E-government is dead: long live public administration 2.0. Inf. Polity **17**, 239–250 (2012)

9. Norris, D.F.: E-Government 2020: Plus ça change, plus c'est la même chose. Public Adm. Rev. **70**, S180 (2010)
10. Bertot, J., Estevez, E., Janowski, T.: Universal and contextualized public services: digital public service innovation framework. Gov. Inf. Q. **33**, 211–222 (2016)
11. Savoldelli, A., Codagnone, C., Misuraca, G.: Understanding the e-government paradox: learning from literature and practice on barriers to adoption. Gov. Inf. Q. **31**, S63–S71 (2014)
12. Norris, D.F., Reddick, C.G.: Local e-government in the United States: transformation or incremental change? Public Adm. Rev. **73**, 165–175 (2013)
13. Weerakkody, V., Janssen, M., Dwivedi, Y.K.: Transformational change and business process reengineering (BPR): lessons from the British and Dutch public sector. Gov. Inf. Q. **28**, 320–328 (2011)
14. Kraemer, K., King, J.L.: Information technology and administrative reform: will e-government be different? Int. J. Electron. Gov. Res. (IJEGR) **2**, 1–20 (2006)
15. Nograšek, J., Vintar, M.: E-government and organisational transformation of government: black box revisited? Gov. Inf. Q. **31**, 108–118 (2014)
16. Misuraca, G., Viscusi, G.: Shaping public sector innovation theory: an interpretative framework for ICT-enabled governance innovation. Electron. Commerce Res. **15**, 303–322 (2015)
17. Zumstein, D., Hundertmark, S.: Chatbots–an interactive technology for personalized communication, transactions and services. IADIS Int. J. WWW/Internet **15**, 96–109 (2017)
18. Weizenbaum, J.: ELIZA—a computer program for the study of natural language communication between man and machine. Commun. ACM **9**, 36–45 (1966)
19. Dale, R.: The return of the chatbots. Nat. Lang. Eng. **22**, 811–817 (2016)
20. Przeganlinska, A.: State of the art and future of artificial intelligence. Policy Department for Economic, Scientific and Quality of Life Policies, Brussels (2019)
21. Brandtzaeg, P.B., Følstad, A.: Why people use chatbots. In: Kompatsiaris, I., et al. (eds.) INSCI 2017. LNCS, vol. 10673, pp. 377–392. Springer, Cham (2017). https://doi.org/10.1007/978-3-319-70284-1_30
22. Mehr, H., Ash, H., Fellow, D.: Artificial intelligence for citizen services and government. Ash Center, Harvard Kennedy School (2017)
23. Lommatzsch, A.: A next generation chatbot-framework for the public administration. In: Hodoň, M., Eichler, G., Erfurth, C., Fahrnberger, G. (eds.) I4CS 2018. CCIS, vol. 863, pp. 127–141. Springer, Cham (2018). https://doi.org/10.1007/978-3-319-93408-2_10
24. Eggers, W.D., Schatsky, D., Viechnicki, P.: AI-augmented government: using cognitive technologies to redesign public sector work. Deloitte Center for Government Insights (2017)
25. Bousquet, C.: Five Ways Chatbots Could Transform Government Services. https://datasmart.ash.harvard.edu/news/article/five-ways-chatbots-could-transform-government-services-1033
26. Desouza, K., Krishnamurthy, R.: Chatbots move public sector toward artificial intelligence. https://www.brookings.edu/blog/techtank/2017/06/02/chatbots-move-public-sector-towards-artificial-intelligence/
27. Ministry of Justice of the Republic of Latvia: Register of Enterprises opens the first public administration virtual assistant in Latvia – UNA. http://www.tm.gov.lv/en/news/register-of-enterprises-opens-the-first-public-administration-virtual-assistant-in-latvia-una
28. OECD: UNA – the first virtual assistant of public administration in Latvia. https://oecd-opsi.org/innovations/una-the-first-virtual-assistant-of-public-administration-in-latvia/
29. Tilde: Tilde Virtual Assistant makes talking to the government effortless. https://www.tilde.com/news/tilde-virtual-assistant-makes-talking-government-effortless-3

30. World Summit Awards: UNA – The First Virtual Assistant of Public Administration in Lativa selected as the Best National Digital Solution for International World Summits Awards in the Category "Government & Citizen Engagement". UNA – The First Virtual Assistant of Public Administration in Lativa selected as the Best National Digital Solution for International World Summits Awards in the Category "Government & Citizen Engagement". World Summit Awards, Riga/Salzburg (2018)
31. Tilde: The virtual assistant UNA developed by Tilde helps win The International Quality Awards 2018! https://www.tilde.com/news/virtual-assistant-una-developed-tilde-helps-win-international-quality-awards-2018
32. Latvian Public Broadcasting: How to set up a company in Latvia. https://eng.lsm.lv/article/economy/economy/how-to-set-up-a-company-in-latvia.a215329/
33. Urban Innovation Vienna: WienBot. https://smartcity.wien.gv.at/site/en/wienbot/
34. Wien.at Redaktion: WienBot - der digitale Assistent der Stadt Wien [WienBot - the digital assistant of the city of Vienna]. https://www.wien.gv.at/bot/
35. World Summit Awards: WienBot – a chatbot for the city of Vienna. https://www.worldsummitawards.org/winner/wienbot-a-chatbot-for-the-city-of-vienna/
36. Stadt Bonn: GovBot Bonn. https://govbot.bonn.de/
37. Stadt Bonn: Stadt Bonn - Smartphone-Dienste der Stadtverwaltung Bonn [City of Bonn - Smartphone Service of the city administration Bonn]. http://stadtbonn.de/rat_verwaltung_buergerdienste/buergerdienste_online/smartphone_app/index.html
38. Ehneß, S.: Ein Chatbot für eGovernment [A Chatbot for eGovernment]. https://www.egovernment-computing.de/ein-chatbot-fuer-egovernment-a-696809/
39. PublicPlan: GovBot - Dialogisches E-Government mit Chatbots | publicplan GmbH [GovBot - Dialogical e-Government with Chatbots | Publicplan GmbH]. https://publicplan.de/produkte/govbot-dialogisches-e-government-mit-chatbots
40. PublicPlan: Typische Anwendungsfälle | publicplan GmbH Typical applications | publicplan GmbH. https://publicplan.de/produkte/govbot/typische-anwendungsfaelle

Digital Transformation in Public Sector Organisations: The Role of Informal Knowledge Sharing Networks and Social Media

Shefali Virkar[(⊠)], Noella Edelmann, Nicole Hynek, Peter Parycek,
Gerald Steiner, and Lukas Zenk

Danube University Krems, 3500 Krems, Austria
{shefali.virkar, noella.edelmann, nicole.hynek,
peter.parycek, gerald.steiner,
lukas.zenk}@donau-uni.ac.at

Abstract. It is estimated that during the period 2020–2025, about 30% of the employees at the Austrian Ministry of Defence will retire. This raises the question of how to encourage employees to share informal knowledge in order to successfully embrace organisational change in increasingly digitised environments with a view to retaining them long-term. Through the development of a three-part empirical study, this research paper investigates the role played by informal knowledge sharing networks and social media in expediting digital transformation within a public sector organisation. Our findings show that the public sector stands to benefit from informal knowledge sharing, and that both a permissive organisational culture and the provision of clearly demarcated 'knowledge sharing spaces' are fundamental in this respect.

Keywords: Informal knowledge sharing · Social media ·
Digital transformation

1 Introduction

Knowledge has always been at the heart of economic growth, political power, and social well-being. However, the rapid global proliferation of the new Information and Communication Technologies, their advanced ability to gather and manipulate large amounts of data and information, has placed knowledge at the heart of business innovation, strategic decision-making and thus represents an economic asset that needs to be strategically managed [1]. For businesses and governments alike, accessing and harnessing knowledge lying latent in employees by creating appropriate networks and channels for its transmission is being viewed as more and more critical to innovation and organisational success. In parallel, the popularity of social media, originally seen and used for entertainment and youth activities, has also significantly contributed to a change in business models [2], making new technology-based operating environments and continuous change the new norm, rather than the exception, for the contemporary organisation.

© IFIP International Federation for Information Processing 2019
Published by Springer Nature Switzerland AG 2019
P. Panagiotopoulos et al. (Eds.): ePart 2019, LNCS 11686, pp. 60–72, 2019.
https://doi.org/10.1007/978-3-030-27397-2_6

Web 2.0, social media and networks also play a significant role in the digital transformation of the public sector where, for example, Mergel [3] argues that the use of social media in the public sector can be considered to be the "fifth wave" of Information and Communication Technologies and sees social media as supporting government organisations' "mission". Measurements and evaluation are important aspects in implementing social media, and it is important to identify the factors that lead to success that are important for interaction and engagement [4, 5]. The use of social media in public sector not only requires a strategy, it must be used on a day-to-day basis, it use monitored and observed so that problems or operational deficiencies can be corrected [6]. Whilst it is important to understand what motivates employees to contribute to innovation, adapt to new HR policies and use social media, it is also important to measure and evaluate to what extent current activities are helping to achieve the desired or set aims.

The purpose of this research paper is to investigate, through an empirical study, the role played by informal knowledge sharing networks in expediting digital transformation within a public sector organisation. In particular, the paper will focus on the opportunities afforded by social media, in the guise of a new so-called third generation of communication tools, to help public sector actors successfully negotiate this transition. The research paper is structured as follows: The second section presents the literature review that addresses the global trends in governmental transformation and knowledge sharing. In the third section, the research design of the study is discussed. The fourth section presents essential empirical findings. These results are critically analysed in Sect. 5. Strategic recommendations based on the research results are derived in Sect. 6.

2 Literature Review

We live in 'knowledge societies' and work in 'knowledge economies' [7, 8], and for businesses and governments alike, knowledge is a central strategic resource; it is critical to organisational success, and needs to be effectively managed through the adoption of a series of activities and practices known collectively as *knowledge management* [1]. Within the broader context of knowledge management, *knowledge sharing* may be defined as any activity that involves the exchange of information, skills and expertise between people or within and across organisations and institutions [9]. More particularly, Ipe [1] defines knowledge sharing as "the act of making knowledge available to others within the organisation" [p. 341], that is, converting knowledge into a form that can be understood, and used by other individuals and collectives, or the wider organisation [10]. Organisational knowledge sharing may be uni-, two-way, or multidirectional [9], is involved in the dissemination of innovative ideas [11, 12] and is thus central to creating economic value and benefit from competitive advantage [13].

Knowledge sharing within organisations can occur through both formal and informal channels [1, 14, 15]. Formal knowledge sharing is usually the outcome of activities via outlets institutionalized by management that are explicitly designed to acquire, aggregate, structure, and disseminate knowledge; including through scheduled meetings, brainstorming sessions, training programmes, highly-organised work teams, and technology-based infrastructure designed to facilitate the exchange of information, know-how, and expertise [14]. Informal knowledge sharing, however, involves the exchange of knowledge and transfer of practices via informal socialization mechanisms that exist alongside all institutionalized forms of knowledge sharing; including spontaneous conversations, interactions based on personal relationships – both friendship and business – and social network dynamics occurring within the context of informal settings [1, 14, 15]. Almahamid [16] maintains that the process of knowledge sharing within an organisation is key to its ability to respond quickly and proactively to situational change in an unpredictable business environment.

Social relationships and the networks they constitute have a direct influence on the effectiveness and efficacy with which individual actors and collectives create, acquire, transfer, absorb and apply knowledge [17, 18]. Such networks may be referred to as *knowledge networks*, defined by Phelps et al. [17] as "… a set of nodes – individuals or higher level collectives that serve as heterogeneously distributed repositories of knowledge and agents that search for, transmit, and create knowledge – interconnected by social relationships that enable and constrain nodes' efforts to acquire, transfer, and create knowledge" [p. 1117]. Knowledge networks may be considered as informal transmission channels of knowledge between both individuals and firms activated by occasions like incidental meetings, or the need for favours or services [18], they are social relationships or loose linkages among different knowledge who nonetheless possess certain commonalities or common attributes [19]. Despite the assumption that employees primarily search in databases to find relevant information, various studies show that it is about five times more likely that employees turn to other colleagues than using impersonal sources like databases [20, 21]. This implies that the right kind of knowledge network is necessary to facilitate the search and transfer of knowledge. The qualities of networks, according to Augier & Thanning Vendeĺo [18], have two implications for the management of knowledge networks: first, knowledge networks are difficult to manage, control and access in the traditional sense given the loose interlinkages between different actors; secondly, it is difficult to predict in advance which knowledge will be needed by a particular part of the network, and even when identified, that knowledge may exist in a different place than expected. Cross et al. [22] found that four relational qualities facilitate effective knowledge sharing [p. 105]: knowing what another person knows and identifying sources of information and expertise (overview), being able to gain timely access to a knowledge source (access), the willingness of the knowledge source to engage in proactive problem solving with the knowledge seeker as against merely dumping information (engagement), learning interactions are carried out in a safe and permissive environment (safety).

Knowledge sharing also occurs in virtual organisational settings [16, 23, 24], and Hsu et al. [23] identify trust, self-efficacy, and outcome expectations as factors influencing the willingness of individuals to share knowledge within the virtual space. In more recent years, many have argued that the use of social media tools in digital networks, are key for interactivity, collaboration, co-creation, re-shaping the relationships between actors in organisations across all sectors [4, 25–27]. The public sector benefits from knowledge sharing; it helps the public sector find "innovative new ways to deliver public value" [6], and consequently it has become commonplace for governments to advocate the use of social media. The rise of social media allows for the emergence of new forms of open collaboration, coproduction, partnerships and collective action [5, 6, 28], to increase organisational transparency, participation or engagement, support a community or develop an identity, or help public sector organisations learn what is being said about them [29]. Many public administrations already use social media channels to disseminate content (usually for marketing or PR purposes), but they can be used for other external purposes too, such as providing information, communicating with citizens, for co-creating content, or designing or delivering new services. Mergel [2] suggests that a change of paradigm in public administrations can be seen, that social media supports the move from "need-to-know" to "need-to-share" information, a paradigm that includes dimensions such as openness, conversations, inclusion, co-creation, and real-time feedback cycles. Social media can also be used for internal purposes too, making it easier to collaborate and communicate within and between departments, to help staff in their work [30, 31]. To ensure the success of social media in an organisation, government or public administration, it is important to remember that the use of social media requires resources and must be accepted by the staff in an organisation. If the use of social media is to support knowledge networks, the actors involved and the sharing of knowledge, then the implementation of social media should not be seen as an IT project but as the need for a cultural shift within the organisation so that technology can make a difference [31].

3   Research Design

To examine the central research problem, and to test the associated hypothesis, a sequential mixed-methods research design was used. This comprised of, first, a systematic review of relevant literature [32]. The results of this review were then used to guide the development of qualitative data collection tools (a co-creation workshop, a framework for qualitative interviews, and a stakeholder workshop). Research data collected by these tools was then used to inform the creation of a quantitative research component (a questionnaire, Implicit Association Test, Social Network Analysis).

In order to conduct a comprehensive review of relevant scholarly and practitioner literature, researchers made use of one database of peer-reviewed literature (Scopus). Further databases were used to incorporate additional publications from diverse sources, that also includes knowledge from practitioners, i.e. one specialist search engine (Google Scholar), and one database of full-text books (Google Books). A systematic conventional search string launched within the 'title', 'abstract' and 'keywords' fields was used to query the Scopus Database for peer-reviewed, scholarly literature. A conventional key word search also used to obtain full-text sources of material previously discovered using Scopus, to identify clusters of publications authored by the same person, and to discover new citations of pertinent material from via the Google Scholar search engine. Simultaneously, a similar keyword search was used to trawl the Google Books database, with the aim of uncovering new material from both single-author books and chapters within edited volumes, and to access books and material from books identified in previous literature searches by other search engines.

From the research literature, qualitative and quantitative data collection approaches were developed to gain a deeper insight into the knowledge management strategy at the

Austrian Ministry of Defence. Three consecutive individual studies were carried out during the qualitative phase in order to gradually accumulate and integrate the topics and meanings of the concept of knowledge transfer from different perspectives of different actors and stakeholders from outside and inside the ministry. In the first phase, a co-creation workshop was held at the Danube University of Krems with 23 participants at the Department for E-Governance and Administration. The aim of this workshop was to develop a deeper understanding of this particular organisation's system dynamics and was used as a pre-study for later interviews and stakeholder workshops held at the Ministry of Defence. Broad questions asked concerned current topics on knowledge transfer in various companies. One of the main topics mentioned during the workshop focused on corporate culture. During the second phase, qualitative interviews about knowledge management were conducted with four stakeholders from different departments and Communities of Interest (COI) at the ministry. Two theoretical models - knowledge components by Probst et al. [33], and knowledge sharing in organisations by Ipe [1] - were used to inform the guided interviews. The guiding questions concerned knowledge sharing between individuals, focusing on the motivation to share their knowledge, which opportunities and channels are provided to do so, the perceived culture of the working environment and to what extent they are supported from others and the organisation to share their knowledge. In the third phase, a final workshop was held with stakeholders of the ministry to develop a general overview of relevant factors necessary to prepare a questionnaire and an Implicit Association Test (IAT), and to identify the relevant actors and relations for social network analysis.

Based on the findings of the workshop, three main topics were identified: *Personal Intentions* (motivation and attitudes toward informal knowledge sharing); *Interpersonal Relations* (e.g. overview of expertise); and *Organisational Support* (the degree to which an organisation facilitates knowledge sharing). A questionnaire was created, and a customised Implicit Association Test developed, based on the collection of relevant top-level concepts and stimuli. The questionnaire addressed socio-demographic aspects, motivation and support for knowledge sharing, and contained relational questions to measure interpersonal relations. Central to this study are the following questions: *To what extent are you motivated to share your informal knowledge? What motivates you to share your informal knowledge? What discourages you from sharing informal knowledge? To what extent are you encouraged within your department or community to share your informal knowledge? To what extent is informal knowledge sharing promoted in your department or community? How is informal knowledge sharing prevented in your department or community?*

The online test consisted of the standard version of the Implicit Association Test [34, 35] to analyse to what extent the concepts "share knowledge" and "retain knowledge" as well as "good" and "bad" are associated. For the concept "share knowledge", the stimuli *openness, general usage, communication,* and *distribute knowledge* were used; for the concept "retain knowledge" the stimuli *reticence, self-interest, secret,* and *hoard knowledge*; and for "good" and "bad" the stimuli proposed by Nosek et al. [36]. From 04 May 2017 to 06 June 2017 one link to the survey, that included the online test and questionnaire were sent to three departments and two Communities of Interest (COI). In total, 116 persons were invited via email, and 59 persons (men = 52, women = 4) completed the whole survey. On average the employees worked for 21.75 (SD = 10.21) years in the Ministry of Defence. In the sample, most of the employees have completed a higher level of education, over 50% of the participants graduated from university. One third of the respondents indicated that they had obtained school leaving examination and 17% state that their highest educational attainment is a Vocational Education and Training (VET) qualification. The percentage of informal knowledge sharing (46%) compared to formal knowledge sharing (54%) in the Ministry of Defence was quite high and indicated the importance of studying informal knowledge sharing in more detail.

Legal restrictions foreclosed the possibility of carrying out a detailed social network analysis needed to investigate the informal knowledge sharing between the participants. Instead, knowledge relations between the participants' functions were included in the questionnaire to analyse the general knowledge flow between hierarchical roles as well as items for relational qualities. To integrate these different methods and questions, the empirical part of the study will test the following derived hypotheses:

Hypothesis 1. Employees will have a tendency to share their informal knowledge within the same hierarchical functions.
Hypothesis 2. There exists a positive correlation between relational qualities and the personal intention (explicit and implicit) to share informal knowledge.
Hypothesis 3. The use of electronic channels of communication, and in particular social media, will increase as office environments get digitised.
Hypothesis 4. The degree of physical proximity between departments and Communities of Interest determines the nature of the communication channels used to share knowledge. The greater the physical distance, the more frequent the use of electronic channels.
Hypothesis 5. The degree of physical proximity between departments and Communities of Interest determines the nature of the situations in which knowledge is shared; the smaller the distance, the more popular face-to-face interactions are.

4 Empirical Results

The final report submitted to the ministry [37] concluded that members of staff with different functions, based within different departments and Communities of Interest exhibited homogeneous positive personal intention toward knowledge sharing. Based on this result, the impact of interpersonal relations and organisational support on informal knowledge sharing between constituent actors is critically explored here in detail.

4.1 Interpersonal Relations

Two dimensions of knowledge sharing networks within the Austrian Ministry of Defence pertaining to interpersonal relations were investigated: the knowledge flows between different hierarchies, and to the extent to which people rate the relational qualities. Based on previously articulated hypotheses the following results are discussed:

Result 1. The ministry expected that their employees would share their informal knowledge within the same hierarchical functions, as they assumed that people with similar organisational functions share their knowledge with each other. As expected, a tendency towards knowledge sharing between the same hierarchical functions was revealed. However, most relational ties were collected between different hierarchical functions. As opposed to homophily theories, even employees with significantly different hierarchical functions passed on their knowledge.

Result 2. Data collected also shows that ministry employees rated all four relational qualities identified by Cross et al. [22] very highly (on average between 4.35 to 4.67 on a 5-point Likert Scale; From 1 "does not apply" to 5 "applies"). This means that employees have a good overview of others' expertise (they know what others know), have access to others with the relevant information (they can contact relevant colleagues), they rate their colleagues as engaged (they are willing to answer professional questions proactively), and feel safe to ask for advice (they can ask others openly). Correlations between personal intention and each relational dimension, as well as the sum of all relational dimensions were calculated. As expected, a significant correlation between explicit motivation and the sum of all relational qualities was found ($r = .32$), but there was no significant correlation between the implicit attitude and the relational qualities ($r = .16$). Focusing on a single dimension of relational qualities (safety), we found a significant correlation between explicit motivation and safety ($r = .27$), as well as explicit motivation and overview ($r = .32$).

Result 3. Besides the individually perceived qualities of relational qualities, channels used to share informal knowledge were examined. Almost all of the employees were found to share their knowledge via face-to-face communication. Around half of the respondents use telephone and email. Far fewer people stated that they use different kinds of media to share their informal knowledge.

Result 4. Based on the questionnaire, most of the people stated that they share informal knowledge during meetings (83%), in the office (68%), or during breaks while drinking coffee or smoking a cigarette (58%). Hence, against our expectations, the results show no significant differences regarding the communication channels. Only minor differences could be detected such as the preference of employees in departments to share their knowledge through face-to-face communication (100% for collocated departmental members as compared to 91% within COIs) and the preference of employees in communities of interest to share their knowledge through short message systems (54% for collocated departmental members as compared to 41% within COIs).

Result 5. The results show that both employees in departments and communities of interest prefer to share their knowledge in face-to-face situations. Nevertheless, the preferences for specific situations had a greater variance than the communication channels. Members of departments prefer to share their knowledge during meetings (92% for collocated employees compared to 68% for members of COIs) and in their office (76% for collocated employees as compared to 55% for COI members); while members of communities of interest indicated to share their knowledge in situations such as lunch (41% as compared to 22% for collocated employees) and events (32% compared to 16% for collocated employees) was twice as high as members of departments.

4.2   Organisational Support

This part of the empirical enquiry examined the extent to which employees feel supported by their organisation to share their informal knowledge. Although employees are motivated to share their informal knowledge, there is a lack of organisational support to do so. Our calculations revealed that employees rated their motivation to share informal knowledge on average with 4.2 on a 5-point Likert Scale ("To what extent are you motivated to share your informal knowledge?"; From 1 "not supported at all" to 5 "highly supported"). Compared to the explicit motivation, the mean value of the perceived support by the organisation is lower with 3.5 on a 5-point Likert Scale ("To what extent are you supported to share your informal knowledge?").

Nevertheless, for the purpose of the study, a positive correlation between the personal intention (explicit motivation and implicit attitude) and the perceived support to share knowledge by the organisation was assumed. As hypothesized, a significant positive correlation between explicit motivation and the perceived support ($r = .42$) was found, but no significant correlation between implicit attitudes and perceived support. A positive correlation was also assumed between the interpersonal relations and the organisational support. Regarding the accumulated value of interpersonal relations (information flow), no significant correlation was found, however, a correlation between a single dimension of relational qualities, safety, and the organisational support ($r = .36$) was found.

5   Discussion

Based on earlier discussions of scholarly literature, and on the basis of the findings from this study, a number of recommendations pertaining to knowledge creation, knowledge sharing, and the use of social media within public organisations may be derived. The advent of new information and communication technologies has dramatically altered the environments within which private and public organisations operate and has placed several new demands on the individual actors and collectives that make up these larger entities. Knowledge is central, and organisation's constituent elements must know how and when to respond rapidly and appropriately to external changes and fluctuations; employees have to share informal knowledge within modern public organisations.

Digital transformation, when spoken of within the context of public administration, may occur in two distinct ways: either through the transformation of internal processes, or through the transformation of the external relationships between governments and other political, economic and social actors [38]. The organisation must actively support the formation of knowledge networks amongst its constituent elements and with external actors. To generate new knowledge, and to match information to those who need it, formal and informal channels of communication need to be devised that bring knowledge seekers together with knowledge sources. Here, the importance of *tacit knowledge* - operational skills and know-how that are acquired through personal or practical experience [1] - must not be ignored. A wealth of information, skills and experience is locked up in individuals and collectives as tacit knowledge. Often knowledge sources are reticent to share this sort of knowledge as it can be difficult to impart and can be regarded as a form of personal wealth or power. The organisation must adopt a strategy to encourage employees and groups to share this latent potential with others, a strategy that must include knowledge networks and the opportunities offered by new technologies.

Public organisations are shaped by the interactions, rules and norms, behaviours of their internal systems, and cognitive patterns of their inhabitants. The organisation evolves through the mutual interactions of its participants and the stakeholders involved, and digital technology can be used to shape new forms of organisational functions, increase public sector legitimacy, and integrate the functions between public agencies. Institutional support must be given to the formation of knowledge networks within the organisation, particularly those concerned with informal knowledge sharing and weak ties. An overt demonstration of institutional backing is likely to motivate employees from across departments and sub-units to seek out, impart, and exchange informal or tacit knowledge. A four-fold strategy for effective knowledge sharing may be derived from [22]: the development of an internal system that enables employees to quickly determine who holds the required knowledge, skillset, or expertise; the maintenance of an internal information technology infrastructure that connects knowledge seekers with knowledge sources, instantaneously and (often) in real-time; the initiation of an institutionalized or semi-institutionalised constructive and sustained dialogue between knowledge sources and knowledge seekers to promote meaningful knowledge sharing; and the creation of a 'safe' and permissive environment to encourage informal knowledge sharing. It may be concluded, therefore, that both a permissive organisational culture, and the clear designation of virtual and physical 'enabling spaces' for informal knowledge sharing are fundamental prerequisites of effective knowledge exchange or transfer.

The high relevance of face-to-face communication leads to us to question the types of situations within which employees are able to effectively share their knowledge. Allen [20] shows that physical distance affects the frequency of communication between employees, and thus spatial arrangements of buildings can influence informal knowledge sharing and physical proximity enhances not only the communication between attendants but also their use of virtual communication.

Public organisations and social media do not fit easily. There are huge lags between the rate at which technology is developing and the government implements and digitisation does not always match the internal processes well. Mergel [30] points out that the main problem may be that the characteristics of social media are very different to the characteristics of public administrations, and these can often lead to conflicts and difficulties. Merely pressurising organisations and public administrations to digitize processes may lead to simply converting processes from analogue to digital, which may neither be the best strategy nor result in the adequate processes being chosen for this transformation. The process of digital transformation is therefore more than an "(IT)-project" and not about finding an IT-solution to an IT-problem. An organisation needs to think about what the results and aims to be achieved should be and what users need, as digital transformation requires changing government processes, involves flexible HR policies, overcoming cultural hurdles and agile leadership that allows experimenting.

Mergel [2] notes that further barriers to the use of social media in the public sector can be the costs, the distribution of government power, organisational and cultural challenges, operating procedures, informational challenges and legal challenges. Serrat [31] argues that barriers to a successful implementation can include the demographics of an organisation, a reliance on outdated hardware, software or information systems but also factors external to the organisation (e.g. legal and privacy issues). But there may also be systematic challenges, e.g. the need for a change in organisational processes so that they adapt and accommodate new forms of interaction and task fulfilment, a change in the rules, standards, requirements and resource allocation [31]. Such barriers can be reduced through the implementation of a social media strategy, the implementation of policies, adequate staffing and staff guidelines regarding their use of social media. It can be challenging for a government public administrations to integrate new social media application(s) or tool(s) into the (daily) routine of knowledge creation and dissemination, it may also be hard to motivate employees to share their knowledge and do more than is defined in the established job descriptions [31], but it also clear that governments should not miss the opportunities afforded by social media.

The successful implementation of social media in an organisation depends on the people who use it rather than on the technology itself. Staff needs to learn how to use new tools and applications, but also new roles and regulations may have to be defined: social media makes it easy to mix private and official functions and guidelines for their use will have to implemented. In order for social media to support the organisation, [30] and [31] suggest that it works best when implemented in a context characterised by high trust, collaboration and knowledge intensity; that is, in an environment where there are no barriers to social media, a culture that favours cooperation, and ensuring that tools and applications are adopted at an early stage. It is also important to decide what contents are to be made available, as not all content is suitable for all social media channels and applications. Not only may content be bound to data protection regulations and privacy policies, but it may also depend response times required, whether content has to be adapted for the specific channel and what the further use or dissemination may be.

6 Conclusion

New technologies present the unique opportunity to bridge old divides of space and time. Digital technologies are able to bring together people and collectives separated by physical and temporal distances to generate and share new knowledge. For this study, two main areas of knowledge sharing in the organisation were analysed: (1) interpersonal relations: employees were asked to rate their interpersonal knowledge relations; and (2) organisational support: the extent to which employees feel supported by their organisation to share informal knowledge was analysed. A better overview of the expertise within the organisation and an organisational culture that provides the social legitimization to openly ask questions seems to have a positive impact on knowledge sharing.

Our study revealed that the efficacy of new technologies as tools to facilitate informal knowledge sharing between public sector actors, and by extension their ability to cope with digital transformation, will depend to a significant extent on the degree to which the use of these tools is aligned with existing internal workflow processes and organisational culture. There are several benefits to be gained through the implementation of social media in particular, for example, providing access to external stakeholders and managing external relationships. However, their introduction should support the organisation's internal communication patterns, thereby making them more effective, faster and gaining feedback. An important aspect of deciding about the use of social media is the use of strategy that considers which tool to use, whether they are suitable for the content to be transmitted and/or stored, length of communication, the response times. The organisation has to adapt to specific cultural characteristics of the social media tools and all channels chosen have to be maintained equally well. The use of guidelines will make it necessary to consider questions such as: what is the aim to be achieved? Who will use it? What contents will it transport? What tools or platforms will be used? What is the time framework? What resources are available? What parts of the organisation are involved? Have the aims been reached? [39].

At the same time, first- and second-generation channels of communication must not be forgotten. Evidence from the empirical study presented in this paper suggests that people still make use of traditional methods of communication such as face-to-face interactions or the telephone to exchange knowledge and to forge networks. In devising a communications or knowledge sharing strategy, the 'old school' technologies must also be considered for inclusion. Finally, the implementation and use of social media in public sector organisations must be monitored and evaluated. The impact of new tools on informal organisational knowledge sharing needs to be evaluated. Such evaluations may be quantitative and/or qualitative, can be conducted at the beginning, the end, or during the implementation of the new tools. Several indicators can be used for this, and although the focus is usually on the measurement of online activities and interaction, it is equally important to consider the network effects that may not always be visible but have an impact on the transfer of knowledge between public sector knowledge actors.

References

1. Ipe, M.: Knowledge sharing in organizations: a conceptual framework. Hum. Res. Dev. Rev. **2**(4), 337–359 (2003)
2. Mergel, I.: Social media adoption: toward a representative, responsive or interactive government? pp. 163–170. ACM Press (2014)
3. Mergel, I.: Social Media in the Public Sector: A Guide to Participation, Collaboration and Transparency in the Networked World, 1st edn. Jossey-Bass, San Francisco (2012)
4. Criado, J.I., Rojas-Martín, F., Gil-Garcia, J.R.: Enacting social media success in local public administrations: an empirical analysis of organizational, institutional, and contextual factors. Int. J. Public Sector Manag. **30**(1), 31–47 (2017)
5. Mickoleit, A.: Social Media Use by Governments (OECD Working Papers on Public Governance No. 26) (2014)
6. Linders, D.: From e-government to we-government: defining a typology for citizen coproduction in the age of social media. Gov. Inf. Q. **29**(4), 446–454 (2012)

7. Hara, N.: Communities of Practice: Fostering Peer-to-Peer Learning and Informal Knowledge Sharing in the Work Place. Springer, Heidelberg (2009). https://doi.org/10. 1007/978-3-540-85424-1
8. David, P.A., Foray, D.: Economic fundamentals of the knowledge society. Pol. Futures Educ. 1(1), 20–49 (2003)
9. Janus, S.S.: Becoming a Knowledge Sharing Organization: A Handbook for Scaling Up Solutions Through Knowledge Capturing and Sharing. World Bank Group, Washington, D.C. (2016)
10. Kuusinen, K., Gregory, P., Sharp, H., Barroca, L., Taylor, K., Wood, L.: Knowledge sharing in a large agile organisation: a survey study. In: Baumeister, H., Lichter, H., Riebisch, M. (eds.) Agile Processes in Software Engineering and Extreme Programming - 18th International Conference, XP 2017, Cologne, Germany, May 22-26, 2017, Proceedings, pp. 135–150. Springer, Switzerland (2017)
11. Lin, H.-F.: Knowledge sharing and firm innovation capability: an empirical study. Int. J. Manpower 28(3/4), 315–332 (2007)
12. Armbrecht Jr., F.M.R., et al.: Knowledge management in research and development. Res. Technol. Manag. 44(4), 28–48 (2001)
13. Hendriks, P.: Why share knowledge? The influence of ICT on the motivation for knowledge sharing. Knowl. Proc. Manag. 6(2), 91–100 (1999)
14. Taminiau, Y., Smit, W., de Lange, A.: Innovation in management consulting firms through informal knowledge sharing. J. Knowl. Manag. 13(1), 42–55 (2009)
15. Lawson, B., Petersen, K.J., Cousins, P.D., Handfield, R.B.: Knowledge sharing in interorganizational product development teams: the effect of formal and informal socialization mechanisms. J. Prod. Innov. Manag. 26(2), 156–172 (2009)
16. Almahamid, S.: The role of agility and knowledge sharing on competitive advantage: an empirical investigation in manufacturing companies in Jordan. In: Proceedings of the 19th Annual Conference of the Production and Operations Management Society (POMS), 9–12 May 2008, La Jolla, California, pp. 9–12 (2009)
17. Phelps, C., Heidl, R., Wadhwa, A.: Knowledge, networks, and knowledge networks: a review and research agenda. J. Manag. 38(4), 1115–1166 (2012)
18. Augier, M., Thanning Vendelo, M.: Networks, cognition and management of tacit knowledge. J. Knowl. Manag. 3(4), 252–261 (1999)
19. Buchel, B., Raub, S.: Building knowledge-creating value networks. Eur. Manag. J. 20(6), 587–596 (2002)
20. Allen, T.J.: Managing the Flow of Technology: Technology Transfer and the Dissemination of Technological Information Within the R&D Organization. MIT Press Books, Cambridge (1984)
21. Waber, B., Magnolfi, J., Lindsay, G.: Workspaces that move people. Har. Bus. Rev. 92(10), 68–77 (2014)
22. Cross, R., Parker, A., Prusak, L., Borgatti, S.P.: Knowing what we know: supporting knowledge creation and sharing in social networks. Org. Dyn. 30(2), 100–120 (2001)
23. Hsu, M.-H., Ju, T.L., Yen, C.-H., Chang, C.-M.: Knowledge sharing behavior in virtual communities: the relationship between trust, self-efficacy, and outcome expectations. Int. J. Hum.-Comput. Stud. 65(2), 153–169 (2007)
24. Chiu, C.-M., Hsu, M.-H., Wang, E.T.G.: Understanding knowledge sharing in virtual communities: an integration of social capital and social cognitive theories. Decis. Support Syst. 42(3), 1872–1888 (2006)
25. Knox, C.C.: Public administrators' use of social media platforms: overcoming the legitimacy dilemma? Admin. Soc. 48(4), 477–496 (2016)

26. Mergel, I.: Social media institutionalization in the U.S. federal government. Gov. Inf. Q. **33** (1), 142–148 (2016)
27. Bertot, J.C., Jaeger, P.T., Grimes, J.M.: Using ICTs to create a culture of transparency: E-government and social media as openness and anti-corruption tools for societies. Gov. Inf. Q. **27**(3), 264–271 (2010)
28. Mergel, I.: Open collaboration in the public sector: the case of social coding on GitHub. Gov. Inf. Q. **32**(4), 464–472 (2015)
29. Loukis, E., Charalabidis, Y., Androutsopoulou, A.: Promoting open innovation in the public sector through social media monitoring. Gov. Inf. Q. **34**(1), 99–109 (2017)
30. Mergel, I.: A framework for interpreting social media interactions in the public sector. Gov. Inf. Q. **30**(4), 327–334 (2013)
31. Serrat, O.: Social media and the public sector. In: Serrat, O. (ed.) Knowledge Solutions, pp. 925–935. Springer, Singapore (2017). https://doi.org/10.1007/978-981-10-0983-9_105
32. Kitchenham, B.: Procedures for Performing Systematic Reviews. Joint Technical Report – Keele University Technical Report TR/SE-0401& NICTA Technical Report 0400011T.1, June 2004 (2004)
33. Probst, G., Raub, S., Romhardt, K.: Wissen managen: Wie Unternehmen ihre wertvollste Ressource optimal nutzen. Gabler Verlag/GWV Fachverlage GmbH, Wiesbaden, Wiesbaden (2010)
34. Greenwald, A.G., Banaji, M.R., Nosek, B.A.: Statistically small effects of the Implicit Association Test can have societally large effects. J. Person. Soc. Psychol. **108**(4), 553–561 (2015)
35. Steiner, G., Geissler, B., Schreder, G., Zenk, L.: Living sustainability, or merely pretending? From explicit self-report measures to implicit cognition. Sustain. Sci. **13**, 1–15 (2018)
36. Nosek, B.A., Banaji, M., Greenwald, A.G.: Harvesting implicit group attitudes and beliefs from a demonstration web site. Group Dyn.: Theory Res. Practice **6**(1), 101–115 (2002)
37. Zenk, L., Edelmann, N., Virkar, S., Hynek, N., Parycek, P., Steiner, G.: Informal Knowledge Sharing: Towards a Resilient Knowledge Network in Agile Organizations, Report to the Bundesministerium für Landesverteidigung und Sport (BMLVS), Republic of Austria, 29 December 2017 (2017)
38. Luna-Reyes, L.F., Gil-Garcia, J.R.: Digital government transformation and internet portals: the co-evolution of technology, organizations, and institutions. Gov. Inf. Q. **31**(4), 545–555 (2014)
39. Edelmann, N., Rinnerbauer, B., Eibl, G.: Leitfaden zur Nutzung sozialer Medien in der öffentlichen Verwaltung. Soziale Medien Leitfaden-Version 1.0. https://www.ref.gv.at/ref.gv.at/cms/fileadmin/user_upload/Soziale_Medien_Leitfaden_1-0_20180129.pdf. Accessed 21 Mar 2019

Designing Proactive Business Event Services
A Case Study of the Estonian Company Registration Portal

Helena Kõrge[1]([✉]), Regina Erlenheim[2], and Dirk Draheim[3][iD]

[1] Department of Information Society Services Development,
Ministry of Economics and Communication, Suur-Ameerika 1, 10122 Tallinn, Estonia
helena.korge@mkm.ee
[2] Software Science Department, Tallinn University of Technology,
Akadeemia tee 15a, 12618 Tallinn, Estonia
regina.erlenheim@taltech.ee
[3] Information Systems Group, Tallinn University of Technology,
Akadeemia tee 15a, 12618 Tallinn, Estonia
dirk.draheim@taltech.ee

Abstract. In the last decade, effectiveness, efficiency and quality have been main objectives in the transformation of government services. Citizen orientation can be seen as the crucial driver behind these objectives. A contemporary theme in all of this is about proactive services. Proactive services switch the service delivery from reactive to proactive, thereby, promising a yet unforeseen level of quality. In this paper, we ask how to successfully design proactive business event services in the Estonian company registration portal. We investigate current problems of this e-service as encountered by Estonian entrepreneurs. We conduct qualitative interviews with experts from the government and micro-business owners that use the registration portal. Based on the findings, we give a set of recommendations for designing proactive business event services in the public sector.

Keywords: E-government · Proactive services · Life events · Service design

1 Introduction

All major life and business events, such as acquiring education, getting a job, starting a family, or starting a company, demand for interactions with the government via various separately developed services that are provided by different state agencies or local governments. Thus, the citizen needs to communicate with multiple authorities and needs to visit various web-portals to get things done. Due to the overall demand for government services to become more efficient and customer-oriented, countries with more advanced e-governments such

© IFIP International Federation for Information Processing 2019
Published by Springer Nature Switzerland AG 2019
P. Panagiotopoulos et al. (Eds.): ePart 2019, LNCS 11686, pp. 73–84, 2019.
https://doi.org/10.1007/978-3-030-27397-2_7

as Estonia [1], New Zealand [2–4], and Taiwan [5–7] have started to look into providing *proactive services* based on and triggered by life and business events. A proactive service groups together several services related to the same life event or business event, so that, for the service user, they appear as a single service that ideally functions automatically or with a minimum of interaction.

Proactive services are a contemporary topic in e-government service provision. As early as in 2011, the *e-Government Program of Taiwan 2011-2016* [5] contains proactive services as a strategic element:

"Proactive One-stop Service: We are simplifying service processes and integrating interagency services from a life cycle and overall service perspective, which let us provide the public with one-stop end-to-end government services." [5] $\qquad$ (1)

In Estonia, the notion of proactive service entered regulations. Since May 2017, it appears in regulation no. 88 (Principles for Managing Services and Governing Information) as follows:

"§2(3) Proactive services are the direct public services provided by an authority on its own initiative in accordance with the presumed will of persons and based on the data in the databases belonging to the state information system. Proactive services are provided automatically or with the consent of a person." [8] $\qquad$ (2)

Despite all of this, only a few studies exist on the subject; and theories on proactive services are emerging only recently. In this paper, we aim at determining the necessary requirements for successfully designing proactive business event services. Estonia strategically aims at developing proactive services, compare with [1,8]. One behalf of this, it is planned to renew the already existing *company registration portal* (CRP) by 2025. An objective of our research is to support the designers of the new CRP services, so that the new CRP would adhere better to the needs of the users. We claim that many of the findings are of general nature, so that they can be useful also for other countries that want to develop proactive services.

We target the following *overall* research question:

- How to design proactive business event services for the new Estonian company registration portal?

In service of the *overall* research question, we aim at answering the following *auxiliary* research questions:

- What requirements should proactive business event services meet?
- What features stakeholders expect from the future service?

For the purpose of this research, we have conducted in-depth semi-structured interviews with experts from the four public agencies that are involved as stakeholders in the renewal of the company registration portal, i.e., the *Ministry of Finance* (MoF), the *Ministry of Economics and Communications* (MoEC), the *Ministry of Justice* (MoJ), the *Centre of Registers and Information Systems* (CRIS) and, furthermore, with three owners of micro businesses who use the company registration portal.

We start with a discussion of related work in Sect. 2. In Sect. 3, we provide an overview of the Estonian company registration portal. In Sect. 4, we aim at answering the *auxiliary* research questions. In Sect. 5, we aim at answering the *overall* research question. We briefly discuss future research directions in Sect. 6 and finish with a conclusion in Sect. 7.

2 Related Work

In the emerging notion of *proactive service*, two established concepts of e-government service design are amalgamated, i.e., the concept of *life/business events* and the concept of *proactivity*. Estonian regulations distinguish between *proactive services* and *event services*, where the concept of *event service* is used to gather certain aspects of proactive services, compare also with (2), as follows:

> "§2(4) Event services are the direct public services provided jointly by several authorities so that a person would be able to perform all the obligations and exercise all the rights conferred on the person due to an event or sit- (3) uation. An event service compiles several services (hereinafter component service) related to the same event into a single service for the user." [8]

Henceforth, we rather do not want to use the term *event service* and want to speak about *proactive services* only. However, we still want to talk about *proactive business event services* as opposed to *proactive life event services*. Also, our interviewees use the term *event service*.

Wimmer [9] and Wimmer and Tambours [10] explain *life events* or *life episodes* as an important service design metaphor that helps to increase citizen orientation of e-government services. The events in this metaphor include not only "human" life events but also *business events* that are also called *business situations* in [9,10]. The orientation towards life/business events is a convenient requirement elicitation tools for e-services, but not only; beyond that, it provides a metaphor for structuring e-services portals. Orientation towards life/business events is an essential ingredient of proactive service design [6,7,11–14].

In [15], Vintar and Leben report on the prototypical implementation of a life-event portal for the Republic of Slovenia. The quality of the Slovenian life-event portal has also been analyzed by Vintar et al. [16], compare also with [17].

The case study of e-government in Singapore [18] by Srivastava and Teo reveals that proactive provision of information is a main factor in increasing citizens' trust in e-government services.

For Dunleavy et al. [19] pro-activity is part of transcending *new public management*. Here, proactivity is about anticipating citizens' needs, e.g., *"using feasible algorithms, agencies can then proactively try to match their services to meet citizens' needs or the key risks to policy"* [19]. In [20], Linders identifies *"proactive information dissemination"* [20] as a key ingredient in moving from a stage of customer-to-government (C2G), or *"citizen sourcing"* [20], to a stage of government-to-customer, or *"government as platform"* [20].

Linders, Liao and Wang [6,7] explain that proactive services are about transforming e-service delivery from a *pull to push* model. They identify administrative effectiveness and efficiency, quality of e-services and, on behalf of this, quality of life for citizens as the objectives for introducing proactive services. They report on three cases of e-government initiatives in Taiwan: (i) the so-called *e-housekeeper* initiative, an integrated messaging platform of the government agencies, (ii) the proactive citizen hotline of the city of Taipei [21], and (iii) a pilot program in decreasing digital divide.

In [11,12], Sirendi and Taveter conduct a concept study on proactive service design, including a prototypical implementation, for the family benefits system of the *Estonian National Social Insurance Board*. A main objective of the proactive service design in [11,12] is user centricity as a key rationale of service design [22–25]. In [13], Sirendi et al. analyze two concrete e-government services with respect to current shortcomings and their potential for proactive service design. The first is about providing services for parents of disabled children in the Estonian e-services portal[1]; the second is the Australian mobile web-application *Ask Izzy*[2] that provides services and support for the homeless. On the basis of this analysis, guidelines for introducing proactive e-services are created.

Schuppan and Köhl [14] consider research in proactive services (*proactive government*) in [14], as relevant for meeting citizens' expectations towards e-government services and e-government service portals.

3   The Estonian Company Registration Portal

Estonia is strong in providing public e-services for businesses. Almost everything can be done online – quick and easy – starting a business, declaring taxes, changing data etc.[3] However, the provision of business services is decentralized and distributed over multiple agencies and portals. In order to fulfill all of their legal duties, business owners need to move between several platforms and registries, each with a different design and requirements. One of the most used platforms is the company registration portal of the *Centre of Registers and Information Systems* (CRIS), that provides a secure and convenient platform for entrepreneurs to start a business, submit documents and change information to the e-business register. The system holds information on all legal persons registered in Estonia. It allows private persons to start a company and legal persons to establish new

---

[1] www.eesti.ee.

[2] https://askizzy.org.au/.

[3] https://e-estonia.com/.

enterprises. All Estonian citizens can log into the CRP with their ID-cards or mobile IDs and, soon, also with smart IDs[4]. The CRP is available since 2007; but it is not required to use the CRP for starting a company, i.e., it is still possible to do this the conventional way via a notary; although, this is much more expensive and time- consuming (it takes around five days to set up a company instead of two hours).[5]

Figure 1 shows the current, rather simple process of establishing a private limited company – the most common type of business in Estonia. Upon entering the portal, the user needs to start an application for registering a new enterprise. He needs to specify its type (private limited company, sole proprietorship, limited partnership, general partnership, or non-profit). Then, the user needs to provide additional information such as the name of the business, its statute, persons involved, or the main area of activity. The application must be signed digitally, and state fee needs to be paid electronically. Upon that, an entry into the business register is made.

However, the overall process is not as simple as it appears on first sight – and this deserves some remarks. In addition to the CRP registration, companies need to fulfill more obligations with respect to other agencies and portals such as registering in the e-taxation portal, getting a VAT number or registering their employees. If the area of business is subject to specific regulations as, e.g., in the construction industry or the food industry, a business need to submit also a notice or needs to apply for a license in the *register of economic activities*. Furthermore, registering a company in the CRP is only possible if all the persons that have been involved in its establishment (members of the management board, founders etc.) are able to digitally sign the establishing application and the respective documents – otherwise, the registration has to be done with the notary.

4   Results

We have conducted in-depth semi-structured interviews with the Estonian deputy governmental CIO from the *Ministry of Economics and Communications* (MoEC), a project manager from the *Ministry of Finance* (MoF), an e-governance team leader from the *Centre of Registers and Information Systems* (CRIS), and a further expert from the *Ministry of Justice* (MoJ). Furthermore, we conducted three additional interviews with owners of micro businesses who use the CRP, in order to understand the needs and expectations of one of its main target groups. The interviews have been conducted in November 2018. All but one interview have been conducted one-on-one, face-to-face. One interview has been conducted via email. All interviews have been conducted in Estonian to simplify communication and to avoid translation errors. Afterwards, the interviews have been transcribed and translated.

---

[4] As of May 2019, there are around 127.600 active enterprises and 9.500 apartment associations in Estonia.

[5] https://www.rik.ee/en/international/e-business-register.

We analyzed the interviews with respect to five areas: (i) the state of business service provision, (ii) the functionality of the CRP, (iii) event-based service provision, (iv) level of bureaucracy and (v) barriers to further improvements.

One of the main issues confirmed by all interviewees is that services are distributed over multiple agencies and platforms, which makes the service provision less user-friendly for entrepreneurs. The interviewee from the MoF claimed that, due to the many websites, entrepreneurs can easily get confused about where to find the desired information: *"The main problem is that services are dispersed and that is not user-friendly. The entrepreneur has to orientate himself in different websites and sometimes does not even know where to go or does not know all his obligations."*

A few interviewees brought out that the CRP works pretty well, but that it is old. The interviewee from the MoEC was rather critical and claimed that the portal is outdated: *"It is not great – according to today's standards. It was built in 2008 or something. It is old and can become much better. But it is going to be great, they are moving towards it."*

With respect to event-based logic, the interviewees seemed to have a good idea of what can be achieved with this. The interviewee from the CRIS explained how event-based service provision can help to offer personalized services: *"The idea is that the environment is so clever that it can provide services that are important to that company. For example, I am interested in Harju county or enterprises with more than a million Euro turnover. With these indicators, we can provide a very personalized approach to utilizing all the information in order to gauge the best contact and relevance to the business."*

Then, we asked the entrepreneurs about the level of bureaucracy. In general, the interviewees do not feel that the state asks too much information. At the same time, since proactive service provision has not been discussed widely,

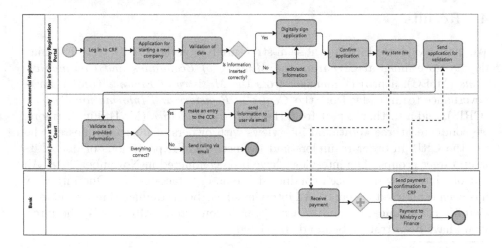

Fig. 1. *As-is* model of starting a company in the Estonian company registration portal.

people generally do not know how things could be done differently. However, two interviewees mentioned that both of them have already forgotten some deadline, which indicates that the notification system could be improved.

With respect to barriers to the introduction of proactively, three project members mentioned the importance of data security. This indicates that it needs extra attention on that. One project member mentioned that a similar in the past project suffered organizational issues such as lack of clear communication. This should be kept in mind for any project that aims at introducing proactive services. The interviewee from the MoE stated: *"The Data Protection Inspectorate (DPI) is the key player in creating event services. Things need to be talked through on how to do thing. Data protection must be in the focus."*

Not all characteristics of good service design [22–25] have been implemented in the CRP. There is need for a change. However, the issues can be fixed by providing proactive event-based services. As a conclusion, we summarize benefits of implementing proactive business event in Table 1.

Table 1. Benefits of implementing proactive business event services.

Benefit	Explanation
Improved business environment	Proactive and automated services allow entrepreneurs to focus and to invest more time and effort into their core competencies, i.e., freeing them from dealing with administrative obligations
Better user experience	A precondition of proactive event-based service provision is better cooperation of state agencies and their information systems. Better interoperability of state information systems [26, 27] allows for designing a convenient one-stop-shop service
Once-only principle [28, 29]	Duplication of data is reduced. Entrepreneurs do not have to submit the same data several times, as cross-usage of data increases
Better data quality	Since state agencies automatically gather data from companies, the change also increases the data quality. This enables policy makers to make decisions based on more accurate data. Anonymous data should be shared with them as well, so that entrepreneurs can also benefit from this
Increased awareness of service provision	Information and services can be found in a single place which makes life easier for all associations
Better overview of companies	Since all the information is in a single place, entrepreneurs have a better overview of the current status of their company

Table 1 lists the benefits of proactive services with respect to service quality. There might be some further, more indirect benefits on behalf of the improved service quality. First, the convenient and simple business environment could attract more people to become entrepreneurs. Second, it is advantageous for the reputation of Estonia: using an innovative approach such as proactive services is in line with Estonia's standing as a leading-edge IT-country. Furthermore, the resulting simpler business environment could attract foreign capital and more e-residents [30, 31].

5   Recommendations

When it comes to the introduction of proactive e-services, it is important that all stakeholders interact with each other throughout the project to gain a mutual understanding of their needs. For a proactive business event service, in order to be effective, a single sign-on authentication process should be used. Furthermore, the *once-only principle* (TOOP) [28, 29] should be followed. All technical aspects take considerable time; that is why it is recommended to tackle these issues early. At the same time, it is important to keep data security in mind, which plays a large role in creating interactive portals. It is advised to involve a data security officer early. The portal should have a scalable design so that new features can be easily integrated. Furthermore, it is advised to have a state-wide agreement that clarifies which services are grouped under which event. This enables easier communication between the involved state agencies and enables a clear schema for users. A similar agreement should be used for the *triggering points* of proactivity. With respect to this, is also advised to divide business services into three categories: (i) services that are provided automatically, (ii) services that allow for opting out, and (iii) services that require to opt in. If the state could divide all services into such categories in its regulations, the implementation of proactive services would become much smoother.

Figure 2 proposes a *to-be* process model of starting a company in the CRP, compare also with the *as-is* process in Fig. 1. As the first step, the user needs to provide basic information (company name, area of activity etc.). Then, the system asks whether it may gather information from other state databases. If not, the user can proceed with the application as shown in the *as-is* process in Fig. 1. Such opt-out from proactive service provision is important – at least if the system is in its early phases. In case that a foreigner wants to start a company, such opt-out is essential. Otherwise, i.e., it the user agrees, the system queries multiple other databases and registries. The system checks whether any company stakeholders have any business bans. If not, the system automatically makes a request to the *Estonian Tax and Customs Board*'s (ETCB) system to open an e-taxation account and freeze state fee payment from the bank account provided to the ETCB. The payment will not be made immediately, i.e., not before the user digitally signs the application. As the next step, the system checks whether the company operates in a field that is subject to special requirements and must be registered in the *Register of Economic Activities* (REA). If so, it provides a possibility for making the necessary amendments. The system moves on to a validation and, possibly, correction of the data. Then, the system asks the user to digitally sign. Then, the system sends a notification to the bank to unfreeze the state fee. Then, it sends another request to create a company bank account. After the company bank account is created, the system sends a request to the e-business register for entering a new company. Here, it is necessary to agree with the private sector, i.e., the banks, to keep the system as functional as possible.

6 Future Directions

Proactive services have been described as a paradigm shift *from pull to push*. A closer look reveals that this is a slightly odd metaphor. In established portals, the citizen pulls the service from the government, whereas, with proactive services, the government pushes the service to the citizen. But, in that narrative, a change of perspective happens, i.e., from the citizen to the government. If the story is told, consistently, from the citizen's perspective, the essence of the proactive service paradigm should be coined as *from pull to pushed*. Of course, *from pull to pushed* does not sound so nice any more. But that is exactly the point: What we see, based on previous experience [32], is, that we should care to consider the user not merely as a *consumer/customer*, but also as a *citizen*. There is a need for deep and discoursive [33] research of user adoption of proactive services. In user adoption studies it can easily happen that we are biased in favor of project success, i.e., we consider user concerns as critical for the project but sometimes stop in analyzing the concerns *behind* the concerns [34].

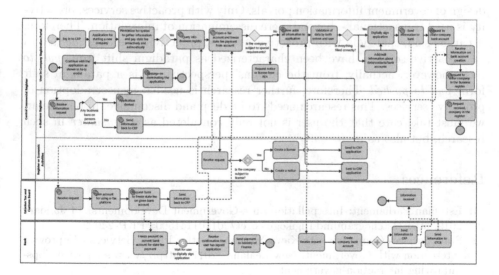

Fig. 2. *To-be* model for starting a company in the Estonian company registration portal.

As a concrete next step in this direction, we will conduct a survey[6] on the impact of digital initiatives. We are interested, in how much and in what respect digital transformation will impact our societies, governments, economies, and daily lives and work. Among other recent digital initiatives, we will ask this, in particular, with respect to proactive services, including emerging topics such as smart business processes [35–37] and automatic decision making (ranging from basic administrative tasks to automatic court case decisions).

7 Conclusion

In this paper, we investigated the current situation in business e-service provision in the Estonian company registration portal, in order to be able to understand the requirements for designing proactive business event services. The current situation shows direct negative factors such as a high level of bureaucracy and little user-centricity. Seven interviews with stakeholders have been conducted to learn about these issues, i.e., with four members of government authorities plus three micro business owners, who are considered as main beneficiaries of the system. The interviewees provided relevant feedback on stakeholders' needs and for requirements of future proactive services.

Life events are an established metaphor that helps to increase the citizen orientation of e-government services and portals. As such, they are not about triggering services. It can be said, that only with proactive services, life events become *live*. Proactivity is an established e-government best practice in the design of government information portals. Only with proactive services, proactivity is used transactional – beyond mere dissemination of information. Therefore, it can be said, that only with proactive services, proactivity becomes *active*.

Proactive services have been characterized as paradigm shift from *pull to push*, however, actually, from the citizens' perspective, it is a paradigm shift form *pull to pushed*. Therefore, further research is needed in user adoption of proactive services. This research needs to be deep and discoursive, in particular, we must take care that the user is not only considered as a *consumer* in such research, but also as a *citizen*.

References

1. Estonian Parliament: Interpellation on e-Government Developments, 14 January 2019. http://stenogrammid.riigikogu.ee/et/201901141500#PKP-24022
2. State Services Comission - Te Kawa Mataaho: Better Public Services - Improving Interaction with Government, New Zealand (2017). http://www.ssc.govt.nz/bps-improving-interaction-government
3. State Services Comission - Te Kawa Mataaho: Service Innovation Work Programme, New Zealand (2019). https://www.digital.govt.nz/digital-government/strategy/5-focus-areas-for-digital-change/service-innovation-work-programme/

---

[6] Together with Capgemini Germany (Business & Technology Solutions Public Sector), Mitshubishi UFJ (Research & Consulting).

4. State Services Comission - Te Kawa Mataaho: SmartStart a new type of service, New Zealand (2018). https://www.digital.govt.nz/showcase/smartstart-a-new-type-of-service/
5. National Development Council: E-Government Program of Taiwan: 2011–2016. National Development Council (2011)
6. Linders, D., Wang, C.M.: Proactive e-governance: flipping the service delivery model in Taiwan. In: Proceedings of the 7th International Conference on Theory and Practice of Electronic Governance, ICEGOV 2013, pp. 154–157. ACM (2013)
7. Linders, D., Liao, C.Z.P., Wang, C.M.: Proactive e-governance: flipping the service delivery model from pull to push in Taiwan. Gov. Inf. Q. **35**(4, Suppl.), 68–76 (2018)
8. Estonian Government: Principles for Managing Services and Governing Information, Regulation no. 88. Riigi Teataja - State Gazette, 31 May 2017. https://www.riigiteataja.ee/en/eli/507072017004/
9. Wimmer, M.A.: A European perspective towards online one-stop government: the eGOV project. Electron. Commer. Res. Appl. **1**(1), 92–103 (2002)
10. Wimmer, M.A., Tambouris, E.: Online one-stop government. In: Traunmüller, R. (ed.) Information Systems. ITIFIP, vol. 95, pp. 117–130. Springer, Boston (2002). https://doi.org/10.1007/978-0-387-35604-4_9
11. Sirendi, R., Taveter, K.: Bringing service design thinking into the public sector to create proactive and user-friendly public services. In: Nah, F.H., Tan, C.-H. (eds.) HCIBGO 2016. LNCS, vol. 9752, pp. 221–230. Springer, Cham (2016). https://doi.org/10.1007/978-3-319-39399-5_21
12. Sirendi, R.: Designing proactive public services as sociotechnical systems by using agent-oriented modelling. In: Proceedings of ECDG 2016 – The 16th European Conference on Digital Government, Academic Conferences and Publishing International, pp. 308–316 (2016)
13. Sirendi, R., Mendoza, A., Barrier, M., Taveter, K., Sterling, L.: A conceptual framework for effective appropriation of proactive public e-services. In: Proceedings of ECDG 2018 - The 18th European Conference on Digital Government, Academic Conferences and Publishing International, pp. 213–221 (2018)
14. Schuppan, T., Köhl, S.: One stop government: stalled vision or a matter of design? Empirical findings from social services in Germany. In: Proceedings of the 50th Hawaii International Conference on System Science, pp. 2448–2457. Association for Information Systems (2017)
15. Vintar, M., Leben, A.: The concepts of an active life-event public portal. In: Traunmüller, R., Lenk, K. (eds.) EGOV 2002. LNCS, vol. 2456, pp. 383–390. Springer, Heidelberg (2002). https://doi.org/10.1007/978-3-540-46138-8_62
16. Vintar, M., Kunstelj, M., Leben, A.: Benchmarking the quality of Slovenian life-event portals. In: Löffler, E., Vintar, M. (eds.) Improving the Quality of East and West European Public Services, pp. 208–221. Ashgate (2004)
17. Kunstelj, M., Vintar, M.: Evaluating the progress of e-government development: a critical analysis. Inf. Polity **9**(3–4), 131–148 (2004)
18. Srivastava, S., Teo, T.: Citizen trust development for e-government adoption: case of Singapore. In: Proceedings of PACIS 2005 - The 9th Pacific Asia Conference on Information Systems, pp. 721–734. Association for Information Systems (2005)
19. Dunleavy, P., Margetts, H., Bastow, S., Tinkler, J.: New public management is dead - long live digital-era governance. J. Public Adm. Res. Theor. **16**(3), 467–494 (2005)
20. Linders, D.: From e-government to we-government: defining a typology for citizen coproduction in the age of social media. Gov. Inf. Q. **29**(4), 446–454 (2012)

21. Chen, D.Y., Huang, T.Y., Hsiao, N.: Reinventing government through on-line citizen involvement in the developing world: a case study of Taipei city mayor's e-mail box in Taiwan. Public Adm. Dev. **26**(5), 409–423 (2006)
22. Shostack, G.L.: How to design a service. Eur. J. Mark. **16**(1), 49–63 (1982)
23. Shostack, G.L.: Designing services that deliver. Harvard Bus. Rev. **84115**, 133–139 (1984)
24. Kimbell, L.: Designing for service as one way of designing services. Int. J. Des. **5**(2), 41–52 (2011)
25. Stickdorn, M., Schneider, J.: This is Service Design Thinking - Basics, Tools, Cases. Wiley, Hoboken (2012)
26. Kalja, A.: The first ten years of X-road. In: Kastehein, K. (ed.) Estonian Information Society Yearbook 2011/2012, Ministry of Economic Affairs and Communications of Estonia, pp. 78–80 (2012)
27. Paide, K., Pappel, I., Vainsalu, H., Draheim, D.: On the systematic exploitation of the Estonian data exchange layer X-road for strengthening public private partnerships. In: Proceedings of ICEGOV 2018: The 11th International Conference on Theory and Practice of Electronic Governance. ACM (2018)
28. Wimmer, M., Marinov, B.: SCOOP4C: reducing administrative burden for citizens through once-only - vision and challenges. Jusletter IT, February 2017
29. Wimmer, M., Tambouris, E., Krimmer, R., Gil-Garcia, J., Chatfield, A.: Once only principle: benefits, barriers and next steps. In: Proceedings of DG.O 2017 - The 18th Annual International Conference on Digital Government Research, pp. 602–603. ACM (2017)
30. Tammpuu, P., Masso, A.: Transnational digital identity as an instrument for global digital citizenship: the case of Estonia's e-residency. Inf. Syst. Front. **21**, 621–634 (2019)
31. Kotka, T., del Castillo, C.I.V.A., Korjus, K.: Estonian e-Residency: benefits, risk and lessons learned. In: Kő, A., Francesconi, E. (eds.) EGOVIS 2016. LNCS, vol. 9831, pp. 3–15. Springer, Cham (2016). https://doi.org/10.1007/978-3-319-44159-7_1
32. Muldme, A., Pappel, I., Lauk, M., Draheim, D.: A survey on customer satisfaction in national electronic ID user support. In: Proceedings of ICEDEG 2018 - The 5th International Conference on eDemocracy & eGovernment, pp. 31–37. IEEE (2018)
33. Habermas, J.: Moral Consciousness and Communicative Action. MIT Press, Cambridge (1991)
34. Schein, E.: Organizational Culture and Leadership. Wiley
35. Draheim, D.: Business Process Technology - A Unified View on Business Processes. Workflows and Enterprise Applications, Springer, Heidelberg (2010). https://doi.org/10.1007/978-3-642-01588-5
36. Draheim, D.: Smart business process management. In: 2011 BPM and Workflow Handbook. Workflow Management Coalition, pp. 207–223 (2012)
37. Mendling, J., Baesens, B., Bernstein, A., Fellmann, M.: Challenges of smart business process management: an introduction to the special issue. Decis. Support Syst. **100**, 1–5 (2017)

Crisis and Emergency Management

ICT-Enabled Citizen Co-production in Excluded Areas – Using Volunteers in Emergency Response

Sofie Pilemalm(✉)

Linköping University, 582 28 Linköping, Sweden
sofie.pilemalm@liu.se

Abstract. One of many contemporary public-sector challenges is the increasing socio-economic gaps and excluded areas in many cities worldwide. This study explores ICT-enabled citizen co-production using volunteers as first responders in excluded areas near Stockholm, the capital of Sweden. The study indicates that these volunteers can make a major difference if arriving first at an emergency site, e.g. saving lives by administering CPR and extinguishing fires before they spread. Major challenges relate to individual versus collective engagement, gender aspects and language barriers. Current ICT support, in the form of text messages or a basic app, is deemed sufficient but, for the initiative to expand and enable long-term effective engagement, calibrated solutions matching competence, role and language with incident and area are needed. In a public-sector innovation context, the study highlights the need for future research on digitalized co-production with an explicit focus on the ICT artifact and its co-creation artifact as catalysts for change. In relation to this, this study confirms previous research arguing for the merging of policy science and information systems research in an era of rapid digitalized public-sector transformation, but adds that they need to be complemented by perspectives from sociology, e.g. on gender and ethnicity, in initiatives involving citizens in excluded areas.

Keywords: Public-sector innovation · Co-production · Citizen engagement · ICT

1 Introduction

The public sector is undergoing rapid transformation in response to increasing global challenges, e.g. in terms of natural disasters, migration streams, increased socio-economic gaps, urbanization, aging populations, war and terrorism, financial cutbacks and resource shortages [1]. Digitalization has paved the way for various initiatives built around citizen engagement, as one (of many) means to address several of them. This has sometimes been referred to as "do-it-yourself government" as an emerging culture within public-sector innovation [2]. It has been explored using different perspectives and theoretical lenses; for example, co-production [3].

In terms of socio-economic gaps, the tendency in many western countries is towards growing segregation, whereby an increased number of urban sub-areas are characterized by poverty and social exclusion, sometimes to an extent where societal

P. Panagiotopoulos et al. (Eds.): ePart 2019, LNCS 11686, pp. 87–101, 2019.
https://doi.org/10.1007/978-3-030-27397-2_8

structures are deemed absent and replaced by parallel structures, and where criminality increases [4, 5]. In such areas, research reveals poorer health and school results, higher unemployment, and, not least, a larger number of emergencies than for the rest of the population [6]. For instance, those exposed to intentional urban fires in Sweden more often live in socio-economically disadvantaged sub-areas [4]. In emergency response, volunteerism and citizen engagement initially expanded rapidly within large-scale crisis management [7]. Over the past decade, organizing citizen volunteers as first responders has also gained attention in relation to frequent accidents on a smaller scale [7]. In Sweden, which has been progressive in developing the concept, the idea was first applied in sparsely populated rural areas where civil citizens are often closer to an incident site than professional response organizations [8, 9]. More recently, it has spread to socially vulnerable municipalities and excluded sub-areas in large cities. The concept is enabled by modern ICT, such as people having access to mobile devices with GPS positioning, which can be integrated with the emergency response organizations' systems for dispatching resources. This study focuses on a brand-new initiative using citizen volunteers as first responders in collaboration with the municipal fire services, in two municipalities outside the capital of Stockholm. The initiative is aimed at improving safety and the effectiveness of first response, and reducing the consequences of emergencies in areas exposed to high rates of crime and accidents. The initiative is studied here as an example of ICT-driven public-sector innovation under the lens of co-production.

1.1   Study Aim and Objectives

The aim of this study is to explore the concept of engaging citizens as volunteer first responders in socially vulnerable areas. Specifically, the objectives include:

- Describing the recruitment and tasks of the volunteers.
- Identifying the distinct features of the ICT artifact as a catalyst for the initiative.
- Identifying the perceived benefits, challenges and needs of the volunteers.

The intended audience is researchers and practitioners in emergency response, those involved in public-sector innovation and citizen co-production initiatives in general, and in excluded areas specifically. The study should have international relevance since volunteerism is growing globally and since our society shares the challenges, even if various countries' structures, regulations and legal mechanisms differ.

2   Background

2.1   Public-Sector Innovation and Co-production

Public-sector innovation can be traced back to the 1960s. Recent decades, however, have seen an increasing trend of replacing random initiatives with more systematic work and planned innovations, as a response to pressing societal challenges in an era when the public sector's own resources are constrained [10]. It can take various forms and involve public–public, public–private, and/or public–third-sector partnerships. One form concerns *citizen engagement,* which is described from various perspectives, sometimes depending on research discipline. It is possible to speak about *co-production,* where citizens are involved in the delivery of public policies and services, as part of the conception, design, steering, and management of services [3, 11]. From the perspective of e-government, it has also been described as a form of "do-it-yourself government" or "we-government," referring to "the re-emergence of citizen coproduction" and where citizens act as partners rather than customers in the delivery of public services, in order to make them more viable and effective [2]. In comparison with earlier forms of e-government, we-government implies that a certain group of citizens takes on certain tasks from the authorities, not only for themselves, but also for their co-citizens. This, in turn, requires that their ICT artifacts are integrated with the authorities' own information systems (IS). Speaking in terms of IS development and research, co-production and we-government can thus be related to concepts of co-creation, co-design, and participatory design (PD) [3, 10–12]. Of particular relevance to the study, it has been argued that designing for and co-creating with vulnerable groups is a key priority to advance and benefit the contemporary service field [13]. In a wider perspective, citizen co-production opens up opportunities for interesting mergers of research disciplines; for example, policy science and IS, a cross-fertilization which has recently been pointed out in relation to government and a public sector undergoing change [14–16]. The study therefore applies intertwined co-production/we-government/IS perspectives and relates these to the on-going discussion.

2.2   Study Context: Citizen Co-production in Excluded Areas

It is sometimes claimed that the social contract between citizens and the authorities is crumbling [17]. This is especially notable in an increasing number of urban sub-areas characterized by segregation, ethnic diversity and few opportunities for inclusion in society, where residents experience insecurity and a lack of trust in the authorities and perceive themselves as having little possibility of influencing their environment or lives [4]. Unemployment is usually higher than average, resulting in low socio-economic status, and recruitment to criminality is correspondingly growing, especially among young people [18]. Accidents also tend to strike according to patterns related to such aspects as gender, ethnicity, class, and living area [19]. In this study, these areas are referred to as socially vulnerable areas or excluded areas. This trend is global and in need of handling. Increased citizen engagement could be one way forward.

The study takes place in the context of Swedish emergency response, referring to *actors, technologies, procedures and rules, which aim to save lives and minimize human suffering and material damage in emergencies such as traffic accidents, fires and medical matters.* In Sweden, various initiatives have been undertaken over the past decade to improve efficiency and overcome long distances by the involvement of various societal resources in day-to-day emergency response, in collaboration with the professional operative response organizations (fire services, ambulance services, and the Public Safety Answering Point (PSAP)). Examples include cross-sector collaboration using entirely new occupations, for example, security guards or civil volunteers, as first responders. In the latter, the concept first spread to sparsely populated rural areas in northern Sweden, where the response organizations are located a long distance from small villages. There is thus a large chance that the volunteers will arrive first at the emergency site, providing basic first aid while waiting for professional resources [8, 9]. Over the past few years, similar initiatives have emerged in urban areas, above all located near Stockholm and Gothenburg. Stockholm has a population of about 2 million people if the surrounding municipalities are included, with a rapid expansion in recent decades, due to both urbanization and refugee immigration, not least in 2012–2015.

3 Methods: The Studied Initiative and Action Research

The studied initiative is taking place in two municipalities outside Stockholm with about 100 000 inhabitants each. Here, a major Swedish Fire Response Association has started an initiative that recruits citizens living in socially vulnerable/excluded areas as volunteer first responders. The volunteers are provided with one day of basic training in such areas as first aid, heart-and-lung rescue (CSPR), extinguishing small fires, and acting in single traffic accidents. They also receive a basic backpack containing a first aid kit, reflective vests, pocket masks and hand-held fire extinguishers. The aim of this initiative is twofold; firstly, to create a sense of presence, security and social relations in these areas, to decrease the incidence of intentional fires (mostly in cars), assaults and vandalism. Secondly, if an emergency takes place, to have the volunteers act as first responders for certain alerts. The idea is not to have the volunteers replace the professional response organizations, but rather for them to carry out first response while waiting for the professionals, in order to reduce the response time. To receive alerts, volunteers have to be less than five kilometers away from the emergency site, and acting on the alert is always voluntary. By early 2019, about 80–90 civil volunteers had been recruited and trained in various areas across these municipalities.

The overall study design has the character of action research meaning that the researchers aim to develop and improve the initiative together with the participating actors [20], including the volunteers. This study reports from the first phase (April 2018 to January 2019). Three researchers have been involved in this phase. The author of this paper was involved in all data collection described below.

3.1 Data Collection: Semi-structured Interviews and Focus Groups

The study was performed as a qualitative interview study including four semi-structured interviews and one focus group interview with five respondents (Table 1). In semi-structured interviews, a template or themes are usually applied to guide the interview but no strict adherence to the template is required and respondents are allowed to make other associations during the course of the interview. Focus groups work similarly but enable group dynamics and collective views on a particular phenomenon from a group whose members have experience or knowledge concerning the topic in question [21]. A snowball sample approach [21] was chosen since the initiative is new, emerging and undergoing expansion. For instance, when the study started in spring 2018, only about 10 civil volunteers were in the system and it was deemed important to interview those who had responded to alerts.

First, a focus group interview was held with a fire team consisting of one fire chief and three firefighters. Another fire chief joined for the second half of the interview, and continued responding to questions when the team had to respond to an incoming emergency alert. The focus group lasted in total for 90 min. All focus group respondents played a role in the volunteer initiative. This was followed by interviews with the instigator of the initiative and the current project leader, who took over from the instigator (both had a background as firefighters), and two civil volunteers who were residents of excluded areas and had acted on several alerts. Each interview lasted about one hour.

For all the data collection, templates that had been used in the earlier project on volunteers in sparsely populated areas [9] were used. However, they were revised to suit the current initiative and urban setting. The templates were also somewhat adapted depending on whether someone from the fire services or a civil volunteer was being interviewed. All interviews were audio-taped and transcribed. For the analysis, a thematic approach was used [21], clustering data into overall themes based on the empirical data and in line with the action-research approach, with a focus on development; for example, benefits, challenges and needs. The author of this paper performed the data analysis and received feedback from one of other researchers on the identified themes.

Table 1. Respondents participating in the study.

Focus group	Fire chief (1 + 1)	Firefighters (3)		5
Interviews	Project instigator (1)	Project leader (1)	Volunteers (2)	4
Total number of respondents				9

4   Results

The identified themes are presented in the following. The ICT artifact will receive specific attention but is integrated under the various themes.

4.1   Recruitment of Volunteers

As mentioned, there are several motivations lying behind this project, of which the most important is to create a sense of presence and security in the studied areas to improve collaboration with the response organizations, and to reduce crime, above all incidents of arson in cars and buildings. A related motivation is gender related, with the hope that women will improve their prospects for integration into Swedish society by becoming volunteers. There is also the hope of a more effective response if an emergency arises, but this is not as pronounced because the initiative is taking place in an urban area where the response times for professional response organizations are relatively short.

In the recruitment process, the fire services have deemed it important to engage people who have a certain social status in the sub-areas. An example could be the priest of a certain church. Another idea is to build on family and social relations; for example, if your relative is a volunteer first responder, you may think twice about setting a car on fire nearby. It has also been shown to be crucial that volunteers who are active in a certain area speak its dominant language and can acts as interpreters, since many people in these areas do not speak Swedish:

> *A problem was also that everybody believed the entire block was going to burn to the ground. Everybody who lives there ran to their balconies and were about to jump because they thought they were going to die. There were huge problems and no interpreter in place, no one from the fire station. Then I thought, what the hell, it's time to find out if I can be of any help.* (Volunteer 1)

The responders from the fire services described how they have used local interest associations, the municipalities and related real-estate companies for recruitment campaigns. The volunteers confirmed that they received information about the initiative from their respective real-estate companies. The interest has generally been much higher than the fire services expected; they had wanted to start on a small scale. One of the fire chiefs provided an example in which an entire Syrian Orthodox association of about 200 women signed up their interest. This forced the fire services, which pay for all related expenses, to initially turn down many of those who were interested.

An initial fear was that they may recruit those who are involved in criminality. Before volunteers undergo training, therefore, they are first checked with the police to discover if they have a criminal record. To date, this fear appears to be groundless:

> *Even though it is possible that an individual is known to be a criminal by those living in the area but not by us and we recruit them, then they might feel increased trust in us for creating social benefits... Or it will have the reverse effect* [on trust] *....it's a break even....Those into heavy criminality spreading fear will not show interest; they have so much capital violence to manage, a full-time assignment...* (Project leader)

4.2 Dispatching of Volunteers and First Response Tasks

There are two ways of dispatching the volunteers, depending on sub-area. In some areas they are dispatched by text message lists (Swedish abbreviation: SMS), in which case their mobile phone's GPS functions are connected to the fire services' system for handling incoming alerts. If the type of emergency is one of those described below, the volunteers will receive an SMS if they are on the list and within a radius of five kilometers of the emergency. The SMS displays the position coordinates, the address (road, but not specific number), municipality and type of emergency (Fig. 1). A commercial app adapted for the purpose, which is used in other areas, has somewhat more functionality. The principle for dispatching (radius in kilometers) is the same, but the volunteers receive a push notice together with an alert signal. In addition, the app includes a map and when the alert is due a red button is placed in the map, indicating the emergency site. Through this button, the volunteers (receivers of the alert) can also communicate with each other and provide updated information on the emergency (Fig. 2). In both cases, it is the fire services back office systems that provides the GPS coordinates, the addresses and the information of the emergency, i.e. the volunteers receive the same basic information as the professional first responders.

Fig. 1. SMS-dispatched ICT solution for volunteers. The example displays outdoor fires in vehicles.

Fig. 2. Dispatching of volunteers through the app

The volunteers are dispatched to the following types of emergencies: outdoor fires (e.g. vehicle), fires in building, heart failure, single traffic accidents and drownings. The emergency should not be risky for them (e.g. uncontrolled fires or a shooting) and they should be able to carry out first response using their small backpack equipment kit. The volunteers perform a range of tasks at the emergency site but those reported as most frequent by the volunteers are: extinguishing small fires, checking if the fire has spread and in this case informing the fire services, and backing bystanders and keeping them at a distance when the latter arrives. They have also acted in some single traffic accidents and after assaults (but here they must never intervene but await the police) with basic first-aid tasks (band aids, stopping minor bleeding) and providing comfort. There are heart failure alarms but these are less frequent. One of the volunteers says he has only acted on two heart failure alarms over a period of about a year.

The volunteers receive a debriefing by fire service personnel immediately after a response operation, but no follow ups. But, as stated by one of the volunteers, "the fire station is always open". The volunteers are collectively insured by the fire association.

4.3 Perceived Benefits

It is deemed too early to say whether the major aim of the initiative has been fulfilled. However, it is clear that there is great engagement on the part of the volunteers, and a desire to create a safer neighborhood rather than to receive financial compensation. Also, when something does happen, volunteers sometimes arrive before the fire services and a single first response can make a major difference, as illustrated by the following quotes:

I was at home and received an alert concerning a fire near a health center. Thought that they wanted to test me to check how I function. I was the first person at the site, it was a car on fire. I extinguished it completely. (Volunteer 1, first alert).

Was at home, 200 meters from me, went there, they are screaming from the balcony that he's died. Seven floors up. He was on the floor, not breathing, I started heart and lung rescue. He comes back, starts breathing. Two minutes later, the ambulance arrives. He is alive. (Volunteer 1, heart failure alert).

Again, communication and acting as an interpreter are central, as well as having knowledge about the area and knowing the people who live there. This is something the fires services and volunteers agree upon:

I believe very much in this. Above all, they might have knowledge of the area and who is the leader, so to speak. When the police take action, the outcomes are often not that good. (Fire chief, focus group, volunteers backing crowds of people)

I have learnt how to "back" a crowd of people. I know the language, I can tell them that this smoke is a cancer risk. (Volunteer 1).

4.4 Challenges

The major perceived challenge is having volunteers actually responding to alerts and going to the incident site. Massive interest in recruitment is not the same thing as actually patrolling the neighborhood or taking action when something happens. There are a few enthusiasts who respond to many alerts, but they are often the only ones responding to that particular alert, making first response an individual task. The project leader believes that a potential explanation is that few volunteers know any firefighters and that "the fire services work in an end room". This might result in hesitancy about intervening in an emergency. He also poses the question of whether economic compensation would after all play a role, and argues that it might have been better to start on a larger scale:

I think I would have started on a larger scale. More volunteers from the very beginning [training/equipping]… to kind of create a feeling of local and not individual engagement.

A related challenge concerns gender aspects. There was a hope that the initiative would pave the way for women to move into society, and many women did express interest. However, one year later, all the active volunteers are men and the project leader expresses uncertainty when considering how a female volunteer would be seen;

for example, when backing people. Also, a common notion among all the fire service respondents is that communication and learning is top down; i.e., the fire services train the volunteers and tell them what to do, but there is no mechanism for the volunteers to provide feedback or share their knowledge. The project instigator is somewhat self-critical about this:

> This is true, and we devoted no time to them teaching us. It's an important point, that this should go both ways...It's not completely unproblematic having a group of more or less ethnic Swedes going to XXX [sub-area] and telling people "this is how it works".

As the initiative progressed, Facebook (FB) groups were started in various sub-areas of the municipality. However, there is much more activity in those groups that are based in more well-off areas, where the majority of volunteers are of Swedish ethnicity. Neither of the two volunteers in the interviews have joined a FB group.

Another perceived challenge is, again, language. It is not optimal to send just any volunteer, but rather one who knows the particular language of those involved in an emergency or the dominant language in the given sub-area. There is also the general challenge of evaluating the concept, both qualitatively and in terms of efficiency; for example, lives saved, response times, and monetary value. Since this is an initiative in progress, no such plans had been made at the time of this study. However, they are important for motivating the spread of the concept among municipalities and for decision-making by politicians, among others.

4.5 Needs

The fire-service respondents agree that the major need is to expand the initiative, in terms of having more volunteers acting as safety persons/first responders, making it locality rather than individual based, as expressed by the project leader in January 2019:

> As things are now, the project has not really expanded to the extent that we want it to. I think that with the technical prerequisites that we have and with the design that technology makes possible...it should be possible to expand more. The technology, at the moment, does not limit us.

The volunteers also see the need to expand, and one of them suggested that they partake in the recruitment process; for example, by engaging colleagues at their workplace so that they could go on alerts together, knowing each other beforehand. Apart from this, the volunteers did not express many needs, even though they were asked explicitly. One of them mentioned a warmer jacket and that exercises are good.

A concrete need, however, concerns the ICT solution. The volunteers being interviewed relied on the SMS lists and mentioned that they sometimes receive the wrong address from the rescue services, a problem they share with the fire services (since it is the back office systems that sometimes send incorrect coordinates or information e.g. indicating roads), thus delaying response time:

> I don't always know exactly what building or tenement. With a straight address, it would be perfect. In...[sub-area] there are two roads that are often mixed up in the SMSs. Not even the fire station always knows. [Volunteer 2]

In the app version, this have partly been addressed by the supplier adding an additional map to navigate among e.g. roads that cross or run in parallel, and the volunteers would thus like to have an extended app version that includes a map and inbuilt GPS guidance to the emergency site. Also, the project leader mentioned the importance of the app but that some structure, templates and matching is needed to send the "right" volunteer to the "right" site, reaching different roles, competences and language groups:

> If a certain group of immigrants becomes so dominant that we cannot reach that group, then we would need an app that could reach that specific group.

5   Discussion: Digitalization as an Enabler of Public-Sector Innovation and Co-production

Public-sector innovation is rapidly transforming our society at a global level, as are initiatives directed specifically towards citizen engagement and co-production [2, 3]. The emerging trends all feature digitalization and modern ICT as an enabler. Nevertheless, as argued by [9], there are relatively few studies (in emergency response, [7] is an exception), that focus explicitly on the direct relation between co-production and ICT artifacts, even though it has been pointed out that ICT can support co-production [22]. Even fewer, if any, studies focus explicitly on the ICT artifact itself, as a catalyst of the co-production. This study's findings illustrate the need to bridge this gap. At first glance, the initiative seems broad and the ICT artifact plays a less than central role, with a basic SMS solution working sufficiently in most cases, even though maps and GPS guidance have been requested. However, data analysis indicates that, for the initiative to be successful and expand, the design of the ICT artifact can contribute significantly. Future app solutions should be able to handle calibration of the volunteer concept; for example, matching availability, competence, role, and language with a specific emergency situation and/or sub-area, by adding functions allowing for dynamic resource dispatching. In order for the whole system to work, there is the corresponding need to do a thorough analysis of the necessary features and interfaces in the fire services back office systems who are to provide this information. Also the overall infrastructure need to be handled, not the least since the office systems sometimes send the wrong address and/or inexact coordinates. In terms of service design, an emergency response process can be divided into two parts, the service-providing process and the services supporting process [23]. Two pay attention to both these processes, including giving correct information to mobile solutions with attractive, easy-to-handle interfaces, and to improved communication between the fire services and the volunteers, may also contribute to more volunteers acting on the alerts. This in its turn includes the necessity to involve additional stakeholders of e.g. the fire services, the PSAP, the suppliers of the back-office systems, and possibly the ambulance services.

Also, in many sub-areas there are frequent alerts but few volunteers responding to them. A more secure solution with function allowing withdrawal if an emergency should turn into something that is dangerous to the volunteers (e.g. toxic fumes, gunfire) is added, this may reduce fear about responding to an alert and stimulate long-term engagement. In relation, similar studies in rural areas [9] have shown that the volunteers, even when collective insurances are provided, are not sufficiently protected by the current Swedish legal system. To address policy and liability issues seem even more important in areas exposed to high rates of criminality risk, and may also influence the volunteer engagement in a positive way.

From a wider public-sector perspective, the bi-directional influence of technology and various forms of governance has been recognized for over a decade and pointed out recently [24, 25]. Relating this to the research field of IS, the discipline has often drawn upon other disciplines when needed [26]. Several recent studies have claimed the benefits of and need for a cross-fertilization of policy science and IS research perspective, relating explicitly to emerging forms of government in an era of digitalization [14–16]. This study's finding are in line with this research since digitalization/ICT development needs to consider e.g. regulations and laws on what volunteers are allowed to do and what information the alerts can and cannot include. Below, this discussion is taken further, arguing for a wider integration of research perspectives, when turning to excluded areas and initiatives involving the residents living there.

5.1 Citizen Engagement, Co-production and Co-creation in Excluded Areas

Socially vulnerable and/or excluded areas are not new phenomena, in either western or non-western countries, and parallel societal structures and gang criminality have been studied for a long time [5, 27]. As socio-economic gaps are expanding rapidly, related challenges now also include countries where thus far they have not been so tangible. Sweden is a typical example. The country took many immigrants during the refugee streams of 2012–2016, and is currently struggling to provide them with opportunities for integration and access to the Swedish labor market. Relating this to co-production, citizen engagement initiatives from "the inside", where a community's own residents are recruited to handle criminality and to work with (instead of against) the police have long existed, for example, in shantytowns across the world; albeit not without challenges. Still, [28] argues that more research on city neighborhoods affecting the will to engage in co-production, is needed. Their own study concludes that:

> The answer is...straightforward. Neighbourhoods do make a difference in explaining co-production. However, the social capital, rather than the social status, of the neighbourhood explains the difference between neighbourhoods (p. 105).

This notion may contribute to explaining parts of this study's results, where the volunteers seem willing to engage but less secure about acting as a safety person or first responder. When making a brief comparison with other parts of Sweden, in rural, sparsely populated areas dominated by people of Swedish ethnicity, a different picture emerges (a full comparison is not possible since these studies have spanned longer time periods with more volunteer respondents). Here, volunteerism is a collective effort based on long-term social relations, sometimes also including the victims of accidents. Volunteers never go on an alert alone, and they have been more active in both putting explicit requests to the fire services; for example, for trauma support (while one of the volunteers in this study claimed that this is not needed because he had seen worse things in his home country). They also suggested added functionality to their dispatch ICT solutions, sometimes even implementing their own functions [9].

In relation to this, co-production is often related to co-creation [3], but as increasing numbers of ICT applications are easily available off-the-shelf from commercial suppliers, co-creation of the artifact itself is often forgotten. This is evident also in this study where the commercial app that some-sub areas use has not been created together with users, and do not include the functions for GPS navigation, calibration, language and withdrawal as suggested in Sect. 5 above. This can be compared to [9], in which a mobile app prototype was developed together with end-users (semi-professionals and volunteer first responders in rural areas) along with the surrounding infrastructure (e.g. training, equipment, legal aspects), even though commercial applications for the purpose existed. This resulted in additional and partially different functions, based on user needs and in line with other features of the collaborations, which might contribute to a more efficient first response and long-term engagement. Co-creation, and corresponding IS development approaches that include user involvement, lean on the active participation of users, when developing both the ICT artifacts themselves and the surrounding infrastructure [12, 29]. In particular, PD, which has clear political and ideological roots, has been applied to provide exposed societal groups with an opportunity to influence their own situation and environment; for example, in urban planning, in third-world countries, and among charities working for homeless people [30]. Gender relations have also been highlighted by the PD community; for example, how they affect power structures in design groups [31]. The need to achieve the co-creation/PD of ICT support is also highlighted by this study. But this implies that you have volunteers to work with in the first place. To date, relatively few volunteers go on the alerts and women volunteers do not exist at all. It was also perceived as difficult to access the volunteers as study respondents (they did not want to be interviewed, which may have been due to such issues as language barriers). The challenges are in line with a recent study on six co-design sessions, suggesting that vulnerable user groups cannot be approached in the same way as in conventional user involvement processes, and proposing alternative design frameworks and inter-sectionalist perspectives [32]. Leaning on co-creation, co-design and PD such frameworks and methods for user involvement should thus be considered in future expansion of the collaboration and design of related infrastructure and ICT artefacts. It is also plausible that the initiative would benefit from adding research perspectives from others disciplines, to expand the knowledge base and enable participation. Examples may include sociology, inter-sectionalist perspectives, and criminology. The author of this study has previously argued that there is a need for pronounced inter-disciplinary development teams in the case of emerging collaborative forms of public-sector innovation, including cross-sector collaboration and the use of volunteers [8]. Adding the above competences to more traditional systems (or business) development teams seem important in the context of the current study.

6 Conclusion and Future Work

This study set out to explore the concept of citizen co-production engaging them as volunteer first responders in socially vulnerable areas with a focus on aspects including the benefits, challenges and needs, and with the ICT artifact as a catalyst. The study concludes that volunteers with basic equipment and training can make a significant difference if they arrive first at an emergency site. The major challenge is actually having them respond to an alert and go to the site. Other challenges relate to gender and to increasing the opportunities for immigrant women in Swedish society, to language barriers, and to changing the one-way communication from the fire services to the volunteers into a two-way flow. The ICT solutions provided are basic and accessible because they are installed on the volunteers' own mobile phones. Still, they are central to engagement, allowing for the dispatching of volunteers who are near to an emergency. Current solutions work sufficiently well, but for optimal usage and expansion of the initiative, ICT solutions supporting dynamic resource allocation (role, competence, language, situation), communication among volunteers and withdrawal functions are suggested.

Previous research has argued that the need to mix perspectives from IS research with policy science becomes particularly pressing in a public sector where new government forms relying on digitalization – for example, governance, policy networks, co-production/we-government, and citizen engagement – are rapidly emerging [14, 16]. In particular, policy and liability issues needs to be addressed in the emerging volunteer first responder initiatives. An additional conclusion drawn from this study is that additional inter-sectional perspectives and disciplines, not least from the field of sociology, become equally important, in this and similar initiatives, in a society where they are likely to increase. Sweden is perceived as progressive in terms of organized, long-term, civil citizen engagement in emergency response while most international studies tend to focus on issues such as on-site volunteers, large-scale crisis management and crowdsourcing [9]. As pointed out by [9], the types of emergencies have both similarities and differences but to be able to use the same volunteers in them would be beneficial, since they would be accustomed to the ICT solutions and work procedures. This indicates that this study could provide inspiration for similar initiatives but also in relation to large-scale crisis management. A limitation of the study is that only two volunteers were interviewed and thus the perspective from the fire services is most prevalent. At the same time, the pictures painted by the fire services and the volunteers overlap in many respects, somewhat compensating for this.

In future work, the app will be further developed and also connected to fire detectors in a number of selected tenements, to also include unintentional fires, for which excluded areas are also over-represented [18]. Research and co-creation/co-design will be continued with specific attention to vulnerable groups, e.g. in workshops and focus groups, to reach more volunteers, the municipalities, the fire services, the PSAP, and other relevant stakeholders, in order to address the challenges and needs identified in this study. The gender and ethnicity aspects will be addressed by involving a researcher who has studied them previously in IS, public-sector, and emergency-response contexts. Qualitative and quantitative variables will be identified, in order to be able to evaluate the initiative and its transferability to other, similar contexts, both in Sweden and internationally. At a more general level, it is of specific interest to look further into how the original concept, first developed in sparsely-populated, rural areas, can be transferred to urban contexts, and what modifications, for example, in training and the handling of challenges, should take place.. In relation to large-scale crises, future research could focus on this double use of volunteers, in Sweden not the least since the government is currently planning for large-scale digitalized coordination of volunteers, in the after-math of the 2014 and 2018 widespread wild forest fires.

Acknowledgements. This study has been made possible by financial support from the Swedish Civil Contingencies Agency and the Swedish Fire Research Board.

References

1. Haddow, G., Bullock, J., Coppola, D.P.: Introduction to Emergency Management, 5th edn. Butterworth-Heinemann, Waltham (2013)
2. Linders, D.: From e-government to we-government: defining a typology for citizen coproduction in the age of social media. Gov. Inf. Q. **29**(4), 446–454 (2012)
3. Alford, J., O'Flynn, J.: Rethinking Public Service Delivery: Managing with External Providers. Palgrave Macmillan, Hampshire (2012)
4. Guldåker, N., Hallin, P.-O.: Spatio-temporal patterns of intentional fires, social stress and socio-economic determinants: a case study of Malmö, Sweden. Fire Saf. J. **70**, 71–80 (2014)
5. Chalfin, A., McCrary, J.: Criminal deterrence: a review of the literature. J. Econ. Lit. **55**(1), 5–48 (2017)
6. David, E., Enarson, E.: The Women of Katrina: How Gender, Race, and Class Matter in an American Disaster. Vanderbilt University Press, Nashville (2012)
7. Díaz, P., Carroll, J.M., Aedo, I.: Coproduction as an approach to technology-mediated citizen participation in emergency management. Future Internet **8**(3), 41 (2016)
8. Pilemalm, S.: Participatory design in emerging civic engagement initiatives in the new public Sector: applying PD concepts in resource-scarce organizations. ACM Trans. Hum.-Comput.-Interact. **5**(1), 5–26 (2018)
9. Ramsell, E., Pilemalm, S., Andersson Granberg, T.: Using volunteers for emergency response in rural areas: network collaboration factors and IT support in the case of enhanced neighbors. In: Proceedings of the 14th International Conference on Information Systems for Crisis Response and Management (ISCRAM), Albi, France (2019)
10. AvBason, C.: Leading Public-Sector Innovation: Co-creating for a Better Society, 2nd edn. The Policy Press, Bristol (2018)
11. Ostrom, E.: Crossing the great divide: coproduction, synergy, and development. World Dev. **24**(6), 1073–1087 (2016)
12. Schuler, D., Namioka, A. (eds.): Participatory Design: Principles and Practices. Lawrence Erlbaum Associates Inc., Hillsdale (1993)
13. Ostrom, A.L., et al.: Moving forward and making a difference: research priorities for the science of service. J. Serv. Res. **13**(1), 4–36 (2010)
14. Melin, U., Wihlborg, E.: Balanced and integrated e-government implementation: exploring the crossroad of public policy-making and information systems project management processes. Transform. Gov.: People Process Policy **12**(2), 191–208 (2018)

15. Janowski, T., Pardo, T.A., Davies, J.: Government information networks: mapping electronic governance cases through public administration. Gove. Inf. Q. **29**(1), 1–10 (2012)
16. Gil-Garcia, J.R., Dawes, S.S., Pardo, T.A.: Digital government and public management research: finding the crossroads. Public Manag. Rev. **20**(5), 633–646 (2018)
17. Wijkström, F., Zimmer, A. (eds.): Nordic Civil Society at a Cross-Roads: Transforming the Popular Movement Tradition. Nomos, Baden-Baden (2011)
18. Urinboyev, R.: Migration and parallel legal orders in Russia. Aleksanteri Insight-Expert Opinion Series 4, (2016)
19. Sefyrin J., Pilemalm, S.: "It's more important to be fast than to be informed": gender, age, disability and ethnicity in relation to IT in the Swedish Rescue Services. In: Proceedings of the 13th International Conference on Information Systems for Crisis Response and Management (ISCRAM), Rio de Janeiro, Brazil (2016)
20. Denzin, N., Lincoln, Y.S.: Entering the Field of Qualitative Research: Strategies of Qualitative Inquiry. Sage Publications, Thousand Oaks (1998)
21. Myers, M.: Qualitative Research in Business and Management. Sage Publications, Thousand Oaks (2009)
22. Verschuere, V., Brandsen, T., Pestoff, V.: Co-production: the state of the art in research and the future agenda. VOLUNTAS: Int. J. Volunt. Non-Profit Organ. **23**(4), 1083–1101 (2012)
23. Kling, R., McKim, G., King, A.: A bit more to IT: scholarly communication forums as socio-technical interaction networks. J. Am. Soc. Inf. Sci. Technol. **54**(1), 47–67 (2003)
24. Shan, S., Wang, L., Li, L.: Modeling of emergency response decision-making process using stochastic Petri net: an e-service perspective. Inf. Technol. Manag. **13**(4), 363–376 (2012)
25. Loukis, E., Janssen, M., Dawes, S., Zheng, L.: Evolving ICT and governance in organizational networks: conceptual and theoretical foundations. Electron. Mark. **26**(1), 7–14 (2016)
26. Watson, R.T., Kelly, G.G., Galliers, R.D., Brancheau, J.C.: Key issues in information systems management: an international perspective. J. Manag. Inf. Syst. **13**(4), 91–115 (1997)
27. Klein, M., Maxson, C.: Street Gang Patterns and Policies. Oxford University Press, Oxford (2006)
28. Thijssen, P., van Dooren, W.: Who you are/where you live: do neighborhood characteristics explain co-production? Int. Rev. Adm. Sci. **82**(1), 88–109 (2015)
29. Hillgren, P., Seravalli, A., Emilson, A.: Prototyping and infrastructuring in design for social innovation. CoDesign **7**(3–4), 169–183 (2011)
30. Halskov, K., Brodersen Hansen, N.B.: The diversity of participatory design research practice at PDC 2002–2012. Int. J. Hum.-Comput. Stud. **74**, 81–92 (2015)
31. Balka, E.: Participatory design in women's organizations: the social world of organizational structure and the gendered nature of expertise. Gender, Work Organ. **4**(2), 99–115 (1997)
32. Dietrich, T., Trischler, J., Schuster, L., Rundle-Thiele, S.: Co-designing services with vulnerable consumers. J. Serv. Theory Pract. **27**(3), 663–688 (2017)

Digitalizing Crisis Management Training

Monika Magnusson[1]([⊠]) [iD], Geir Ove Venemyr[2], Peter Bellström[1] [iD],
and Bjørn Tallak Bakken[2]

[1] Karlstad University, 651 88 Karlstad, Sweden
{monika.magnusson,peter.bellstrom}@kau.se
[2] Høgskolen i Innlandet, 2418 Elverum, Norway
{geir.venemyr,bjorn.bakken}@inn.no

Abstract. The ongoing digital transformation in government has enabled
innovative changes in operational processes and service. However, while e-
services and social media are widely adopted, earlier studies indicate that this
transformation is still being awaited in other areas, such as crisis or disaster
preparedness. Recent events such as the 2018 wildfires in several parts of
Europe, as well as empirical research, highlight the need for more (systematic)
training of local governments' crisis management teams. Conventional training
methods are time- and space-dependent and require long-term planning, making
it complicated to increase the extent of training. In this interdisciplinary study,
we report on the results from the Swedish-Norwegian CriseIT project that aimed
to develop information systems (IS) for crisis management training. The purpose
of the article is to describe information systems designed to support local
governments' crisis management training and to discuss how these artefacts
could improve crisis management training practices.

Keywords: Crisis management training · Crisis training software ·
Computer-based training · Disaster management · Design science research

1 Introduction

Global warming and terror attacks are just two examples of phenomena that have put
crisis preparedness at the top of the agenda of government agencies world-wide. Crisis
exercises are considered a key component for increasing preparedness [28]. Prior
studies have detected problems with conventional training such as lack of time and
other resources for planning and executing exercises and concerns that exercises are
performed too seldom and/or with too few members of the organization [13]. Other
problems include inadequate assessment of the effectiveness of training, difficulties in
defining a suitable training content, providing feedback, and transferring the lessons
learnt to future crises [23]. Researchers have also identified a lack of systematic
approach to training [28] and too little focus on longitudinal learning processes [26].

In this article, we propose information systems (IS), developed in the Swedish-
Norwegian R&D project CriseIT, as a complement to conventional crisis or disaster
management training methods. In-depth interviews in the CriseIT project with 19
respondents from 16 organizations handling societal crisis at local, regional and
national levels showed that the organizations wanted more training, especially for the

© IFIP International Federation for Information Processing 2019
Published by Springer Nature Switzerland AG 2019
P. Panagiotopoulos et al. (Eds.): ePart 2019, LNCS 11686, pp. 102–113, 2019.
https://doi.org/10.1007/978-3-030-27397-2_9

strategic level [11]. Regrettably, the organizations found this difficult to accomplish in practice, due to a lack of resources and the current training methods. For managers to devote half a day or more to an exercise and for safety coordinators to set a date, construct a crisis scenario etc. can be challenging tasks. Scenarios are often planned from scratch and the ability to collaborate in planning and reuse of exercises are requested by the organizations [12]. In smaller municipalities, a safety coordinator, sometime working part-time with the assignment, might be solely responsible for organizing the organizations' training [14]. Few of the organizations organized any individual training.

Lukosch et al. [10] suggest that computer-based training, in comparison to traditional time- and space-dependent training, offers higher flexibility (efficacy) and improved resource-efficiency. Whether these advantages are being realized in practice remains to be seen. Studies of ongoing usage, effects and learning outcomes from computer-based training are rare, as are user need analyses [13], indicating that the field of computer-based crisis management training is still in its infancy.

Organizations interviewed in the CriseIT project were aware that different IS for crisis training existed on the market, but few had used them. Neither were the national, and freely provided, systems WIS (Sweden) and CIM (Norway) used for training to any considerable extent. Limited functionality for training and low usability were mentioned as possible explanations. Instead, crisis training exercises were often planned, executed and documented using regular office software. In this article, we argue for the need for new IS for crisis management training in local government. These digital tools should support both trainers and trainees and be well grounded in the user contexts, if they are be useful and adopted. As current training practices are well functioning in many aspects, the IS should complement, not replace conventional training. The overall objective of the IS artefacts presented is to enable expanded crisis management training, in a systematic and resource-efficient manner. The purpose of the article is to *describe information systems artefacts designed to support local governments' crisis management training and to discuss how these could improve crisis management training practices.*

We use the concept 'crisis management training' to represent both training for individual roles in a crisis, and collaborative exercises, for "unplanned natural or man-made events with a sudden and severe negative impact on human live [sic], the functioning of society and/or the physical environment" ([24], p. 61).

2 Literature Review

The fact that crises are rare often means that few in an organization's crisis management team have actual experience of handling them. Sinclair et al. [22] argue that "[...] emergency management training must include mechanisms that substitute for the practice and experience afforded by working life in most organizations. This involves exercising" (p. 59). Exercises also serve other purposes, such as testing the viability of the response network [19] the crisis management or disaster plan [18] or fostering relationships between key personnel [24]. Based on experiences from over a hundred exercises in twelve municipalities during a ten-year period, van Laere and Lindblom

[26] argue for a continuous training pro-gram with recurrent exercises in various formats to spur the long-term development of an organization's crisis management capacity. They suggest three development phases: (1) obtaining role understanding; (2) developing skills and practices; and (3) mastering self-evaluation and adaption.

Despite the seeming consensus in earlier research about the necessity of training, earlier studies also indicate that there is a lack of a systemic approach to training [28]. Such an approach can be found in the management training methodology developed from a meta-analysis of training and development studies by Eduardo Salas et al. [21]. Salas et al. [21] stress the importance of viewing training "as a system", and not a once-off event. The methodology was intended for general 'management' training, but can also be used for emergency training [27]. Seven basic phases were defined by Salas et al. [21], see Fig. 1. Phase 1, *Student Need Analysis*, involves determining who needs training (audience), and what should be trained (content). In Phase 2, *Educational Competencies*, general skills-based competences for crisis management are described and compared with the skill inventory information from Phase 1. The analysis in the first two phases indicates the direction of the rest of the learning process. Phase 3, *Learning Objectives*, consists of specifying measurable training goals. After the training goals have been set, simulation scenarios are developed in Phase 4, *Trigger Events Exercises*. The scenarios and events provide opportunities to influence behaviour and practice within the relevant field of competence. In Phase 5, *Performance Measures*, process and performance measurements are developed. Without measuring performance, it is impossible to improve behaviour or competence, provide feedback, or document learning. In Phase 6, *Performance Diagnosis*, the measurements from Phase 5 are compared with the training goals defined in Phase 3 to assess if the training is effective. Finally, Phase 7, *Developmental Feedback*, involves the development of constructive feedback based on performance and process data. Feedback allows the scheme to be called training and not just simulation.

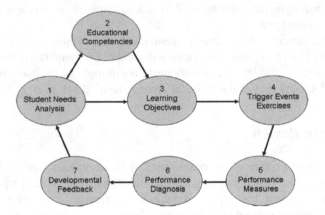

Fig. 1. Stages for the successful implementation of simulation based training in management education (Salas et al. [21], p. 565).

Information systems can positively affect an organization by improving its efficacy, efficiency and/or effectiveness [6]. Higher efficacy refers to improvements in volumes or quality of the output, while improved efficiency is a measurement of the output in relation to the resources used (ibid.). Effectiveness, finally, refers to the system's contribution to the purpose of higher-level systems. If and how computer-based training indeed increase efficacy, efficacy and effectiveness remains to be seen. Among the earlier research studies from the IS field we found useful in our work are the conceptual framework for understanding training issues in Sniezek et al. [23], the generic systems modules presented by Reuter et al. [20]. Also, the flexible and user driven simulation exercises presented in Yao et al. [29], the PANDORA system for co-located, distributed or synchronous training [4] and the IS for tabletop exercises presented by Asproth et al. [3] and Araz et al. [2]. Furthermore, we have studied the participatory design process described by Lukosh et al. [10], and the serious gaming solution for individual training presented by Van de Ven et al. [25]. Moreover, Garzón and Acevedo [7] have done a meta-analysis of the impact of AR on students' learning effectiveness. These and other studies have guided the design processes presented later in the article.

3 Method

This study reports results from the R&D project CriseIT. CriseIT run in the border region of Värmland and Innland, during 2016–2019. The main aim was to improve crisis preparedness in the regions by developing IS in close collaboration between public organizations, universities, enterprises and non-government organizations (NGOs).

The overall research approach can be described as design science research (DSR) as the aim was to design IS artefacts. Four IS prototypes or what Hevner et al. [9] call instantiations have been developed: *a training process management tool* (T1), *an individual training tool* (T2), *a web-based collaborative training tool* (T3) for 'tabletop-like' exercises and *an operational decision support system* (T4) for 3D-based training. The prototypes are presented in the next section. Although used in the IS field for more than 30 years, there are diverse views and application of the DSR paradigm [17]. Numerous articles present theoretical and conceptual guidelines for DSR (e.g. [9, 16]). However, the body of somewhat diverse guidelines, frameworks and objectives, makes it difficult to present DSR studies without conflicting with some of the rules [17]. The DSR process model from Peffers et al. [16] represents the overall approach for our work, although the detailed DSR processes have varied between the different artefacts. Furthermore, we adhere to the seven well-known guidelines for DSR presented by Hever et al. [9]. Through in-depth interviews with respondents from organizations at all levels in both countries and by using user-centered development methods, we especially emphasized the guideline of establishing problem relevance. Also, we have adopted the 'cycle view' of DSR first presented as three designs cycles in Hevner et al. [8]. We believe that while the model of Peffers et al. [16] guides the researchers' activities, the design cycle view helps the researchers to concretize the activities, e.g. in mapping the environment for the artefact(s) to be produced. In addition, the design cycle view well illustrates the iterative approach we used in our design processes.

4 The Design Processes

The cross-sector focus in this study, together with the aim of finding generic solutions for local and regional governments, meant that multi-actor design processes needed to take place. The methodology of Salas et al. [21] (Fig. 1) was used to guide the design of the artefacts as were research on decision-making in crisis situations [e.g. 5]. Furthermore, methods for change analysis and development of 'work-system' have guided the design process (e.g. [1]). Also, the results from earlier studies on crisis management training and IS for crisis training served as a starting point. Beynon Davies' [6] extension of the model for information system success developed by DeLoan and McLean in 1992 has served as a guide for evaluations of the artefacts.

For both *the training process management tool* (T1) and *the operational decision support system* (T4) an agile approach to system development, inspired by Scrum, was used. T1 was developed through a series of 10 time-boxed iterations, called sprints. This iterative process secured a user-oriented approach, and the sprints enabled creative and synergetic meetings with the team members. Similarly, the development of T4 took place in increments or iterations, with feedback from prospective users and crisis management experts after each increment/iteration. Both T1 and T4 had been evaluated by several students groups, of which many also are practitioners, and by project stakeholders, and show promising results, for example in ensuring a systematic approach to exercises. T1 was evaluated in approximately 15 field studies (cf. [9]) in crisis handling organizations for the planning of crisis training activities. The evaluations provided feedback on utility, systems quality, ease-of-use and other parameters. T4 has so far mainly been evaluated with a focus on overall utility, interface/ease-of-use and identifying defects in what Hevner et al. [9] label functional testing. The project CriseIT2 will more systematically evaluate the artefact and further demonstrate its utility with respect to training effectiveness, ease of use (both when used locally and distributed), and costs.

For *the individual training tool* (T2) and *the collaborative training tool* (T3), an interdisciplinary research team performed in-depth, semi-structured interviews with 19 security coordinators and other personnel responsible for civil contingency management at local (municipal), regional, and national government levels in both countries. The interviews were important for the mapping of the user context, and for the identification of problems and perceived opportunities with an increased digitalization of crisis management training.

Furthermore, 17 workshop were organized. A majority of the stakeholders involved worked at municipalities on either side of the border, often as safety coordinators. Problems, opportunities and systems requirements were identified and prioritized by the stakeholder, and system prototypes were evaluated. Primarily two target groups were identified, trainers and trainees, i.e. safety coordinators responsible for planning and executing exercises and crisis management teams in local and regional government agencies that need to train/exercise. The workshops and interviews revealed that the planning processes differ somewhat from one situation to another although several respondents stressed the importance of a systematic approach to ensure quality. For example, while there are national guidelines as well as an agreement among the respondents that the purpose and goals of an exercise should be established first, the respondents admit that is common to start defining the scenario before the purpose has been determined. The problems, opportunities and requirements identified are described in Magnusson et al. [12] and will only be briefly presented here. As for problems, several organizations experienced problems connected to organizational constraints in personnel, budget, or insufficient IS support. In addition, the expenditure of time in planning and executing current training methods were problematic, as were the lack of a systematic approach, especially to the follow-up of exercises. Some respondents found it complex to design exercises and to know the needs of training audience. Several respondents considered it difficult to keep up the organizational knowledge due to employee-turnover. New (digital) IS for crisis training were thought to enable both individual training and collaborative exercises, co-located and distributed, synchronous and asynchronous, on any device, and in short sessions. This increased flexibility, together with multimedia or gaming features, was seen as an opportunity to get more actors/trainees involved and/or to train more often. Also, new IS were considered to facilitate collaboration and reuse of exercises material, thus contributing to more resources-efficient training. Several risks and potential disadvantages of IT tools were also acknowledged, including that digital training would replace conventional training, and that technical problems would arise. Also, 17 distributed screen-sharing prototyping sessions took place in which users' needs and objectives were identified, refined and validated in what Hevner et al. [9] describe as functional testing. T3 prototypes were also evaluated through what Hevner et al. [9] label structural testing in three "walk-through" sessions with target users. Later, T3 was evaluated in 4 minor field studies (cf. [9]) with approximately 2–10 participants in distributed, asynchronous exercises. A mixed group of researchers and practitioners participated in the first two exercises. The next two exercises in T3 were planned and executed in real settings in the application context. One exercise was cross-border. T2 was evaluated in the functional testing of interfaces and field studies for utility and ease-of-use in more than 30 planning or training sessions. T2 and T3 will also be further evaluated during the Interreg CriseIT2 project.

5   The Artefacts

Four software prototypes were developed. T1 and T4 were developed in Norway; T2 and T3 in Sweden. While the prototypes were largely developed in this order, the development processes overlapped somewhat. There were several reasons for constructing four separate tools. First, one of the tools, T1, already existed as a prototype that was refined and adapted to the target group in the project. Second, two of the tools, T1 and T4, are to be commercialized and two, T2 and T3, are open/free to use. Finally, as the tools are still under construction, and in different development stages, the separation into four different prototypes was deemed most practical. In the future, it is possible that all or some of them will be integrated with each other (e.g. T1 with T2 and T3, or T2 with T3). Next, we present the four prototypes.

T1: The Training Process Management Tool MeTracker. T1 guides the planner and offers supporting questions and suggestions to ease the planning process. In the first step, the user can create a new training process, edit, or copy established processes. Step 2 guides the user through a Training Need Analysis (TNA) for the training organization. A Main Training Objective (MTO) is established for a longitudinal training process (a series of exercises) and operationalized in Training objectives (TO). Training objectives are categorized into different generic areas of expertise (situational awareness, leadership and organisation, collaboration, decision-making and communication). TOs are then further operationalized by Evaluation Points (EP). In step 3, the training sessions and exercises are planned in detailed Activities. Activities will vary in form and duration, from basic seminars and workshops, to tabletop and input-response exercises, and full-scale exercise(s). Step 4 results in an overview of the planned activities and how the TOs are covered. It is also possible to edit, copy or establish new activities. Step 4 has several options for detailed observation (e.g. photos or video clips) and evaluation based on the predefined criteria. Step 5 is used for the final evaluation, presentation of results and to formulate lessons learned, recommendations and training reports (see Fig. 2). This includes a graphic visualization of present, wanted and achieved status, linked to each area of expertise involved in the training process. All input collected in T1 is stored, and master documents are prepared and issued on the basis of this information. The system provides templates for reports, etc.

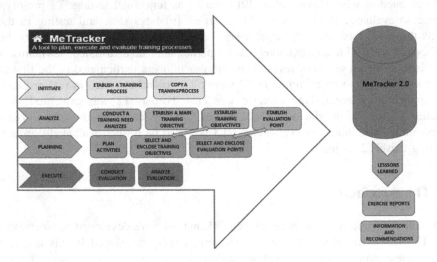

Fig. 2. The MeTracker system.

With its holistic view of the training process and systematic stepwise approach, T1 is based on well-known theoretical frameworks for management training [21]. It supports all the phases in Salas et al., although it does not include functionality for the actual training assignments or exercises. By defining long-term goals and regarding training as a processes consisting of several training activities, as well as enabling reuse, T1 is well in line with the recommendations in van Laere and Lindblom [26]. The guidance of the process, the built-in support for training need analysis, etc., all provide a good foundation for improved quality (efficacy) as well as resource efficiency and doing the right things (effectiveness) (c.f. [6]).

T2: The Individual Training Tool. The individual training tool (T2) was developed to enable individual training, and has two main user groups: trainers and trainees. The tool is a responsive web application that make it possible to plan and conduct individual training sessions independently of time and place, provided that the device used has an Internet connection. T2 is still an early prototype, however it is still possible to create, share, copy, edit and search existing training assignments. An assignment could for example include a short learning material (text, video etc.) as an introduction, followed by a quiz or open-ended questions. The individual crisis training tool (T2) can be mapped as a useful tool to support Phases 2, 4 and 5 in Salas et al. [21]. It could thus be used to facilitate understanding of the (individual) role, something that van Laere and Lindholm [26] suggested to be a vital part of building up crisis management skills in organizations. The T2 tool offers good possibilities for increased individual training, i.e. improved efficacy (cf. [6]).

T3: The Collaborative Training Tool. The T3 tool was developed for collaborative training sessions independently of time, place and device. Like T2, the T3 tool is a (responsive) and free web-based application. In addition, T3 has two main user groups – trainers and trainees – and therefore has interfaces for both creating (planning) and conducting collaborative training sessions. T3 is built for 'tabletop-like', discussion-based exercises. The trainer or a group of trainers plan and create an exercise for a collaborative training session. Various manuals and guidelines from authorities at different levels in both countries were important in the design of our artefacts (e.g. [15]). While planning and creating an exercise, the trainer adds modules (sections) which in turn contain the actual content of the exercise such as text describing what had happened and tasks/challenges for the trainees. The tasks are to be solved in collaboration by the exercise team. So far, only text ('comments') has been used as input from the trainees but other data formats will also be tested in the future. Modules can be asynchronous or synchronous, i.e. the trainees may perform some or all of the tasks at different points of time, although within a given timeframe. The trainer decides when each module should be accessible to the trainees by giving them a date and time stamp when they should be visible. If necessary, the trainer can intervene in the exercise by communicating with the trainees in chat rooms, changing the modules, their order or pace. Figure 3 illustrates the collaborative training tool. By clicking on the plus sign to the right, the module is expanded and its content is shown.

The crisis training tool for collaborative exercises (T3) mainly supports Phase 4 but also Phase 5 in Salas et al. [21] and recurrent exercises/series of exercises, as recommended by van Laere and Lindblom [26]. Last but not least, a free and flexible tool such as this, offering distributed and asynchronous exercises, should increase the volume of training at a low cost, thus improving both efficacy and efficiency (c.f. [6]).

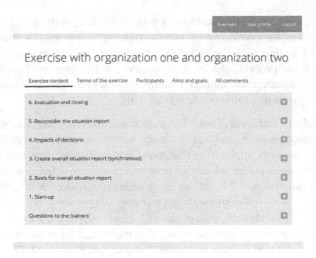

Fig. 3. The collaborative training tool.

T4: The Operational Decision Support System (O-DSS). The O-DSS is based on Microsoft's Hololens Technology (https://www.microsoft.com/en-us/hololens), which is an application of Augmented Reality (AR). It is designed to assist decision makers in crisis management situations to acquire shared situation awareness, as well as to serve as an environment for training decision making at the operational level. T4 support training on decision support, communication, collaboration etc., distributed or co-located. User interaction occurs through an interface that allows the user to look at the simulated environment through a "virtual overlay" on the real world outside. Using HoloLens goggles, a large map, the size of a standard classroom, is projected "around" the participant. The map consists of a "Disaster Town/Municipal". Participants can orientate themselves in the map by moving their heads and walking around "in the map". Some glasses have a "Game Master" feature that allows the carrier to add objects to the map (police car, fire truck, medical car, etc.). Scenarios such as landslides and forest fires are included. Users can manipulate the simulated environment in various ways without using any other "gadgets" than their fingers and hand movements. The O-DSS allows up to four players or decision makers, who can form teams at will or join predefined teams. Each player may make decisions in order to manage an incident, usually involving allocating resources of the right type and volume to the site of the incident. Color-coding of the dome indicates status. For example, red code means that the situation is critical and resources are needed immediately. Points may be rewarded to both team and individual players, in accordance with the successfulness of their allocations. The equipment operates without any PC attached, and connects wirelessly to the internet. This tool has been used for tabletop and input-response exercises and has been tested for both tactical "on-scene command" and for staff training at operational levels. Like T3, this tool mainly supports the fourth phase in Salas et al. [21] but also the fifth and sixth phases, as it is possible to record the training sessions and use the recording for after-action reviews and improved feedback.

6   Discussion and Conclusions

The purpose of this article is to describe information systems designed in the CriseIT project to support local governments' crisis management training and to discuss how these artefacts could improve crisis management training practices. The IS presented contribute to the computer-based training field by providing novel examples of how the entire crisis training process can be systematically supported from analysis of training needs to follow-up of lessons learnt, while also offering functionality that enable collaboration and reuse. Furthermore, both the role of the trainer and the trainee are supported, by highly flexible training software. We suggest that the IS presented here may improve crisis management training in local and regional government agencies by:

- Enabling more frequent training/exercises incl. repetition [T2, T3], thus improving the potential for increased crisis awareness and maintaining knowledge (cf. [26]).
- Facilitating the involvement of more external actors and (internal) trainees, also for preparing new employees in-between exercises [T2] or training of individual roles.
- Increasing flexibility in training/exercises with the potential to participate in training/exercises anywhere (if Internet access) and anytime (within defined time spans) in shorter sessions [T2, T3].
- Enabling cross-organizational, collaborative planning and the reuse of exercises, providing templates, auto-generating reports, offering lists of common exercise goals, etc. [T1, T3], thereby making planning more resource-efficient and increasing the variety in exercises.
- Structuring the planning process and guiding the order of activities [T1, T3], thus ensuring quality.
- Offering in-depth support for training need analysis [T1], thereby using resources wisely and ensuring that essential knowledge gaps are filled.
- Making exercises more immersive and varied [T4].
- Providing richer (training) data, and thereby improved evaluations [T1, T2, T3, T4], thus supporting follow-up, and feedback to the trainees as well as transfer of learning.

This paper serves as an introduction to the IS designed in the CriseIT project. These constitute the first components of a digitally supported crisis management training model aimed to complement conventional crisis training methods. The individual tool and their design process will be presented in more depth in forthcoming studies. The tools will also be further evaluated and developed in the CriseIT 2 project. In addition, educational material, methods and guidelines to support the usage of the software (in planning/design of training/exercise as well as during the execution training/exercise) are being developed. Furthermore, all tools, except T1, have only had limited evaluations. The bullet list above are thus mainly visions of technology impacts at this stage. A natural next step is to test them thoroughly with local governments and their partner organizations.

Acknowledgements. This research was partly funded by EU/Interreg, Sweden-Norway program (20200721).

References

1. Alter, S.: The Work System Method: Connecting People, Processes, and IT for Business Results. Work System Press, Larkspur (2006)
2. Araz, O.M., Jehn, M., Lant, T., Fowler, J.W.: A new method of exercising pandemic preparedness through an interactive simulation and visualization. J. Med. Syst. **36**(3), 1475–1483 (2012)
3. Asproth, V., Borglund, E.A., Öberg, L.M.: Exercises for crisis management training in intra-organizational settings. In: Proceedings of the 10th ISCRAM2013 (2013)
4. Bacon, L., Windall, G., MacKinnon, L.: The development of a rich multimedia training environment for crisis management: using emotional affect to enhance learning. Assoc. Learn. Technol. **19**, 67–78 (2011)
5. Bakken, B.T., Haerem, T.: Intuition in crisis management: the secret weapon of successful decision makers. In: Sinclair, M. (ed.) Handbook of Intuition Research, pp. 122–132. Edward Elgar, Cheltenham (2011)
6. Beynon-Davies, P.: Business Information Systems. Macmillan International Higher Education (2013)
7. Garzón, J., Acevedo, J.A.: Meta-analysis of the impact of Augmented Reality on students' learning effectiveness. Educ. Res. Rev. (in press). https://doi.org/10.1016/j.edurev.2019.04.001
8. Hevner, A.R.: A three cycle view of design science research. Scand. J. Inf. Syst. **19**(2), 87–92 (2007)
9. Hevner, A.R., March, S.T., Park, J., Ram, S.: Design science in information systems research. MIS Q. **28**(1), 75–105 (2004)
10. Lukosch, H., van Ruijven, T., Verbraeck, A.: The participatory design of a simulation training game. In: Proceedings of WSC 2012 (2012)
11. Magnusson, M., Nyberg, L., Wik, M.: Information systems for disaster management training: investigating user needs with a design science research approach. In: Proceedings ISCRAM2018 (2018)
12. Magnusson, M., Pettersson, J., Bellström, P., Andersson, H.: Developing crisis training software for local governments – from user needs to generic requirements. In: Andersson, B., et al. (eds.) Designing Digitalization (ISD2018 Proceedings) Lund University, Lund, Sweden (2018). ISBN 978-91-7753-876-9. http://aisel.aisnet.org/isd2014/proceedings2018/General/6
13. Magnusson, M., Öberg, L.M.: Crisis training software and user needs–research directions. In: Proceedings of the ISCRAM2015 (2015)
14. Meum, T., Munkvold, B.E.: Information infrastructure for crisis response coordination: a study of local emergency management in Norwegian municipalities. In: Proceedings ISCRAM2013 (2013)
15. Myndigheten för samhällsskydd och beredskap (MSB). Övningsvägledning Grundbok – Introduktion till och grunder i övningsplanering (2016)
16. Peffers, K., Tuunanen, T., Rothenberger, M.A., Chatterjee, S.: A design science research methodology for information systems research. J. Manag. Inf. Syst. **24**(3), 45–77 (2007)
17. Peffers, K., Tuunanen, T., Niehaves, B.: Design science research genres: introduction to the special issue on exemplars and criteria for applicable design science research. Eur. J. Inf. Syst. **27**(2), 129–139 (2018). https://doi.org/10.1080/0960085x.2018.1458066
18. Perry, R.W.: Disaster exercise outcomes for professional emergency personnel and citizen volunteers. J. Contingencies Cris. Manag. **12**(2), 64–75 (2004)

19. Peterson, D.M., Perry, R.W.: The impacts of disaster exercises on participants. Disaster Prev. Manag.: Int. J. **8**(4), 241–255 (1999)
20. Reuter, C., Pipek, V., Müller, C.: Computer supported collaborative training in crisis communication management. In: Proceedings ISCRAM2009 (2009)
21. Salas, E., Wildman, J.L., Piccolo, R.F.: Using simulation-based training to enhance management education. Acad. Manag. Learn. Educ. **8**(4), 559–573 (2009)
22. Sinclair, H., Doyle, E.E., Johnston, D.M., Paton, D.: Assessing emergency management training and exercises. Disaster Prev. Manag.: Int. J. **21**(4), 507–521 (2012)
23. Sniezek, J.A., Wilkins, D.C., Wadlington, P.L., Baumann, M.R.: Training for crisis decision-making: psychological issues and computer-based solutions. J. Manag. Inf. Syst. **18**(4), 147–168 (2002)
24. Steinberger, N.: Organizing for the big one: a review of case studies and a research agenda for multi-agency disaster response. J. Contingencies Cris. Manag. **24**(2), 60–72 (2016)
25. van de Ven, J.G.M., Stubbé, H., Hrehovcsik, M.: Gaming for policy makers: it's serious! In: De Gloria, A. (ed.) GALA 2013. LNCS, vol. 8605, pp. 376–382. Springer, Cham (2014). https://doi.org/10.1007/978-3-319-12157-4_32
26. van Laere, J., Lindblom, J.: Cultivating a longitudinal learning process through recurring crisis management training exercises in twelve Swedish municipalities. J. Contingencies Cris. Manag. **27**, 1–12 (2018)
27. Waller, M.J., Lei, Z., Pratten, R.: Focusing on teams in crisis management education: an integration and simulation-based approach. Acad. Manag. Learn. Educ. **13**(2), 208–221 (2014)
28. Wilson, P.J., Gosiewska, S.: Multi-agency gold incident command training for civil emergencies. Disaster Prev. Manag. **23**(5), 632–648 (2014)
29. Yao, X., Konopka, J.A., Hendela, A.H., Chumer, M., Turoff, M.: Unleash physical limitations: virtual emergency preparedness planning simulation training, methodology and a case study. In: Proceedings from the 11th Americas Conference on Information Systems, AMCIS 2005, Omaha, Nebraska, USA, 11–14 August, AIS Electronic Library (SIDeL), pp. 1642–1652 (2005)

User Perspectives

Who Are the Users of Digital Public Services?

A Critical Reflection on Differences in the Treatment of Citizens as 'Users' in e-government Research

Bettina Distel[1]([⊠]) [iD] and Ida Lindgren[2] [iD]

[1] University of Münster, Leonardo-Campus 3, 48149 Münster, Germany
bettina.distel@ercis.uni-muenster.de
[2] Linköping University, 58183 Linköping, Sweden
ida.lindgren@liu.se

Abstract. Despite the importance of citizens as users of digital public services, e-government research has not explicitly considered different perspectives on citizens as users of said services. This paper sets out to explore the possible variations in which the citizen as a user of digital public services is conceptualized within the e-government literature. Through a qualitative and interpretive approach, we have analysed literature from different fields of e-government research to create an overview of how citizens as users of digital public services are conceptualized in e-government research. The structure of the review departs from, and is framed by, four established value paradigms for e-government management. Our approach reveals that – depending on the perspective taken – the conceptualization of the citizen varies considerably and, as a consequence, may impact the results and contributions of each research perspective. The conception of the citizen as a user of digital public services varies from being a passive recipient of government services, to being an active co-producer of services. This article contributes to e-government theory by unboxing the conceptions of citizens as users of digital public services that are existent in current research on digital public services. In providing a framework that relates these conceptions to previously known value paradigms, the article offers a starting point for taking a multidimensional perspective in e-government research that considers the citizen as a multifaceted and heterogeneous entity.

Keywords: Digital public service · Citizens · Users · e-government · Value ideals · Theory-building

1 Introduction

As part of e-government initiatives worldwide, public services are being provided through digital channels. Repeatedly, citizens are conceptualized as the major beneficiaries of e-government, e.g. [16], including digital public services, by having ubiquitous access to services [3] and a wide range of information. The implementation of digital public services also aims at making communication and interactions between public administrations and citizens more efficient and easier for the citizen; accordingly, much e-government research treats citizens as a unit of analysis, e.g. [8].

© IFIP International Federation for Information Processing 2019
Published by Springer Nature Switzerland AG 2019
P. Panagiotopoulos et al. (Eds.): ePart 2019, LNCS 11686, pp. 117–129, 2019.
https://doi.org/10.1007/978-3-030-27397-2_10

Despite the importance of citizens, as users of digital public services, only few research attempts exist that closely examine who the citizens are and what they expect from e-government initiatives of this kind, e.g. [25, 30, 31]. Instead, e-government research mostly treats citizens as a homogenous group, without specifying subgroups, e.g. [7]. Often, citizens are clustered along rather unspecific, mostly socio-demographic variables, e.g. [24]. Related to public service provision in general, researchers agree that the mutual expectations and behaviors are dependent on the role in which the citizens interact with public administrations [18], e.g. as a citizen, or as a customer. The necessity to view the interactions of citizens and public administrations from different perspectives does not become obsolete by simply conceptualizing the citizen as a 'user' of a digital service. Rather, the differentiation into separate roles must be made for the digitally mediated interactions and for the citizen as a user of these digital services. However, e-government researchers have so far mostly refrained from opening this black box. Whereas the need for understanding who the user is has been acknowledged in other lines of research, e.g. [23], e-government research has not explicitly considered different perspectives on citizens as users. Against this background, this paper sets out to explore the possible variations in which the citizen as a user of digital public services is conceptualized within the e-government literature.

With the term *digital public service,* we refer to public services that are provided through a digital channel [22], typically using Internet-based technology, meaning that the citizens' interaction with public authorities is partly or completely mediated by the technology [17, 20]. The technology used can serve different purposes; a digital public service can refer to a clearly delimited IT-system, but also to larger service processes in which the digital interface towards the citizen is merely a small and limited part of the process [21]. Digital public service denotes a "fuzzy" phenomenon, in the sense that it can take on many different shapes in practice, and is referred to under several different labels in the e-government literature [17, 20]. As argued above, only few researchers attempt to differentiate the user of digital public services but mostly do so by using socio-demographic variables to distinguish users. In an attempt to further our understanding of how the citizen as a user of digital public services is conceptualized, we explore the citizen concept from a value position perspective. We use the work by Rose et al. [29] as a point of departure, who present four different value paradigms visible in e-government research and practice. These value paradigms (professionalism ideal; efficiency ideal; service ideal; and, engagement ideal) highlight the underlying drivers behind implementations of digital public services. However, the framework by Rose et al. [29] does not include how the user (citizen) is understood in each of these value paradigms. In this paper, we discuss the view on citizens as users of digital public services by relating e-government research that considers the citizen's role in digital public service provision to the value paradigms presented by Rose et al. [29]. As a result of this analysis, we present a framework that distinguishes between different views on citizens and highlights the need to understand the citizen as a user of e-government from multiple perspectives.

This paper contributes to our understanding of digital service provision in the public sector. Succeeding in providing digital services is difficult, due to the complex nature of the public sector context, the service processes being digitized, and the technology used to digitize these processes. The framework presented in this paper can be used to further conceptualize this complex phenomenon and hence help both researchers and practitioners to understand digitization of public services in a more nuanced manner.

The paper is organized as follows; first, we present our research approach. Second, we present the different perspectives that we have identified, and discuss the view on the citizen present in these views. We then proceed to a comparative analysis of these strands, concluding with a conceptual framework that gives and overview of these various conceptualizations. We conclude this article with a short summary and outlook for future research.

2 Background

E-government is not a value-neutral endeavour; in fact, the values driving e-government initiatives, such as the implementation of digital public services, is gaining increasing attention in the research literature [6]. In this context, values are understood as the general aims and drivers of a project [29]. Building on both theory and e-government practice, Rose et al. [29] distinguish between four value positions for managing e-Government initiatives; as described in Table 1. For each value position, they focus on the prevalent tradition of public administration, representative values, how the purpose of e-Government is described, and the role of IT for fulfilling these emphasized values. This framework, however, refers to the ideals of public sector managers and the implementation of e-government projects in public agencies. Thus, it is focused on practice rather than on e-government research and does not include any conceptualization of citizens as participants in this implementation process. Especially against the background that citizens are repeatedly treated as the main beneficiaries of e-government projects, a value framework for e-government research should contain this perspective.

Within e-government research, citizens are understood as users of e-government who generate benefits through the use of digital public services [31]. The citizens' use of digital public services is, from this perspective, focused on consuming public services through electronic means: "[…] citizens and businesses can use e-government for three purposes: to access information; to engage in electronic transactions with government; and to participate in government decision making" [25, p. 212]. Accordingly, types of usage are focused on the *search for information and policies, service use*, and *participation* in political processes [11, 25]. Scott et al. [31], for example, refer as well to these categories but name them differently. In their study, users of e-government are grouped into *passive users* who browse content and download forms or documents, *active users* who communicate and interact with public administrations by digital means, e.g. by electronically transmitting a form, and *participatory users* who take part in the political process of opinion forming through electronic channels. Detached from the channel of communication and interaction, respectively, other researchers have attempted to define different roles in which citizens interact with public administrations and that, as a consequence, may define the type of (digital) service use. For example, Thomas [33] argues that citizens can take three different roles: as *customers* who are served by public administrations and 'consume' public services, as *citizens* who

Table 1. Four value positions for e-Government (shortened version of [29], p. 542)

	Professional ideal	Efficiency ideal	Service ideal	Engagement ideal
Public administration tradition	Providing an independent, robust and consistent administration, governed by a rule system based on law, resulting in the public record, which is the basis for accountability	Providing lean and efficient administration, which minimises waste of public resources gathered from taxpayers	Maximising the utility of government to civil society by providing services directed towards the public good	Engaging with civil society to facilitate policy development in accordance with liberal democratic principles; articulating the public good
Representative values	Durability, equity, legality and accountability	Value for money, cost reduction, productivity and performance	Public service, citizen centricity, service level and quality	Democracy, deliberation and participation
e-Government purpose	Provide a flexible and secure digital public record and support standardised administrative procedures	Streamline, rationalise and transform public administration around digital technologies	Improve the availability, accessibility and usability of government services by providing them online	Support deliberative interactions with the public and the co-production of policy

participate in political processes, and as *partners*, when "[…] the broader pursuit of public ends supposedly occur[s] mostly through networks of private and non-profit entities, members of the public, and governments […]" [33, p. 788]. Especially this last aspect of citizens becoming partners of public authorities is so far a lesser studied topic in our field.

3 Research Approach

This work is interpretive and builds on a hermeneutic literature review [6]. We have analysed literature from different lines of research related to e-government in order to create an overview of how the citizen as a user of digital public services is treated and conceptualized in e-government research. The structure of the review departs from the four value paradigms presented by Rose et al. [29]; these four paradigms therefore function as a frame for the analysis. We have included papers on e-government services, public e-services, web-site channels, etc. that deal primarily with the citizens' perspective. We have searched for literature in an 'unstructured' manner; and have aimed for a more exploratory approach, identifying examples of different conceptualizations of citizens as users of digital public services.

In a first step, the articles were analysed with regard to the question of whether they can be assigned to one or more of the four value paradigms by Rose et al. [29]. The conceptualizations and definitions of the citizen and user, respectively, were extracted for each article. This analysis was focused on the question of how the citizen is understood with regard to her role within the public sector and as a user of digital public services; e.g., whether she is actively involved in the provision of public services or rather seen as a passive receiver of services. We extracted the specific perspective on the citizen from each article and compared the articles with each other to gain a better understanding of each individual viewpoint. Only then, the four existing value paradigms were compared in order to understand what types of definitions and conceptualizations of the citizen and user, respectively, exist (see Sect. 4). While in most of the works on which this article is based one view was dominant, these perspectives are not disjoint and one article may be based on more than one conceptualization.

4 Different Perspectives on Citizens as Users of Digital Public Services

The analysis of e-government research reveals that the understanding of citizens as users of e-government corresponds with the types of value positions presented by Rose et al. [29]. In the sections below, we discuss different perspectives on citizens as users of e-government and depart from these four value positions. For each value position, we have found exemplary articles that we use to illustrate the various interpretations of the citizen as a user of digital public services.

4.1 Citizens as Clients and Consumers of Public Services (Professionalism Ideal)

In the first value position presented by Rose et al. [29], the *professionalism ideal*, IT is seen as important infrastructure that can provide an independent, robust and consistent administration in accordance with the law. Important values guiding e-government initiatives include durability, equity, legality and accountability.

Literature associated with this ideal views the citizen more as a client or a customer. Thus, interactions between public agencies and citizens occur in the process of service delivery. Research from this perspective deals, for example, with changing internal and legal structures that occur with the introduction of IT in the public sector. In this view, public agencies do not simply introduce new infrastructure for improving service delivery but "[...] have the power to dictate the rules and regulations, and thus create a legal obligation" [34, p. 158]. Here, the need for citizens to trust their administrations is often referred to, because public agencies cannot only dictate the rules for online activities but also "[...] may be required by law to share information with other agencies or with the citizenry, further intensifying the need for trust in the maintenance of accurate citizen information" [34, p. 158]. Although the need for citizens' trust is recognized in this line of research, the understanding of the citizen is not further defined; the citizen is simply treated as an external entity to the public administration.

4.2   Citizens as Receivers of Public Services (Efficiency Ideal)

The *efficiency ideal* [29] is characterized by wanting to provide lean and efficient administration, reducing waste of public resources gathered from taxpayers. Hence, value for money, cost reduction, productivity and performance are salient values. The dominant view on technology is that IT can be used for automation of administrative tasks.

Much research on e-government has focused on digitalization of public services and internal administrative processes from a government perspective; in fact, e-government research is often criticized for being too supply-side and efficiency oriented [10, 28]. When looking at digital public services from an efficiency perspective, the external user – the citizen – is most often treated as a homogeneous and faceless group of people [9]. An example can be seen in Heeks' [14] description of stakeholder roles in e-government projects, in which he describes six different types of stakeholders within the project management (project manager/team, suppliers operators, champions, sponsors, and owner), but merely two outside the project (clients and other stakeholders). The 'clients' are subsequently described as being one out of two types; *primary clients* are on the immediate receiving end of what the e-government system does or outputs. Sometimes these will be outside the government (e.g. citizens or businesses). Sometimes, though, these will be inside government (i.e. public servants): in this case, there may also be *secondary clients* who will be affected indirectly by the system since they are served by the primary clients (e.g. citizens served by those public servants) [14]. In this line of thinking, the citizen as a user is mostly described in terms of its 'uptake' and 'adoption' of digital public services. The adoption of e-government by users outside the public administration is necessary to ensure the efficiency and effectiveness of administrative actions [3]. This perspective is reflected in the use of maturity models and benchmarking studies that most often focus on the development of digital public services from a public administration viewpoint and do not consider the use of these services from the citizens' perspective.

Although some research exists that addresses the efficiency ideal from the citizens' perspective [1], citizens are most often not further defined and treated simply as users of e-government [12]. From the citizens' perspective, efficiency gains are related to the use of their personal resources: "Based on [...their] capabilities, the individuals decide how they will use these resources in order to achieve their functioning, that is, the result of the effective use of these resources, which, in a last analysis, will lead to their utility, for example, exercise of rights, welfare [...]" [1, p. 243]. Although the use of e-government by citizens can also be viewed from the perspective of efficiency gains, within this ideal the purpose of IT use is more often related to organizational efficiency: "Information technology (IT) is potentially capable of changing government organizational structures and business processes and, if implemented correctly, of producing substantial organizational, technical, and business benefits [...]" [12, p. 121]. As such, interactions between public administrations and citizens take place within the service delivery process and citizens are here also treated as an undefined external entity.

4.3   Clients as Users and Adopters of Digital Public Services (Service Ideal)

In the *service ideal* [29], maximising the utility of government to civil society by providing services directed towards the public good is in focus. Hence, public service, citizen centricity, service level and quality are dominant values. From this perspective, IT enables improved accessibility, availability and quality of services for citizens.

Interestingly, this ideal is mostly prevalent in studies on e-government adoption although the adoption issue is also closely related to debates around efficiency gains for public administrations. The main rationale underlying this ideal is the use of ICT to better serve citizens: "Nevertheless, all the definitions [of e-government] are headed towards a single notion and encompass a generic and unique mission of e-Gov – presenting government systems using information and communication technology (ICT) to serve citizens better [...]" [32, p. 17]. Similarly, Nam [25, p. 211] expresses: "For a government to move toward a citizen-centric, outward-looking approach, understanding citizens' use of e-government and identifying determinants of e-government use has a central importance for both researchers and practitioners." Notably, although the citizens and their adoption behaviour are focused in this ideal, only Nam [25] makes an attempt to better delineate who the citizen or user of e-government services are by differentiating three types of usage (access to information, transactions, participating). In accordance with the general service orientation expressed within this perspective, the use of IT for governmental purposes is pre-dominantly focused on providing services by electronic means. Whereas articles mainly rooted in the efficiency ideal consider IT as a means to increase the public agency's internal efficiency, articles rooted in the service ideal are mainly geared towards providing better services for citizens: "The term electronic (e-) or digital government describes the utilization of information and communication technologies (ICT), predominantly internet-based applications, by administrative institutions to provide citizens and other stakeholders with directions and services related to a wide field of state functions [...]" [11, p. 637].

In addition to the adoption discourse, two further debates in the e-government community can – at least partially – be related to this ideal. The first discussion is on user participation. Here, the involvement of citizens in the development process of digital public services is discussed as a way of attaining two main goals; system quality and democratic decision making. Conceptualizations of the user are often taken from more traditional IS literature on IT development. Thus, researchers in this field state that "[...] all types of users of a new system must be involved in different ways in the design of the relevant parts of a system" [5, p. 120]. Similarly, Iivari et al. [15, p. 111] state that: "[u]sers usually are the best experts on the local work practices to be aligned with and to be supported by a system. Users also are the final 'implementers' of the system and evaluation of the system without any attention to subjective user-oriented criteria, such as perceived usefulness, perceived ease of use, perceived usability and user satisfaction, is seriously limited". In other fields, the question of who the users are has already been addressed and the integration of users in the design process is discussed [23]. Often however, the users remain a largely undefined mass when examining existing studies [15].

The second discussion, on website quality, has its roots in the work on system quality, e.g. in terms of usability. In the e-government field, this is seen in applications of frameworks such as E-S-Qual [27], resulting in e-government context specific quality assessment frameworks such as E-GovQual [26] and quality dimensions for e-service design and evaluation [17]. These frameworks typically construct quality based on several different constructs, e.g. *efficiency, reliability, citizen support* and *trust* [26], and *usability, functionality,* and *technical performance* [17, 26].

An underlying idea for both of these sub-perspectives is that a digital public service should be of high quality, assessed in relation to a set of quality dimensions, and that service of high quality is more likely to be used by the external user – the citizen. Through high usage of these services, the supplying organization can achieve the effectiveness and efficiency goals set in relation to these services. Hence, the user is seen both as the external actor whose behaviour determines the success of the system, but also as an important input in the design process, in which the system's quality is determined.

4.4 Citizens as Co-producers of Public Policy and Service (Engagement Ideal)

The fourth value position, the *engagement ideal* [29], departs from the public administration tradition of engaging with civil society to facilitate policy development in accordance with liberal democratic principles. Democracy, deliberation and participation are dominant values and IT is seen as a networking facilitation, as IT enables communicative interaction between governments and citizens.

Here, we see literature under a multitude of labels that we, in this paper, choose to treat together; e.g. on e-participation and digital divides. The common denominator is the underlying idea that, from a societal perspective, it is necessary that public services are accessible for all citizens, regardless of their personal abilities or preferences. Often, this research relates to the digital divide debate and discusses the relation between socio-demographic variables and the use of digital public services. The digital divide refers to a gap in the society that exists between those who have access to information and those who do not have access to information. This divide is aggravated by the use of technologies. Bélanger and Carter [4] argue that this phenomenon relates (i) to the access to technologies such as the Internet and (ii) to the skills needed to use these technologies. Consequently, researchers in this area define different groups of citizens according to their access to digital public services and their resulting ability to participate in the digital administration, e.g. [2].

With the increased digitisation of public services, scholars with various backgrounds have reported that in addition to the digital divide debate, not all citizens *want* to use e-government services [19]. In this line of literature, the citizen as a user of public services is therefore often discussed in terms of being an agent that actively chooses between different channels for communication with public administrations. An underlying argument is that understanding how citizens decide on channels for interacting with public administrations might ensure the accessibility of public services for all citizens. Accordingly, authors argue that public administrations are responsible for ensuring social inclusion through digital public services: "In its purest form, citizens are all of us. We live our lives; we vote in elections; and we form special interest groups to influence decisions. In this way, the role of government is to create a society that presents for the individual citizen a possibility to live this kind of life" [13, p. 72]. Thus, the citizens are not only treated as users of digital public services or an external entity, but are assigned different roles with varying degrees of involvement – and power [13].

5   Discussion

In this section, the results of our explorative literature analysis in the preceding section is transposed into a framework of different conceptions of citizens as users of digital public services in relation to the four value positions by Rose et al. [29]. In order to better understand how the citizen is treated in each of the value paradigms and the related debates in e-government research, we focused our analysis of exemplary articles (i) on how the citizen is conceptualized, (ii) which role research assigns to the citizen in interactions with public administrations, and (iii) how much attention the citizen is given (see Table 2). When describing citizens, literature from the field of administrative science often focuses on the role they play in the structure of 'public administration' as a whole as well as their way of interacting with public administration [18, 33]. Therefore, our analysis also focuses on these aspects. Lastly, as our analysis is on the conceptual level, we have added the question of what kind of attention is given to the citizen within each research direction.

In our exploration of possible variations of how the citizen as a user of digital public services is conceptualized within the e-government literature, the analysis revealed several interesting aspects. *First*, the four value positions as proposed by Rose et al. [29] differ with regard to the inherent conceptions of citizens as users of digital public services; presented in Table 2. It is noticeable that within each perspective, the citizen is conceptualized differently. For the professionalism ideal, we find examples for the treatment of the citizen as a client or a customer. Within the efficiency ideal, the citizen is understood as a passive receiver of digital services. Both ideals view the citizen as a more passive interaction partner. Similarly, both perspectives reduce the citizens' role in interactions with public administrations to a point of contact within the service delivery process. In contrast to this, research rooted in the service and engagement ideals promotes the active involvement of the citizen not only in the service process, but also in the design and policy process. Citizens are here treated as users and adopters of e-government, as a source of design input (service ideal), and as co-producers of public policy (engagement ideal). In accordance with these conceptions, the citizens receive differing degrees of attention within each ideal. Whereas within the first two ideals the citizen is put in the background and views as a homogenous group, the service and engagement ideals treat citizens as heterogeneous entities. It is only within the latter ideal that the citizen is focused during the entire process. Surprisingly though, none of the analysed articles provided a definition of the

Table 2. Conceptions of citizens as users of digital public services

	Professional ideal	Efficiency ideal	Service ideal	Engagement ideal
How is the citizen conceptualized?	Client/customer	Receiver of digital service	Users and adopters of technology and source of design input	Co-producer of public policy
What is the citizens' role in interactions with public administrations?	Interaction with the citizen takes place in the service process	Interaction with the citizen takes place in the service process	Promotes active interaction with citizens in design process	Promotes active involvement of citizens in policy processes
How much attention does research give to the citizen?	The citizen is put in the background – treated as a homogeneous group	The citizen is put in the background – treated as a homogeneous group	The citizen is focused during the design and implementation processes. Treated as a heterogeneous entity	The citizen is focused during the entire process. Treated as a heterogeneous entity

term 'citizen' and only conceptualized the citizens and her role in interactions with public administrations implicitly.

Secondly and detached from our proposed framework, the attribution of e-government research to one of the ideals by Rose et al. [29] reveals that they were merely implicitly present in the papers. The most prevalent ideal in this regard was the service ideal, i.e. e-government research often deals with the delivery of public services to external stakeholders such as businesses and citizens. While research related to other ideals often is concerned with interactions between citizens and public administrations that occur within the service process, within this ideal the citizen is often treated as a source of input already within the development and design process of public services. Whereas the efficiency and engagement ideal are as well present in the e-government research, we hardly found any examples for the professionalism ideal. This might be due to the fact that the professionalism ideal takes an organizational and processual perspective on e-government, in which legal aspects and changes to internal structures are focused rather than interactions with external partners. Therefore, there are considerably fewer articles for the professionalism ideal in our work than for the other three ideals. Furthermore, the analysis indicates that the perspectives taken in each article are neither disjoint nor mutually exclusive. Rather, they seem to overlap, at least in part, by taking a similar view, or building on each other. For example, we see that the service ideal is often combined with the engagement ideal, e.g. [25] or that aspects of the engagement and efficiency ideal are treated together in one article, e.g. [12]. In addition to the combination of two ideals, we found only two articles that took multiple perspectives on the citizen and explicitly served purposes that can be related to all four ideals [30, 31]. *Finally*, we find that when analysing e-government papers in relation to the value ideals, it became apparent that each article takes a limited perspective on users of (digital) public services and focuses only certain aspects that serve specific research goals. To our knowledge, our article is the first attempt to collect these perspectives and to take a multi-dimensional look at different treatments of the citizen as a user of digital public services.

6   Conclusion and Outlook

This paper aimed to explore the possible variations in which the citizen as a user of digital public services is conceptualized within the e-government literature. Starting from the value framework proposed by Rose et al. [29], we employed an exploratory approach to analyze the existence of these ideals within e-government research and their manifestation in different conceptions of citizens as users of digital public services. In accordance with these ideals, articles from the field of e-government research differ with regard to their conception of citizens as users of digital public services. These differences are reflected in three aspects; (i) the conceptualization or definition of the citizen, (ii) the role citizens play in the respective research perspectives, and (iii) the emphasis placed on the citizen in the provision of digital public services (see Table 2).

This study contributes to e-government research by opening the lid of the black-box containing the 'citizen' as a user of digital public services. While a majority of studies in e-government consider the citizenry to be a homogenous group of people, our approach reveals that the citizen can be conceptualized in a variety of ways. As a consequence – depending on the perspective taken – different conceptualizations may impact the results and contributions of e-government research. For each of the identified perspectives, it is important to understand how the citizen or the user is treated, and to open the discussion to other perspectives. A too limited treatment of the citizen, as a user of digital public services, may hinder a deeper understanding of when and why citizens chose (not) to interact with the government through digital channels.

References

1. De Araujo, M.H., Reinhard, N.: Categorization of Brazilian internet users and its impacts on the use of electronic government services. In: Janssen, M., Scholl, H.J., Wimmer, M.A., Bannister, F. (eds.) EGOV 2014. LNCS, vol. 8653, pp. 242–252. Springer, Heidelberg (2014). https://doi.org/10.1007/978-3-662-44426-9_20
2. Becker, J., Niehaves, B., Bergener, P., Räckers, M.: Digital divide in eGovernment: The eInclusion gap model. In: Wimmer, M.A., Scholl, H.J., Ferro, E. (eds.) EGOV 2008. LNCS, vol. 5184, pp. 231–242. Springer, Heidelberg (2008). https://doi.org/10.1007/978-3-540-85204-9_20
3. Belanche, D., Casaló, L.V., Flavián, C.: Integrating trust and personal values into the Technology Acceptance Model: the case of e-government services adoption. Cuadernos de Economía y Dirección de la Empresa 15(4), 192–204 (2012)

4. Bélanger, F., Carter, L.: The impact of the digital divide on e-government use. Commun. ACM **52**(4), 132–135 (2009)
5. Bødker, K., Kensing, F., Simonsen, J.: Participatory design in information systems development. In: Isomäki, H., Pekkola, S. (eds.) Reframing Humans in Information Systems Development, pp. 115–134. Springer, London (2011). https://doi.org/10.1007/978-1-84996-347-3_7
6. Boell, S.K., Cecez-Kecmanovic, D.: A hermeneutic approach for conducting literature reviews and literature searches. Commun. ACM **34**, 257–286 (2014)
7. Carter, L., Bélanger, F.: The utilization of e-government services: citizen trust, innovation and acceptance factors. Inf. Syst. J. **15**(1), 5–25 (2005)
8. Carter, L., Weerakkody, V., Phillips, B., Dwivedi, Y.K.: Citizen adoption of e-government services. Exploring citizen perceptions of online services in the United States and United Kingdom. Inf. Syst. Manag. **33**(2), 124–140 (2016)
9. Distel, B., Becker, J.: All citizens are the same, aren't they? – developing an e-government user typology. In: Janssen, M., et al. (eds.) EGOV 2017. LNCS, vol. 10428, pp. 336–347. Springer, Cham (2017). https://doi.org/10.1007/978-3-319-64677-0_28
10. Gauld, R., Goldfinch, S., Horsburgh, S.: Do they want it? Do they use it? The 'demand-side' of e-government in Australia and New Zealand. Gov. Inf. Q. **27**(2), 177–186 (2010)
11. Gerpott, T.J., Ahmadi, N.: Use levels of electronic government services among German citizens. An empirical analysis of objective household and personal predictors. Transform. Gov.: People Process Policy **10**(4), 637–668 (2016)
12. Gil-Garcia, J.R., Chengalur-Smith, I., Duchessi, P.: Collaborative e-Government: impediments and benefits of information-sharing projects in the public sector. Eur. J. Inf. Syst. **16**(2), 121–133 (2007)
13. Hansen, H.S., Reinau, K.H.: The citizens in e-participation. In: Wimmer, M.A., Scholl, H.J., Grönlund, Å., Andersen, K.V. (eds.) EGOV 2006. LNCS, vol. 4084, pp. 70–82. Springer, Heidelberg (2006). https://doi.org/10.1007/11823100_7
14. Heeks, R.: Implementing and Managing eGovernment. An International Text. Sage Publications, London (2006)
15. Iivari, J., Isomäki, H., Pekkola, S.: The user - the great unknown of systems development: reasons, forms, challenges, experiences and intellectual contributions of user involvement. Inf. Syst. J. **20**(2), 109–117 (2010)
16. Jaeger, P.T.: The endless wire: e-government as global phenomenon. Gov. Inf. Q. **20**(4), 323–331 (2003)
17. Jansen, A., Ølnes, S.: The nature of public e-services and their quality dimensions. Gov. Inf. Q. **33**(4), 647–657 (2016)
18. Jos, P.H., Tompkins, M.E.: Keeping it public: defending public service values in a customer service age. Public Adm. Rev. **69**(9), 1077–1086 (2009)
19. Leist, E., Smith, D.: Accessibility issues in e-government. In: Kő, A., Francesconi, E. (eds.) EGOVIS 2014. LNCS, vol. 8650, pp. 15–25. Springer, Cham (2014). https://doi.org/10.1007/978-3-319-10178-1_2
20. Lindgren, I., Jansson, G.: Electronic services in the public sector: a conceptual framework. Gov. Inf. Q. **30**(2), 163–172 (2013)
21. Lindgren, I., Melin, U.: Time to refuel the conceptual discussion on public e-services – revisiting how e-services are manifested in practice. In: Janssen, M., et al. (eds.) EGOV 2017. LNCS, vol. 10428, pp. 92–101. Springer, Cham (2017). https://doi.org/10.1007/978-3-319-64677-0_8
22. Madsen, C.Ø., Kræmmergaard, P.: Channel choice: a literature review. In: Tambouris, E., et al. (eds.) EGOV 2015. LNCS, vol. 9248, pp. 3–18. Springer, Cham (2015). https://doi.org/10.1007/978-3-319-22479-4_1

23. Millerand, F., Baker, K.S.: Who are the users? Who are the developers? Webs of users and developers in the development process of a technical standard. Inf. Syst. J. **20**(2), 137–161 (2010)
24. Molnar, T.: Improving usability of e-government for the elderly. Electron. J. e-Gov. **13**(2), 122–135 (2015)
25. Nam, T.: Determining the type of e-government use. Gov. Inf. Q. **31**(2), 211–220 (2014)
26. Papadomichelaki, X., Mentzas, G.: e-GovQual. A multiple-item scale for assessing e-government service quality. Gov. Inf. Q. **29**(1), 98–109 (2012)
27. Parasuraman, A., Zeithaml, V.A., Malhotra, A.: E-S-QUAL. A multiple-item scale for assessing electronic service quality. J. Serv. Res. **7**(3), 213–233 (2005)
28. Reddick, C.G.: Citizen interaction with e-government: from the streets to servers? Gov. Inf. Q. **22**(1), 38–57 (2005)
29. Rose, J., Persson, J.S., Heeager, L.T., Irani, Z.: Managing e-Government: value positions and relationships. Inf. Syst. J. **25**(5), 531–571 (2015)
30. Rowley, J.: e-government stakeholders - who are they and what do they want? Int. J. Inf. Manag. **31**(1), 53–62 (2011)
31. Scott, M., DeLone, W.H., Golden, W.: Measuring eGovernment success: a public value approach. Eur. J. Inf. Syst. **25**(3), 187–208 (2016)
32. Shareef, M.A., Kumar, V., Kumar, U., Dwivedi, Y.K.: e-Government Adoption Model (GAM). Differing service maturity levels. Gov. Inf. Q. **28**(1), 17–35 (2011)
33. Thomas, J.C.: Citizen, customer, partner. Rethinking the place of the public in public management. Public Adm. Rev. **73**(6), 786–796 (2013)
34. Warkentin, M., Gefen, D., Pavlou, P.A., Rose, G.M.: Encouraging citizen adoption of e-government by building trust. Electron. Markets **12**(3), 157–162 (2002)

Citizens' Motivations for Engaging in Open Data Hackathons

Arie Purwanto[⊠], Anneke Zuiderwijk, and Marijn Janssen

Delft University of Technology, Jaffalaan 5, 2628 BX Delft, The Netherlands
{A. Purwanto, A. M. G. Zuiderwijk-vanEijk,
M. F. W. H. A. Janssen}@tudelft.nl

Abstract. Engaging citizens in open data hackathons provides opportunities for innovation and the generation of new services and products. This paper aims to explore the motivations of citizens who engage in open agriculture data hackathons. We conducted a case study and analyzed data collected from 161 participants of 11 farming hackathons held between 2016 and 2018 in the Netherlands. We found that participants of open agriculture data hackathons have different roles, including business developer, concept thinker, data analyst, data owner, developer, manager, marketer, problem owner, and student. Our analysis shows that citizens are predominantly motivated to engage in open agricultural data hackathons as part of their work. Furthermore, developers and problem owners are mainly motivated by fun and enjoyment. This indicates that it is important for open data policymakers and hackathon organizers to consider different approaches based on citizens' roles when organizing open data hackathons. This paper contributes to the literature by providing insight in the motivations of citizens engaging in open agriculture data hackathons in comparison with hackathons in other sectors, and by mapping citizens' roles to their motivations for engaging in such hackathons.

Keywords: Open data · Open Government Data · Agriculture ·
Citizen engagement · Hackathon

1 Introduction

Open Government Data (OGD) provides opportunities for innovation [1] and for improving the daily life of citizens [2]. One particular example of a sector in which OGD is a promising source of innovation is agriculture. This sector mainly concerns the quality and sustainability of farms and their environment, as well as efficient and smart farming [3]. The use of public agricultural data potentially benefits stakeholders involved in the farming sector. For instance, farmers can improve the precision of farming processes and management by using water quality data, agribusinesses can offer smart farming products based on weather data to help farmers make decisions about when to plant a particular vegetable, and government organizations can be more accurate at giving subsidies to farmers based on fertilizer purchase data. Citizens can engage with the mineral indicator data combined with public participation for keeping their eyes on the environmental and health impacts of farming practices as well. Using

© IFIP International Federation for Information Processing 2019
Published by Springer Nature Switzerland AG 2019
P. Panagiotopoulos et al. (Eds.): ePart 2019, LNCS 11686, pp. 130–141, 2019.
https://doi.org/10.1007/978-3-030-27397-2_11

open agriculture data, citizens can contribute to solving societal challenges in feeding the growing world, environmental sustainability, food safety, and health [4].

The creation of the above-mentioned benefits requires the engagement of citizens in the use of open agriculture data. Engaging with open agriculture data, however, embraces challenging tasks in understanding and processing voluminous data captured from various sources such as sensors installed in tractors and soils, satellite imagery, soil and water indicators, and statistics [3–5]. In addition, knowledge of farming processes, as important parts of the food chain which affect sustainability and consequences on food safety issues and contribute to health, is needed [4]. Therefore, one needs to collaborate with others who possess diverse skills and knowledge required to create value out of agriculture data. Collaboration among citizens in groups to develop new OGD-based products and services is typically facilitated and stimulated in open data hackathons promoted and supported by governments [6].

An open data hackathon is an offline, face-to-face competition sponsored by government agencies in a centralized location that brings together citizens with different backgrounds (e.g., programmers, designers, students) to intensively collaborate in small teams for a short amount of time (e.g., 12 h, 24 h, 2 days) to create artifacts (e.g., ideas, mockups, design, prototypes, applications) using OGD [7, 8]. Typically, at the end of the competition, each team presents the final idea in front of juries, and a winning team usually earns a prize (e.g., money, investment, support). In a hackathon, organizers and sponsors provide nearly all resources and support needed by the teams to work efficiently [7, 9], including catering services, sleeping bags/area, comfortable facilities (gaming device, sports hall), internet connection, electricity (cables), and stationaries. The provision of technical support from open data providers or event organizers is also common for hackathons.

Although research on the socio-technical conditions of OGD utilization, both enabling and disabling factors, has been widely established [10], yet only a handful of studies investigate the drivers of citizen engagement in open data hackathons [11]. Previous research showed that citizens' motivations to participate in hackathons are heterogeneous [12]. For instance, in a Swedish hackathon on public transportation, the motivation is primarily associated with fun and enjoyment [12], while in a Brazilian city hackathon, contributing to solutions of social problems and networking are the main drivers [11]. These studies show the need to differentiate between different types of open data hackathons and instead of black boxing citizen engagement with OGD, the context should be taken into account [13]. This study contributes to existing research by providing insights into citizens' motivations to engage in open data hackathons in the sector of agriculture.

The main research question we aim to answer in this paper is: "Why do citizens engage in open data hackathons in the agriculture sector?" This study is among the first to provide insights on OGD engagement in the agricultural sector. It contributes to research concerning the mapping of citizens' motivations to engage in open data hackathons. The results of the study may help policymakers to formulate a strategy for sustaining open data engagement which takes multidimensional approaches into account.

2   Research Approach

2.1   Case Study Design

Case studies can be used to investigate a real-world situation over which researchers have little or no control [14]. Case study research is the preferred research approach for this study since we aim to answer why citizens engage in open data hackathons which is an ill-understood topic in the OGD utilization context. A multiple-case study design was selected because its evidence is often considered more convincing and, therefore, the overall study is accounted for being more robust compared to a single-case study [15].

The agricultural sector was selected because of its enormous potential to solve problems related to malnutrition, food security, sustainability, and other societal problems [4]. We examined the motivations of 161 citizens for participating in a selection of 11 Dutch hackathons in the agricultural sector held from 2016 to 2018. These 11 cases were selected for the following reasons (1) the authors have access to participant data, (2) the first author of this paper participated in two of the hackathons, namely FarmHack (FH) 6 and FH12 and obtained in-depth insight, and (3) the cases are diverse with regard to the types of outcomes competed in the hackathons (i.e., idea, design, application/prototype, visualization) and the focus of the challenges (i.e., problem-driven, data-driven, or both).

The hackathons were organized by FarmHack.NL, a Dutch company which focuses on developing an ecosystem of coders, hackers, developers, planners, designers, domain experts, civil servants and farmers that enables innovation in the agricultural sector using data and technology. Typically, each hackathon offers different themes as described in Table 1.

Table 1. The overview of eleven cases of Dutch agricultural hackathons organized by FarmHack.NL.

Code	Themes	Outcomes	Focus	Year	Respondents
FH1	Data visualization for potato farmer	Visualization	Data-driven	2016	13
FH2	Drones, satellites and crop protection	Application	Problem-driven	2016	16
FH3	From farmer to city	Application	Problem-driven	2016	12
FH4	Network technology and sustainable livestock farming	Design, application	Problem-driven	2016	13
FH5	AgriVision Hackathon	Application	Data-driven	2017	12
FH6	Manure Hack	Application	Data-driven	2017	22
FH7	Smart Dairy Farming	Application	Data-driven	2017	10
FH8	Fishing Hack	Design, application	Problem-driven	2018	21
FH10	Soil Hack Achterhoek	Application	Data-driven	2018	14
FH11	Tractor Hack	Visualization	Data-driven	2018	6
FH12	National Soil Hack	Idea	Data-driven	2018	22

To participate in the hackathons, as long as seats are available, a citizen is only required to register through FarmHack.NL's website and to complete a registration form. The hackathons were for free and the participants were provided with catering services (i.e., coffee breaks, a breakfast, two lunches, and two dinners), sleeping area, internet connection, electricity (cables), wireless network, stationaries and even a guided tour to sites or museums related to the theme. Each hackathon typically lasted for one and a half days.

Each hackathon was organized as follows. First, on the first day's morning, all participants gathered and received an explanation. Each challenge raised in the hackathon was presented by a team leader who was typically an employee of a sponsoring organization. Then, each team leader discussed the challenge in detail in a small group where interested participants joined. This activity was run twice and participants were free to change group. Next, participants chose and joined a team working for a specific challenge. Thereafter, 'hacking' started in these groups, guided by a framework developed by FarmHack.NL which contained questions that should be answered to achieve the desired solution of the challenge. The framework concerned both the technical aspects, such as data and technology involved and social aspects of the solutions. On the second day of the hackathon, teams had to present their solutions to the challenges, followed by a question and answer session, and ended by the announcement of winners and prizes they won. The prizes were varying across hackathons, ranging from 500 to 20,000 euros.

2.2 Data Collection and Analysis

Multiple sources of evidence were collected from October 2017 to February 2019 at several points in time, as described in Table 2. The collected data include the Farm-Hack.NL webpages, notes taken from unstructured interviews with six participants and observations in two hackathons, and multiple qualitative surveys from participant registration data.

Each type of collected data was analyzed for different purposes. Data from the FarmHack.NL webpages and the observational and unstructured interviews notes were used to describe the characteristics of each hackathon and the variance among the hackathons, while the qualitative survey data were analyzed in three stages. First, the participants' backgrounds and roles were grouped and the reasons for participating were coded based on the framework developed based on our literature review (See Sect. 3). We also included new codes emerged in the data. Then the codes were mapped into a classification of motivations for participating in the hackathons. Finally, the new map of roles and factors were analyzed using simple descriptive statistics (i.e., cross tabulation). The analysis was conducted by the first author and reviewed by the second and third authors. The authors also made the qualitative survey and analysis dataset available online as open research data on 4TU Center for Research Data repository at https://doi.org/10.4121/uuid:879be853-ba9d-463d-a2db-51a076e9ce6e.

Table 2. Data collection strategy.

Data source	Data type
Documents	22 hackathon webpages
Survey	Qualitative survey distributed at 11 Farmhacks (n = 161)
Interviews	Notes from six unstructured interviews
Participant-observations	Notes from FH6 and FH12 observations

3 A Framework for Analyzing Citizens' Motivations to Engage in Open Data Hackathons

In this section, we develop a framework for the analysis of our cases. We do so by searching, collecting and selecting open data literature which investigates factors that influence citizens to engage with OGD or to engage in hackathons using Scopus database. We apply the combination of the following keywords *open data* or *open government data* and *use, engagement,* or *hackathon*. We include six publications which are deemed relevant for this study (see Table 3).

Based on the selected papers, we observed that many factors influence citizens to engage with OGD or to engage in an open data hackathon: intrinsic motivations such as fun and enjoyment and intellectual challenge [12]; extrinsic motivations concerning performance expectancy [13] or relative advantage [16], learning and developing skills, and networking [11, 12]; effort expectancy [13] related to ease of use [17]; social influence [13, 18] including contributing to societal benefits [11, 18]; and data quality [18].

We synthesize the empirical findings and propose a framework of citizens' motivations to engage in open data hackathons. Intrinsic and extrinsic motivations of a participant are viewed based on the source of rewards (internal or external) for engaging in the hackathon [19]. A developer/programmer will enjoy building a prototype/application that solves a problem competed in a hackathon. Even if the problem requires a higher level of challenge compared to the developer's current capabilities/skills, he or she will strive to solve it, because he or she feels that his or her status and reputation is at stake.

Performance expectancy and relative advantage is related to the degree to which an individual perceives that engaging in open data hackathons will help him or her attain gains in job performance [20] or will be advantageous to him or her [21]. The developer can also be motivated by delayed benefits that may be received after participating in a hackathon: learning new skills from teammates or expanding the network with prospective employers or investors.

Table 3. A framework of citizens' motivations to engage in open data hackathons.

Factors	Definition	Constructs	Source
Intrinsic motivation	"doing something because it is inherently interesting or enjoyable" [22, p. 859]	Fun and enjoyment	Juell-Skielse, Hjalmarsson, Johannesson and Rudmark [12]
		Intellectual challenge	
Extrinsic motivation	"doing something because it leads to a separate outcome" [22, p. 859]	Performance expectancy/relative advantage	Wirtz, Weyerer and Rösch [17], Zuiderwijk, Janssen and Dwivedi [13], Weerakkody, Irani, Kapoor, Sivarajah and Dwivedi [16]
		Learning and developing skills	Juell-Skielse, Hjalmarsson, Johannesson and Rudmark [12], Gama [11]
		Networking	
Effort expectancy	"the degree of ease associated with the use of the system" [20, p. 450]	Ease of use	Wirtz, Weyerer and Rösch [17], Zuiderwijk, Janssen and Dwivedi [13]
Social influence	"the degree to which an individual perceives that important others believe he or she should use the new system." [20, p. 451]	Influence from a social relationship	Purwanto, Zuiderwijk and Janssen [18], Zuiderwijk, Janssen and Dwivedi [13]
		Contribute to societal benefits	Gama [11], Purwanto, Zuiderwijk and Janssen [18]
Data quality	"data that are fit for use by data consumers" [23, p. 6]	Accuracy	Purwanto, Zuiderwijk and Janssen [18]

A participant's effort expectancy is related to the degree of ease associated with the use of open data and technology for solving a hackathon's challenge. It also concerns the participant's perceived capabilities/skills required for creating solutions which reciprocally affects the perceived ease of use. The more complex the challenge, the bigger the potential of the participant for being felt bored or anxious which in turn degrades his or her motivation [24].

Participants could be influenced by their social relationships to engage in a hackathon. Supervisors might urge their employees to participate in a hackathon. Social influence can also take form as norms and behaviors established in a hackathon team to accomplish shared goals. As a result, participants will be driven to contribute to the benefits of the team or society by solving a hackathon challenge. Data quality has been associated with technical conditions for OGD utilization [10]. Hypothetically, the higher the quality of data, the more it will be used [25].

4 Results

The qualitative survey data received from the hackathon organizer consists of the potential roles of participants and the motivations they participated in the hackathons. The organizer asked participants to select one or more roles (i.e., business developer, marketer, data analyst, developer, concept thinker, data owner, or others). If the participant's role is not provided in the list, "other" can be selected. We created ten groups of roles which include the original categories and four new groups: Manager, Problem

Owner, Student, and Unknown. Manager concerns participants from managerial positions such as CTO (Chief of Technology Officer) and project managers. Problem owner represents citizens who are practitioners having expertise in the hackathon theme, for example, landscape architect and agriculture advisor. When no role was entered by the participant, we used the label Unknown. If a participant has been assigned more than one role, we group him or her into a role by considering the substance of the reasons for participation. The role group which we assigned might be different than one of the roles that the participant stated. For example, we found a participant who declared that he is a data analyst and concept thinker, but we grouped him as a student because he was a junior in a university. Another example concerns a participant saying that he or she is a business developer, data analyst, developer, and concept thinker, whom we grouped into developer because he or she wanted to use technical expertise in GIS and R programming in the hackathon. Thus, several roles were reassigned.

We evaluated the motivations for participation against the framework described in the previous section. We found that the factors that influence citizens to participate in the hackathon were heterogeneous and a citizen may be motivated by many factors. From the 161 records, we extracted 201 codes representing the reasons. These codes were grouped into the constructs proposed in the framework based on their similarity of meanings. For example, we interpreted a participant's expectancy of the manure market transparency as an aspiration to contribute to societal benefits. Motivations that did not fit in our initial framework, for example, "the conventional farming is not a sustainable system" were grouped into 'Other'. We cross-tabulated the frequency of constructs and arranged them in Table 4. Most participants mention their participation in the hackathons as part of their work (n = 50) such as looking for a job or business opportunity, representing a company, or selling ideas or a product. Personal benefits such as 'winning a prize' and 'pizza' were the least mentioned by participants (n = 2).

Unsurprisingly, the results showed that constructs related to effort expectancy and data quality were not mentioned by participants regardless of their roles since the data and their quality are unknown to participants and so are the efforts required for utilizing them. Although *data* was mentioned frequently in the motivations, most participants conceive that it has the potential to improve the agricultural sector, but never refer to its quality.

4.1 Intrinsic Motivations

Fun and enjoyment are prominent in the developer and problem owner groups. This result indicates that the developers and problem owners enjoyed participating in hackathons specifically because of the topic itself. The developers seemed to enjoy applying technical aspects such as programming. Among these developers, three participants indicated that they enjoy hacking activities by saying "software hacking in the agro sector is my thing," and "I like working in agricultural robotics and IoT." Interestingly, two developers have engaged in a hackathon before and they wanted to continue the hacking experience. The problem owners were interested in the topic of the hackathons because it is something that they have to deal with every day. One of them said the topic was an "interesting subject, in line with my daily practice."

Participants who were driven by intellectual challenge mainly felt challenged to apply and exchange their skills, ideas, knowledge, or expertise.

Table 4. The mapping of citizen roles and motivations to engage in open data hackathons. (The table has been made available on 4TU Center for Research Data repository at https://doi.org/10.4121/uuid:29296049-0222-4df3-9ba7-acdd4949d1b9)

Category/Subcategory of Factor*	BD (n=18)	CT (n=19)	DA (n=25)	DO (n=4)	DV (n=35)	MG (n=10)	MK (n=3)	PO (n=25)	ST (n=13)	NA (n=9)	Total (n=161)
Intrinsic motivations	27.8% (5)	31.6% (6)	36.0% (9)	25.0% (1)	57.1% (20)	50.0% (5)	0.0% (0)	56.0% (14)	23.1% (3)	33.3% (3)	41.0% (66)
Fun and enjoyment	16.7% (3)	10.5% (2)	28.0% (7)	25.0% (1)	37.1% (13)	40.0% (4)	0.0% (0)	32.0% (8)	15.4% (2)	11.1% (1)	25.5% (41)
Intellectual challenge	11.1% (2)	21.1% (4)	8.0% (2)	0.0% (0)	20.0% (7)	10.0% (1)	0.0% (0)	24.0% (6)	7.7% (1)	22.2% (2)	15.5% (25)
Extrinsic motivations	55.6% (10)	42.1% (8)	48.0% (12)	50.0% (2)	45.7% (16)	40.0% (4)	66.7% (2)	36.0% (9)	69.2% (9)	33.3% (3)	46.6% (75)
Working	44.4% (8)	21.1% (4)	32.0% (8)	50.0% (2)	31.4% (11)	40.0% (4)	33.3% (1)	24.0% (6)	30.8% (4)	22.2% (2)	31.1% (50)
Learning and developing skills	5.6% (1)	15.8% (3)	8.0% (2)	0.0% (0)	11.4% (4)	0.0% (0)	33.3% (1)	12.0% (3)	23.1% (3)	11.1% (1)	11.2% (18)
Networking	5.6% (1)	5.3% (1)	4.0% (1)	0.0% (0)	0.0% (0)	0.0% (0)	0.0% (0)	0.0% (0)	15.4% (2)	0.0% (0)	3.1% (5)
Personal benefits	0.0% (0)	0.0% (0)	4.0% (1)	0.0% (0)	2.9% (1)	0.0% (0)	0.0% (0)	0.0% (0)	0.0% (0)	0.0% (0)	1.2% (2)
Social influence	22.2% (4)	31.6% (6)	56.0% (14)	25.0% (1)	17.1% (6)	10.0% (1)	0.0% (0)	32.0% (8)	46.2% (6)	33.3% (3)	30.4% (49)
Social influence	11.1% (2)	5.3% (1)	28.0% (7)	0.0% (0)	8.6% (3)	0.0% (0)	0.0% (0)	4.0% (1)	0.0% (0)	33.3% (3)	10.6% (17)
Contribute to societal benefits	5.6% (1)	10.5% (2)	8.0% (2)	0.0% (0)	2.9% (1)	0.0% (0)	0.0% (0)	16.0% (4)	30.8% (4)	0.0% (0)	8.7% (14)
Teamwork	5.6% (1)	5.3% (1)	8.0% (2)	25.0% (1)	0.0% (0)	10.0% (1)	0.0% (0)	8.0% (2)	7.7% (1)	0.0% (0)	5.6% (9)
Contribute to challenge	0.0% (0)	10.5% (2)	12.0% (3)	0.0% (0)	5.7% (2)	0.0% (0)	0.0% (0)	4.0% (1)	7.7% (1)	0.0% (0)	5.6% (9)
Previous experience	0.0% (0)	0.0% (0)	4.0% (1)	0.0% (0)	5.7% (2)	0.0% (0)	0.0% (0)	4.0% (1)	0.0% (0)	0.0% (0)	2.5% (4)
Others	0.0% (0)	5.3% (1)	8.0% (2)	0.0% (0)	2.9% (1)	10.0% (1)	33.3% (1)	0.0% (0)	0.0% (0)	11.1% (1)	4.4% (7)

Notes: * In % (absolute number of respondents)

BD=Business Developer, CT=Concept Thinker, DA=Data Analyst, DO=Data Owner, DV=Developer, MG=Manager, MK=Marketer, PO=Problem Owner, ST=Student, NA=Unknown

4.2   Extrinsic Motivations

Work is the most influential motivation and stands out in the group of citizens in the roles of business developer, marketer, and student. Participants considered their engagement in the hackathon as part of their jobs. For example, three participants participated to collect data that can enrich their research or thesis. Thirteen participants were motivated to look for a new opportunity either for their companies or careers.

Interestingly, it appears that participants who have a non-technical background (e.g., problem owner) would like to learn more about how data and applications can help them. While those from a technical background (e.g., data analyst, developer) mainly wanted to upgrade their skills or knowledge or learn new techniques or methods.

Only five out of 161 participants said to be motivated by networking. One of them did not specify what kind of network he or she wanted to create, while others wanted to expand to a specific network. A fisherman's technician wanted to create a network with other technicians who can help design a particular trawler. A researcher sought for a network of developers and data analysts for a case study. A data analyst looked for other people who are enthusiastic about agriculture, technology, and data. And, a user interface designer wanted to get in touch with companies to show them what his or her company can do.

Only two participants mentioned personal benefits: a data analyst who wanted a pizza and a developer motivated to win a prize.

4.3   Social Influence

At least four types of social entity were mentioned to be influential to the participants: supervisor (i.e., a participant's team leader), colleague (e.g., data scientist, farmer), company (e.g., FarmHack.NL), and family (e.g., uncle, partner). Usually, a participant influenced by a social relationship would also have other reasons to participate at the same time. For example, a participant who was urged by his or her supervisor to participate, inarguably, means that he or she performs a job in the hackathon.

Different reasons to contribute to societal benefits were observed. One participant wanted a change: more transparency in the manure market, while others wanted to contribute to practical improvement and innovation in the agricultural sector or encourage the involvement of the community. Some participants wanted to contribute to the teams working out for a solution to the hackathon challenges. A data analyst said that he or she wanted to work in a team "to solve a challenging problem." A developer stated that "with my experience in IT, drone technology and precision farming, I think I can make a nice contribution to this challenge." Nine participants were motivated to work in an interdisciplinary team composed of citizens from different background and discipline. By teamworking, participants can learn from each other, exchange or even create new ideas, as well as try to solve a challenge together.

4.4   Previous Experience

Previous hackathon experience was a factor not found in the literature review, but our qualitative survey data showed that it was an important motivation for some participants. Four participants said that they had participated in hackathons before the FarmHacks and wanted to continue participating.

5 Discussion

The results show that most citizens (50 out of 161) appear extrinsically motivated by work-related performance to engage in the open agricultural data hackathons. In contrast, citizens with the developer and problem owner roles (n = 21) are intrinsically motivated by the fun and enjoyment that open data hackathons bring. This finding is in line with previous research investigating the motivations of participants of open transportation data hackathons in Sweden [12], and open city data hackathons in Australia and New Zealand [11].

From the results, we can observe that, on the one hand, most citizens seemed to be driven by only one motive (130 out of 161 participants). On the other hand, some were influenced by multiple motives (31 participants). Citizens who have only one motivation appeared highly motivated because they focus on only one goal in a hackathon, while citizens with multiple motives might want to continually engage in the hackathons until their multiple goals are achieved. Indeed, individuals, such as hackers engaging in free/open source software projects, can be influenced by different, and sometimes contradictory, motivations [19].

Focusing on the multiple motives-driven citizens, we suggest that a pattern of hierarchical relationship exists between motivations, especially social influence and work. A citizen who was asked by his or her supervisor (socially influenced) to engage in a hackathon for delivering support for participants is one of the examples of hierarchical motivation. This implies that participating in a hackathon as part of employment is sometimes determined by social influence as suggested by Zuiderwijk, Janssen and Dwivedi [13].

Work, observed as the main motivation, indicates that most participants prioritize their personal gains. Work also indicates that many companies will likely send their employees to participate in hackathons to look for an opportunity to expand their businesses. Within this frame, we can assume that profit-oriented themes are the most preferred in the context of open agricultural data use. This further indicates that companies are valuing the economic impacts of using open data. Hence, stimulating agriculture companies to become involved in open agriculture data engagement is an important agenda for open data policymakers and hackathon organizers.

6 Conclusion

This paper aims to explore the motivations of citizens who engage in open agriculture data hackathons. Based on a case study of 11 open agriculture data hackathons held between 2016 and 2018 in the Netherlands, we found that participants of these hackathons have different roles, including business developer, concept thinker, data analyst, data owner, developer, manager, marketer, problem owner, and student.

This paper sheds light upon the mapping of factors (i.e., intrinsic motivations, extrinsic motivations, effort expectancy, social influence, and data quality) that drive citizen engagement in open data hackathons based on their roles. In the cases we studied, most of the surveyed citizens were driven by extrinsic motivation, i.e., performing work. They considered their engagement as part of their work performance.

However, among the examined roles, most developers and problem owners appear to be influenced by intrinsic motivation related to the fun and enjoyment of being engaged in the hackathons. Among the analyzed factors, effort expectancy and data quality seem to be uninfluential since no participants mention reasons associated with these factors. This is predictable because the quality of the open agricultural data and the efforts required to utilize the data are unknown to participants.

The above-mentioned conclusions indicate that a pattern of relationship exists between motivations and roles and thus, this study advances the discussion to identify different roles which were not investigated in previous research on the motivations of citizens in hackathons. Our results show that it is important for open data policymakers and hackathon organizers to consider different approaches based on citizens' roles when organizing open data hackathons. Hence, a different strategy should be used to involve, for example, citizens sent by companies compared to developers and problem owners who join the hackathon because they like to discuss the topics of the hackathons.

The limitation of this study concerns the intermediating factors such as personal background (e.g., age, gender) or other situational conditions (e.g., how far the hackathon location is from a participant's house) which might play a role in citizens' motivation but were not taken into account. We suggest that future research explores the relationship between intermediating factors and citizens' motivations.

This paper contributes to the literature by providing insights in the motivations of citizens engaging in open agriculture data hackathons in comparison with hackathons in other sectors, and by mapping citizens' roles to their motivations for engaging in such hackathons.

References

1. Jetzek, T., Avital, M., Bjorn-Andersen, N.: Data-driven innovation through open government data. J. Theor. Appl. Electron. Comm. **9**, 100–120 (2014)
2. The White House. https://www.whitehouse.gov/the_press_office/TransparencyandOpen Government
3. Wolfert, S., Ge, L., Verdouw, C., Bogaardt, M.-J.: Big data in smart farming – a review. Agric. Syst. **153**, 69–80 (2017)
4. Poppe, K., Wolfert, S., Verdouw, C., Renwick, A.: A European perspective on the economics of big data. Farm Policy J. **12**, 11–19 (2015)
5. Janssen, S.J.C., et al.: Towards a new generation of agricultural system data, models and knowledge products: information and communication technology. Agric. Syst. **155**, 200–212 (2017)
6. Susha, I., Janssen, M., Verhulst, S.: Data collaboratives as "bazaars"? A review of coordination problems and mechanisms to match demand for data with supply. Transform. Gov.: People, Process Policy **11**, 157–172 (2017)
7. Concilio, G., Molinari, F., Morelli, N.: Empowering citizens with open data by urban hackathons. In: 7th International Conference for E-Democracy and Open Government (CeDEM), pp. 125–134. IEEE, Krems (2017)
8. Hartmann, S., Mainka, A., Stock, W.G.: Opportunities and challenges for civic engagement: a global investigation of innovation competitions. Int. J. Knowl. Soc. Res. **7**, 1–15 (2016)

9. Briscoe, G., Mulligan, C.: Digital Innovation: The Hackathon Phenomenon. Queen Mary University of London (2014)
10. Safarov, I., Meijer, A., Grimmelikhuijsen, S.: Utilization of open government data: a systematic literature review of types, conditions, effects and users. Inf. Polity **22**, 1–24 (2017)
11. Gama, K.: Crowdsourced software development in civic apps - motivations of civic hackathons participants. In: 19th International Conference on Enterprise Information Systems, Porto, Portugal, pp. 550–555 (2017)
12. Juell-Skielse, G., Hjalmarsson, A., Johannesson, P., Rudmark, D.: Is the Public motivated to engage in open data innovation? In: 13th International Conference on Electronic Government Dublin, Ireland (2014)
13. Zuiderwijk, A., Janssen, M., Dwivedi, Y.K.: Acceptance and use predictors of open data technologies: drawing upon the unified theory of acceptance and use of technology. Gov. Inform. Q. **32**, 429–440 (2015)
14. Yin, R.K.: Case Study Research: Design and Methods. SAGE Publications Inc., Thousand Oaks (2014)
15. Herriott, R.E., Firestone, W.A.: Multisite qualitative policy research: optimizing description and generalizability. Educ. Res. **12**, 14–19 (1983)
16. Weerakkody, V., Irani, Z., Kapoor, K., Sivarajah, U., Dwivedi, Y.K.: Open data and its usability: an empirical view from the citizen's perspective. Inf. Syst. Front. **19**, 285–300 (2017)
17. Wirtz, B.W., Weyerer, J.C., Rösch, M.: Citizen and open government: an empirical analysis of antecedents of open government data. Int. J. Public Adm. **41**, 308–320 (2018)
18. Purwanto, A., Zuiderwijk, A., Janssen, M.: Citizen engagement in an open election data initiative: a case study of Indonesian's "Kawal Pemilu". In: Zuiderwijk, A., Hinnant, C.C. (eds.) The 19th Annual International Conference on Digital Government Research. Association for Computing Machinery, Delft (2018)
19. Lakhani, K.R., Wolf, R.G.: Why hackers do what they do: understanding motivation and effort in free/open source software projects. In: Feller, J., Fitzgerald, B., Hissam, S.A., Lakhani, K.R. (eds.) Perspectives on Free and Open Source Software. MIT Press, Cambridge (2005)
20. Venkatesh, V., Morris, M.G., Davis, G.B., Davis, F.D.: User acceptance of information technology: toward a unified view. MIS Q. **27**, 425–478 (2003)
21. Rogers, E.M.: Diffusion of Innovations. The Free Press, New York (1983)
22. Deci, E.L.: Intrinsic motivation. In: Craighead, W.E., Nemeroff, C.B. (eds.) The Concise Corsini Encyclopedia of Psychology and Behavioral Science, pp. 494–495. Wiley, Hoboken (2004)
23. Wang, R.Y., Strong, D.M.: Beyond accuracy: what data quality means to data consumers. J. Manag. Inf. Syst. **12**, 5–33 (1996)
24. Csikszentmihalyi, M.: Beyond boredom and anxiety: the experience of play in work and games. Jossey-Bass, Inc., San Francisco (1975)
25. Zuiderwijk, A., Janssen, M., Choenni, S., Meijer, R., Alibaks, R.S.: Socio-technical impediments of open data. Electron. J. eGovernment **10**, 156–172 (2012)

Substituting Computers for Mobile Phones?
An Analysis of the Effect of Device Divide
on Digital Skills in Brazil

Marcelo Henrique de Araujo$^{(\boxtimes)}$ ⓘD and Nicolau Reinhard ⓘD

School of Economics, Business and Accounting, University of São Paulo,
Av. Luciano Gualberto 908, São Paulo, SP 05508-101, Brazil
{marcelo.haraujo, reinhard}@usp.br

Abstract. This paper aims to analyze the phenomenon of device divide in the Brazilian context in order to understand how different Internet access devices and sociodemographic factors influence the development of digital skills. The research uses the microdata of 2014 and 2016 editions of a Brazilian nationwide survey named ICT Households survey. The main findings show that mobile devices are widely used by Brazilian Internet users. However, while in upper classes this device plays the role of complementary access to other devices, allowing users to access the Internet using computer and mobile platforms, for lower-income groups mobile is the only means of Internet access, substituting the use of computer equipment. The results also demonstrate that Internet users who access the Internet using both computational and mobile devices exhibit the highest level of digital skills. In contrast, users connecting exclusively via mobile show lower levels of digital skills which might reduce their effectiveness in using the Internet. These outcomes show the relevance of understanding the conditions of Internet access as well as their implication for the development of digital skills and provision of Internet services.

Keywords: Digital skills · Device divide · Digital inequalities · Digital society

1 Introduction

Internet access is increasing worldwide, with more than half the world population (51.2%) using it, reaching a mark of approximately 3.9 billion Internet users [1]. Nevertheless, the question remains if this growth alone contributes to building an increasingly inclusive information society. Growth of internet usage varies between countries, as in developed nations, on average, four out of five people have access to the Internet, in developing countries this rate is approximately 47%, showing that providing universal access to the Internet is still a significant challenge to these countries [1].

The first digital divide studies date back to the mid-nineties and focused exclusively on the dimension of material access to Information and Communication Technologies (ICT), with an emphasis on the dichotomous division between those who have access to the Internet and those who have not [2]. Investigations based on this approach are known as first-order digital divide [2, 3]. However, from the 2000s on, this view of

© IFIP International Federation for Information Processing 2019
Published by Springer Nature Switzerland AG 2019
P. Panagiotopoulos et al. (Eds.): ePart 2019, LNCS 11686, pp. 142–154, 2019.
https://doi.org/10.1007/978-3-030-27397-2_12

exclusion restricted to material access starts being challenged, since digital inequalities remained even after overcoming the Internet access barrier, such as differences in terms of the level of digital skills and/or engagement in ICT use. This group of studies is known as second-order digital divide [3, 4]. Both the first and second order studies on digital divide show that Internet access, as well as the mastery of digital skills and Internet use, are unevenly distributed between Internet users based on different sociodemographic characteristics such as gender, age, geographic area, and social class. As a result, these sociodemographic factors are commonly classified as determinants of digital divide [3, 5, 6].

Even with the widening of the debate on digital divide beyond material access to the Internet, understanding the effects of this dimension is still essential in order to qualify the Internet access, as well as to understand its implications in terms of the online experience [7]. With technological evolution and convergence, connecting to the Internet is no longer an activity restricted to computers, and can be performed by different devices (e.g. cell phones, TVs, game consoles, etc.), providing increasingly ubiquitous and mobile access [7–9].

The relevance of the devices used for Internet access in the debate on digital divide is evidenced by the increase in the number of Internet users connected via mobile devices. In developing countries, these devices are a cost-effective Internet access option for low-income users. However, even if mobile and computer devices can both provide access to the Internet, the types of devices used offer different online experiences, potentially impacting on the use of the Internet and on digital skills development [7, 10], characterizing the existence of a device divide [11, 13].

Although this type of exclusion based on Internet access devices may have implications for the other levels of digital divide, few studies have empirically analyzed the effects of this device divide for the development of digital skills, especially in the context of developing countries. In this sense, this paper aims to delve into this phenomenon in order to highlight how different Internet access devices and sociodemographic factors influence the development of digital skills in a developing country such as Brazil. This research adopts a quantitative methodological approach using the microdata of the 2014 and 2016 editions of a nationwide survey called ICT Households survey, coordinated by the Regional Center for Studies on the Development of the Information Society (Cetic.br), which measures the ownership and use of Information and Communication Technologies by Brazilian citizens.

2 Literature Review

2.1 Device Divide

The diffusion of mobile Internet access is a subject of interest for both academics and policymakers, especially because of the potential role of leapfrogging due to this type of device. Mobile leapfrogging is the process by which new users obtain access to the Internet via mobile devices, without using traditional computer equipment such as the PC [11, 14]. This issue has been the subject of intense debate, as some authors see this leapfrogging effect as beneficial, enabling a rapid and cost-effective reduction of

Internet access gaps and also reducing the need for public policy interventions to deal with the persistent first-order digital divide [14]. On the other hand, a second group presents a critical view of this understanding, arguing that Internet access via mobile devices offers an inferior online experience [7, 10, 11].

In this debate on access devices, most studies have focused on the clash between mobile and computer equipment [7]. Devices such as mobile phones and smartphones offer advantages in convenience, more affordable pricing, mobility, continuous use of the internet (ubiquity), applications that use geolocation, games and streaming services [7, 15]. However, even with technological developments, these devices are not entirely equivalent to computers, due to technical limitations: less memory, lower processing speed, smaller screen, limited typing capabilities. Those features make using the Internet more challenging and complex on the mobile platform, demanding a greater cognitive load on the part of the user [7, 9, 10, 12].

The limitations on mobile affordances may also imply a reduction in the user's level of engagement, especially in activities that require content creation and/or information search [10]. The search for information tends to become a more superficial process and difficult to perform on mobile equipment, whereas on computers such activity tends to be more immersive, allowing a rich search and with more refined results [8]. Regarding creative activities, although they can be conducted on mobile devices, the elaboration of more complex content tends to be more easily performed on the computing platform [7]. While the use of computers favors online capital-enhancing activities, mobile devices are associated with specific activities such as leisure and entertainment and personal security [7–9, 13, 31].

In summary, such findings suggest that mobile-only internet access may affect negatively the development of digital skills. Although few studies have explored this relationship, there is evidence that users of both mobile devices and computers tend to broaden their digital skills spectrum [10]. In this paper, the concept of device divide is operationalized by combining the different Internet access devices, segmenting users in: mobile-only Internet users; computer-only Internet users; and users that connect using both computer and mobile, named multiplatform users [13].

2.2 Digital Skills

Digital skills are defined as the ability to respond pragmatically and intuitively to the challenges and opportunities in exploiting the potential of the Internet and avoid frustrations in its use [16]. In this paper, the focus relies specifically on the skills required to use the Internet (Internet Skills) regardless of the equipment and/or technology employed. Therefore, specific device-dependent skills are not within the scope of the definition adopted [3, 6, 24].

The first instruments developed to measure digital skills took a very limited view of this concept, i.e., considering only the basic and technical skills for using the Internet, such as the ability to use browser software, download and/or upload files [e.g. 4, 17, 18]. With the evolution of Internet use, researchers began to expand the understanding of digital skills, considering both the technical skills and content-related skills (those related to information search, communication and online content production) [6, 19–23]. The digital divide literature presents a wide variety of proposals for measuring digital skills considering their specific domains/dimensions (e.g. communication, informational, creative). One of the main digital skills frameworks is based on the distinction between the purposes of the skills, that is, dividing between the technical skills necessary to use the Internet (medium-related skills) and those related to the content (content-related skills). Regarding technical skills, we highlight the following: (i) operational and (ii) formal skills, while considering the competences related to content, the following stand out: (iii) informational; (iv) communication; (v) content creation and (vi) strategic skills [24].

In this paper, digital skills will be measured considering four specific domains. The first refers to the *operational skills*, consisting of the technical and basic ability to operate the Internet, regardless of the type of device and equipment used. The second is the *informational* skills, the ability to search, select and evaluate the information identified. The third is the *communication skills* consisting of the ability to encode and decode messages and, consequently, to construct, understand and exchange meanings through Internet applications. Finally, the last domain involves *content-creation skills* the ability to create online content with acceptable levels of quality and to publish it online [24].

Empirical studies have shown the role of socioeconomic, generational, geographical and gender inequalities to explain the differences in the digital skills levels of Internet users [2, 5, 6].

Regarding the relation between age and digital skills, the findings have been varied, with results that indicate positive and negative relationships between generational attribute and skills [6]. In general, studies suggest that younger Internet users have a greater ability to perform a large set of online activities, faster, more easily and more fluently, with lower levels of anxiety in the Internet use experience [4]. Although intuitive, some studies question this "superiority" of younger people in the use of the Internet, finding evidence that younger users are more competent only in technical-instrumental skills. On the other hand, in skills that demand information search and content evaluation, older users tend to perform better [20–22, 26].

The findings also point out that the level of education, as well as socioeconomic status (social class), have a positive relation with digital skills. In other words, the greater the socioeconomic status of the Internet users (related to schooling and income), the greater will be their level of digital competence [6, 20–22].

There is no consensus in the literature about gender differences in relation to digital skills. Some authors point out that there is no distinction between genders concerning levels of digital competence [25]. However, others reinforce the stereotype based on gender, in which women are at a disadvantage in relation to the use of the Internet, due to aspects related to technological aversion and higher levels of technophobia, implying lower access rates and less capacity to use the web [27].

3   Methodological Design

Aiming at understanding the phenomenon of the device divide, as well as its implications on the levels of digital skills of Internet users in Brazil, this research uses the microdata of the ICT Households survey coordinated by Cetic.br. The ICT Households survey consists of a nationwide survey conducted annually since 2005 to measure the availability, possession and use of ICT by the Brazilian population aged 10 years and older [28]. In order to ensure international comparability, the design of this survey follows the set of guidelines and methodological definitions described in the Manual for Measuring ICT Access and Use by Households and Individuals, published by ITU [28]. Tables 1 and 2 present the set of ICT households survey variables used in this paper.

In order to perform the data analysis, OLS regression (Ordinary Least Square) was used in order to demonstrate the effect of the different determinants of digital divide (e.g. geographic area, social class, age and gender) and Internet access devices on the domains of digital skills. This multivariate technique allows exploring the linear relationship in a set of explanatory variables with a metric dependent variable [29].

The first set of variables shown in Table 1 are the sociodemographic factors, that is, the personal and positional characteristics commonly considered to be determinants of the digital divide. Although the ICT households survey includes also other demographic attributes, for this research we selected only those that represent inequalities of geographical (area), generational (age), socioeconomic (social class and schooling) and gender, because they are the most frequently cited ones in the literature [2, 5].

Table 1. Demographic factors and device used to access internet (variables)

	Variables	Items/Scale
Demographic factors	Geographic area	1 = Urban; 2 = Rural
	Age groups	1 = 10 to 15 years old
		2 = 16 to 24 years old
		3 = 25 to 34 years old
		4 = 35 to 44 years old
		5 = 45 to 59 years old
		6 = 60 years or older
	Gender	1 = Male; 2 = Female
	Social class (*socioeconomic status*)	1 = Class A and B (higher classes)
		2 = Class C (middle class)
		3 = Class D and E (working classes)
Devices used to access internet	Desktop	1 = Yes; 0 = No
	Laptop	1 = Yes; 0 = No
	Tablet	1 = Yes; 0 = No
	Mobile phone	1 = Yes; 0 = No
	Game console	1 = Yes; 0 = No
	TV set	1 = Yes; 0 = No

Source: ICT Household Survey 2014 and 2016 [28]

The geographical area consists of the location of the respondent's residence, which can be classified as urban or rural, according to the Brazilian Demographic Census. Urban areas are understood as cities (municipalities), villages (districts) or even isolated urban areas, while locations outside this boundary are classified as rural areas. The second variable represents the age group, with respondents of 10 years or more, followed by their gender. Social class represents the concept of socioeconomic status of respondents which is a composite indicator based on the level of education of the head of household, as well as the ownership of the household's durable goods (see [28]). In the published microdata of ICT Households survey, the respondents are classified into four social classes: A (highest), B, C and D and E (lowest). However, because of the low proportion of class A individuals in relation to the other classes, we chose to group classes A and B, reducing this categorical variable to these three classes: A and B (group with greater economic power), C (middle class) and D and E (extract of lower economic power).

Table 2 presents the items used to measure digital skills of the Internet user. Since the ICT Households survey does not have specific items and scales to measure this type of skills, these competencies are measured from a set of proxies with dichotomous scale that represent the activities carried out online by the Internet user in the last three months, as shown in Table 2. In line with the digital divide and digital literacy literature, which adopt the conceptualization of digital skills considering their specific domains/ dimensions, leading to the following ones: (i) operational; (ii) informational; (iii) communication and (iv) content creation [19, 23, 24]. The operationalization of these four domains is given by the sum of the items corresponding to each of these domains.

Table 2. Items used to measure digital skills

Digital skills	Dichotomous items
Operational	Downloading films;
	Downloading songs;
	Downloading games;
	Downloading computer software, programs or applications
Informational	Looking up information on products and services;
	Looking up information on health or healthcare services;
	Looking up information on travel and accommodations;
	Job searches or Sending resumes;
	Looking up information in virtual encyclopedia websites such as Wikipedia;
	Looking up information available in government agencies websites
Communication	Sending and receiving e-mails;
	Sending instant messages, such as chatting via Facebook, Skype or Whatsapp;
	Talking to people using programs such as Skype;
	Taking part in social networks sites, such as Facebook, Orkut or Google+;
	Participating in discussion lists or forums;
	Using microblogs, such as Twitter
Content-creation	Sharing content on the Internet, such as texts, images or videos;
	Creating or updating blogs, Internet pages or websites;
	Posting personally created texts, images or videos on the Internet

Source: ICT Household Survey 2014 and 2016 [28]

4   Characterizing Brazilian Internet Users Sample

For the 2014 and 2016 editions of the ICT Households survey, respectively 19,221 and 20,772 individuals from urban and rural areas in Brazil were interviewed. Since this paper focuses specifically on Internet users, the analysis considered only those respondents who reported having used the Internet at least once in the last three months. Therefore, the sample of this paper is composed by 10,221 (2014) and 11,050 (2016) respondents.

Table 3 presents the demographic profile of the Internet user in Brazil, indicating a predominance of urban users, more than 90% of the sample in both years. This geographical inequality may be due to the scarcity of technological infrastructure available in the rural areas, limiting the provision of this type of service. Regarding age, the results show a concentration of Internet users in the three younger age groups (10 to 34 years), thus reinforcing generational inequality, with the percentage of Internet users being inversely proportional to the age of the respondent [2, 5, 16]. There is a certain balance in the distribution of male and female Internet users, with a higher proportion of women in both years. The distribution of Internet users among the social classes shows a concentration of users in class C (middle class). Between 2014 and 2016 there was an increase in the proportion of Internet users in the lower-income social classes (D and E). These results show the socioeconomic structural inequality, in which lower purchasing power leads to reduced possibility to afford computational devices and/or Internet connection services.

Table 3. Demographic profile of Brazilian internet users (N_{2014} = 10,221; N_{2016} = 11,050)

	2014		2016	
	N	%	N	%
Geographic area				
Urban	9703	94.9	10283	93.1
Rural	518	5.1	767	6.9
Age groups				
10 to 15 years old	1118	10.9	1046	9.5
16 to 24 years old	2426	23.7	2622	23.7
25 to 34 years old	2835	27.7	2999	27.1
35 to 44 years old	1907	18.7	1896	17.2
45 to 59 years old	1501	14.7	1854	16.8
60 years or older	434	4.2	633	5.7
Gender				
Male	4665	45.6	5115	46.3
Female	5556	54.4	5935	53.7
Social class				
Class A and B (upper classes)	4229	41.4	3840	34.8
Class C (middle class)	5173	50.6	5936	53.7
Class D and E (working classes)	819	8.0	1274	11.5
Total	10221		11050	

Regarding the device divide, there was an increase in the percentage of users connecting to the Internet via mobile phones, reaching 93.7% in 2016. Simultaneously, there was a decrease in the use of computers as an Internet access device. While in 2014, respectively, 52.3% and 46% of respondents accessed the web via desktops and laptops, in 2016 these percentages dropped to 32.2% and 33.7%. This trend is sustained when analyzing the combination of different Internet access devices, as between 2014 and 2016, the percentage of computer-only internet users dropped from 22% to only 6%, while the number of mobile-only internet users doubled from 21% to 42%. In this period there was also a reduction among multiplatform Internet users, reduced from 57% to 52%. The growth in the use of mobile phones to access the Internet occurred in all social classes. However, while in classes A and B (upper classes) the percentage of multiplatform users remained stable ($\sim$71%), with about 23% of Internet users accessing only via mobile phone, in classes D and E, the rate of mobile-only internet users jumped from 40% to 71%, with only 22% of multiplatform users. This result suggests that in lower economic classes the mobile phone is the primary means of internet access, being a more affordable option in comparison to computer devices.

Table 4 illustrates the inequality in the digital skills levels of Internet users in Brazil. These results show that, both in 2014 and 2016, online communication is the domain with highest skills in all categories. Among the communication activities, the most frequent ones are sending messages via instant messaging applications (89%) and use of social network sites (76%). Both activities are the ones most often carried out by users of the upper classes and also those with less economic power.

Table 4. Digital skills levels of Brazilian internet users (2014–2016)

Digital skills domain	2014				2016			
	$\overline{X}$	%	SD	α	$\overline{X}$	%	SD	α
Operational [0–4]	1.4	35.8	1.5	0.8	1.2	30.3	1.30	0.7
Informational [0–6]	2.2	36.7	1.9	0.8	2.0	33.5	1.75	0.8
Communication [0–6]	2.8	46.2	1.5	0.7	3.1	51.0	1.35	0.6
Content-creation [0–3]	1.3	42.7	1.0	0.7	1.2	40.7	0.99	0.6

$\overline{X}$ = Sample Mean; % = percentage of activities performed by the Internet user in each digital skills domain; SD = sample standard-deviation; α = Cronbach's Alpha.

5 Analyzing the Effect of Device Divide in Digital Skills

The OLS regression technique was used to understand the factors explaining the differences in digital skills levels of Internet users. The model included, as independent variables, the sociodemographic attributes and the combination of Internet access devices. For increased precision, the model used the metric variable of user age instead of the previously mentioned age group. Table 5 shows the four tested models, demonstrating the effect of the independent variables on each of the digital skills domains. Preliminary data inspection indicated problems of heteroscedasticity of the residuals. To overcome this problem, the Huber-White econometric procedure was used to estimate robust standard errors of the regression [30].

Table 5 summarizes the main results of the OLS regression with robust standard errors, presenting the standardized coefficients for each of the independent variables of the model. We decided to present the standardized coefficients in order to highlight the relative importance of each independent variable to the understanding of the dependent variables' behavior [29].

Table 5 shows a negative relation between the internet users age and their level of digital skills for the operational, communication and content creation domains, indicating that the older the age, the lower is the digital skills level. The only exception is the informational skills, as the more recent results (2016) did not evidence differences in the digital skills level based on the age attribute, although the 2014 data suggested a higher level of informational skills among older users. In summary, although younger users demonstrated superior performance in most skills, the findings allow us to question the premise of innate digital superiority of those users commonly classified as digital natives [26].

Table 5. Effect of sociodemographic factors and device divide in digital skills (*standardized coefficients*)

	Operational		Informational		Communication		Content-Creation	
	2014	2016	2014	2016	2014	2016	2014	2016
Age	-0.21***	-0.26***	0.07***	0.00	-0.06***	-0.08***	-0.13***	-0.14***
Gender (ref. Female)								
Male	0.11***	0.18***	-0.02*	0.01	-0.01	-0.03***	-0.01	-0.01
Geographic Area (ref. Rural)								
Urban	0.03***	0.02***	0.04***	0.05***	0.05***	0.05***	0.03***	0.03***
Social Class (ref. Class A and B)								
Class C (middle class)	-0.12***	-0.03***	-0.18***	-0.10***	-0.19***	-0.13***	-0.11***	-0.07***
Class D and E (working classes)	-0.13***	-0.05***	-0.16***	-0.14***	-0.16***	-0.15***	-0.12***	-0.09***
Device to access Internet (ref. Only mobile)								
Only Computer	-0.05***	-0.02***	0.06***	0.02**	-0.07***	-0.17***	-0.10***	-0.09***
Multiplatform (both computer and mobile)	0.20***	0.21***	0.32***	0.34***	0.25***	0.26***	0,15***	0.17***
R²	0.16	0.17	0.17	0.17	0.17	0.19	0.10	0.09

(***) $p < 0.01$; (**) $p < 0.05$; (*) $p < 0.10$;

These results show that men presented a higher level of operational skills. On the other hand, in the other skills, there was little difference between men and women, suggesting the limitation of the gender attribute to explain differences in content-related skills. Regarding the geographic area, although the coefficients are statistically significant at 1%, it has a small contribution in explaining differences in digital skills levels between urban and rural users.

The results for social class show the discriminatory effect of the socioeconomic attribute. Users with higher socioeconomic status (A and B), with higher income and schooling, are those with a higher level of digital skills. It confirms, therefore, the positive relation of social class with the digital skills identified in the literature. This result reinforces that positional inequalities affect the level of online competence of Internet users, indicating that previous off-line inequalities are maintained and amplified in the digital world [31].

The findings of Table 5 also show that those who access the Internet using both computer and mobile devices (multiplatform) have a higher level of digital skills, indicating that users that connect through both platforms can harness the specific advantages of each type of device, overcoming any limitations in their affordances, and increasing their digital skills [10].

The results also allow us to assess the differences in digital skills between mobile-only internet users and computer-only internet users, showing that those who access the Internet exclusively via mobile phone have a lower level of informational skills. These differences may be a result of both the amount of content made available for the mobile platform and the physical limitations of this type of device (e.g. small screen, limited typing functionality), which make searching and evaluating information more difficult and complex in mobile devices [7, 9, 10, 12]. In contrast, computer-only Internet users have a lower level of operational, content creation and communication skills than those who access the Internet only via mobile devices.

Although contrary to the literature, our results indicate that the higher level of content creation skills among mobile-only users is related to the non-differentiation in terms of the depth and complexity of content produced. After all, even though both platforms enable the creation of online content, it is more challenging to develop complex content (e.g. software development) on mobile devices [10].

Although the literature points out that access via mobile devices is associated with leisure and entertainment activities, such as communication [7, 9, 13], we understand that this positive relationship between the exclusive use of mobile and the ability to communicate can also be explained by the variety of applications available for digital communication, such as social networking applications (Facebook, Twitter, Instagram, etc.) and instant message exchange (WhatsApp, Telegram, Viber, Google Hangouts, etc.). In addition, some of these applications are targeted by zero-rating strategies of mobile operators, in which they do not charge for data consumed in such applications. Consequently, such "free" access encourages the use of these communication applications, especially among those with less economic power.

6   Implications and Final Remarks

The results of this research demonstrate that in Brazil, as in other developing countries, the mobile device plays an important role in the availability of Internet access, being used by more than 90% of Brazilian Internet users. However, while in groups with greater economic power, the mobile phone plays the role of complementary access, adding to other devices (e.g. desktop, laptop, tablet, game console, etc.), in more marginalized groups the mobile is a substitute device for computing equipment, evidencing the role of mobile leapfrogging among these users.

Regarding the effect of the device divide on digital skills, the results demonstrate that Internet users who access the Internet using both computational and mobile devices (multiplatform) are those with the highest level of digital skills. In contrast, those who connect exclusively via mobile displayed lower levels of informational skills due to the physical limitations of this device. Since this is a critical competence for Internet use, lack of informational skills can negatively impact the use of the web in capital-enhancing activities.

In terms of theoretical contribution, the findings of this research contribute to the studies that are based on the hypothesis of stratification, which states that previously existing social inequalities are maintained and amplified in the digital world [16, 31]. After all, users with higher socioeconomic status connect through multiple devices, allowing to develop a higher level of digital competence. In contrast, users in lower-income groups (classes D and E) tend to connect only via mobile, developing lower level of digital skills. In general terms, these results demonstrate the existence of the Mathew Effect (the richer get richer and poor get poorer), refuting the thesis that digital exclusion would be a temporary phenomenon resulting from the diffusion of innovations.

In terms of managerial implications, the findings of this research suggest that public policies aimed at providing Internet access should seek to combine actions that stimulate both access via mobile devices, such as the provision of Internet access via open Wi-Fi networks in public spaces, and also by providing connection via computers in public access centers (e.g. telecenters) and schools. In addition, the results suggest the need to promote training actions, focused on the development/enhancement (up-skilling) of informational skills.

The growing relevance of mobile devices for Internet access also leads to challenges to governments and businesses providing online content and services: due to the increasing percentage of mobile-only Internet users, especially in marginalized groups, it becomes critical to provide e-services in user-friendly interfaces adjusted to the mobile platform or via mobile applications, in order to facilitate online experience and engagement on the part of the users and overcome limitations in the affordances of the mobile. Finally, with the popularization of instant messaging applications (e.g. WhatsApp) and social networks sites in different social classes, we recommend the use of this type of application as communication channels for service delivery and inter-action between government and citizens.

The main limitation of this research lies in the uniform characterization of mobile devices, not considering their wide variety in terms of technical capacity and functionality. Future studies could also explore the relationship between digital skills levels and their implications in terms of Internet use, as well as in terms of tangible outcomes achieved through the mobilization of such digital resources (access, skills and uses).

Acknowledgment. The author(s) received financial support from Coordenação de Aperfeiçoamento de Pessoal de Nível Superior - Brazil (CAPES) funding code 001.

References

1. ITU: Measuring the Information Society 2018 (Volume 1). https://www.itu.int/en/ITU-D/Statistics/Documents/publications/misr2018/MISR-2018-Vol-1-E.pdf. Accessed Feb 2019
2. Dewan, S., Riggins, F.J.: The digital divide: current and future research directions. J. Assoc. Inf. Syst. **6**(12), 13 (2005)

3. Hargittai, E.: The second-level digital divide: differences in people's online skills. First Monday **7**(4) (2002). http://firstmonday.org/ojs/index.php/fm/article/view/942. Accessed Mar 2017
4. Van Dijk, J.: The Deepening Divide: Inequality in the Information Society. Sage Publications, Thousand Oaks (2005)
5. Scheerder, A., Van Deursen, A., Van Dijk, J.: Determinants of internet skills, uses and outcomes. A systematic review of the second-and third-level digital divide. Telematics Inform. **34**(8), 1607–1624 (2017)
6. Litt, E.: Measuring users' internet skills: a review of past assessments and a look toward the future. New Media Soc. **15**(4), 612–630 (2013)
7. Van Deursen, A., Van Dijk, J.: The first-level digital divide shifts from inequalities in physical access to inequalities in material access. New Media Soc. **21**(2), 354–375 (2019)
8. Humphreys, L., Von Pape, T., Karnowski, V.: Evolving mobile media: uses and conceptualizations of the mobile internet. J. Comput.-Mediated Commun. **18**(4), 491–507 (2013)
9. Marler, W.: Mobile phones and inequality: findings, trends, and future directions. New Media Soc. **20**(9), 3498–3520 (2018)
10. Napoli, P.M., Obar, J.A.: The emerging mobile internet underclass: a critique of mobile internet access. Inf. Soc. **30**(5), 323–334 (2014)
11. Mascheroni, G., Ólafsson, K.: The mobile internet: access, use, opportunities and divides among European children. New Media Soc. **18**(8), 1657–1679 (2016)
12. Donner, J., Gitau, S., Marsden, G.: Exploring mobile-only internet use: results of a training study in urban South Africa. Int. J. Commun. **5**, 574–597 (2011)
13. Pearce, K.E., Rice, R.E.: Digital divides from access to activities: comparing mobile and personal computer internet users. J. Commun. **63**(4), 721–744 (2013)
14. Napoli, P.M., Obar, J.A.: Mobile leapfrogging and digital divide policy: assessing the limitations of mobile Internet access. New America Foundation, Washington, D.C. (2013)
15. Mossberger, K., Tolbert, C.J., Hamilton, A.: Broadband adoption| measuring digital citizenship: mobile access and broadband. Int. J. Commun. **6**, 2492–2528 (2012)
16. Dimaggio, P., et al.: Digital inequality: from unequal access to differentiated use. In: Neckerman, K. (ed.) Social Inequality. Russell Sage Foundation, New York (2004)
17. Hargittai, E.: An update on survey measures of web-oriented digital literacy. Soc. Sci. Comput. Rev. **27**(1), 130–137 (2009)
18. Potosky, D.: The internet of knowledge (iKnow) measure. Comput. Hum. Behav. **23**(6), 2760–2777 (2007)
19. Van Deursen, A., Helsper, E.J., Eynon, R.: Development and validation of the internet skills scale (ISS). Inf. Commun. Soc. **19**(6), 804–823 (2016)
20. Gui, M., Argentin, G.: Digital skills of internet natives: different forms of internet literacy in a random sample of northern Italian high school students. New Media Soc. **13**(6), 963–980 (2011)
21. Van Deursen, A., Van Dijk, J.: Improving digital skills for the use of online public information and services. Gov. Inf. Q. **26**(3), 333–340 (2009)
22. Van Deursen, A., Van Dijk, J.: Measuring internet skills. Int. J. Hum.-Comput. Interact. **26** (10), 891–916 (2010)
23. Helsper, E.J., Eynon, R.: Distinct skill pathways to digital engagement. Eur. J. Commun. **28** (6), 696–713 (2013)
24. Van Dijk, J., Van Deursen, A.: Digital Skills: Unlocking the Information Society. Palgrave Macmillan, London (2014)
25. Bunz, U.: A generational comparison of gender, computer anxiety, and computer-email-web fluency. Stud. Media Inf. Literacy Educ. **9**(2), 54–69 (2009)

26. Hargittai, E.: Digital na(t)ives? Variation in internet skills and uses among members of the "net generation". Sociol. Inquiry **80**(1), 92–113 (2010)
27. Hilbert, M.: Digital gender divide or technologically empowered women in developing countries? A typical case of lies, damned lies, and statistics. Women's Stud. Int. Forum **34** (6), 479–489 (2011)
28. CGI (Brazilian Internet Steering Committee): Survey on the Use of Information and Communication Technologies in Brazilian Households: ICT Households 2016. Brazilian Internet Steering Committee, Sao Paulo (2017)
29. Hair, J.F., Black, W.C., Babin, J.B., Anderson, R.E., Tatham, R.L.: Análise Multivariada de Dados, 6th edn. Bookman, Porto Alegre (2009)
30. Hayes, A.F.: Introduction to Mediation, Moderation and Conditional Process Analysis: A Regression-Based Approach, 2nd edn. Guilford Press, New York (2018)
31. Zillien, N., Hargittai, E.: Digital distinction: status-specific types of internet usage. Soc. Sci. Q. **90**(2), 274–291 (2009)

The Role of eParticipation in the Expansion of Individual Capabilities

Marie Anne Macadar[1]([✉]) [iD], Gabriela Viale Pereira[2] [iD],
and Fernando Bichara Pinto[1]

[1] Federal University of Rio de Janeiro, Rua Pascoal Lemme 355,
Rio de Janeiro 21941-918, Brazil
{marie.macadar, fernando.pinto}@coppead.ufrj.br
[2] Danube University Krems, Dr.-Karl-Dorrek-Straße 30,
3500 Krems a. d. Donau, Austria
gabriela.viale-pereira@donau-uni.ac.at

Abstract. This article seeks to understand how eParticipation can boost individual capabilities in an ICT4D context. The analysis has regard eParticipation as a mechanism for expanding capabilities since it increases the democratic and participatory involvement of individuals in society. To this end, we examined the eParticipation field according to Sæbø et al. [18] and Medaglia [11], combining the capability approach from Sen's [21] and Nussbaum's [15] perspectives. Although the literature recognized that the capability approach is particularly difficult to operationalize in practice, we discovered some mechanisms in the eParticipation literature to support our analysis. However, despite its apparent benefits, eParticipation can indirectly contribute toward increasing inequalities among people since it is not available to all. We believe that recognition of the inequalities generated by the digital divide and the subsequent decrease in eParticipation could lead to a better understanding of the ICT4D context and assist in public policy-making.

Keywords: eParticipation · Capability Approach (CA) ·
Information and Communication Technology for Development (ICT4D)

1 Introduction

Medaglia [11] offers an eParticipation definition that faces this category of electronic government as "[...] issues of enabling opportunities for consultation and dialogue between government and citizens by using a range of ICT tools" [11 p. 346]. However, if eParticipation can be a way to foster citizen awareness and participation in public policy decision-making, it can increase inequalities between people with and without ICT access and skills, what jeopardizes the eParticipation philosophy itself[1].

---

[1] Helbig et al. [8] highlight that traditional digital divide factors, such as infrastructure and information availability, must be carefully considered in eParticipation initiatives. Contextual factors also play an important role in this double-edged nature of eParticipation.

© IFIP International Federation for Information Processing 2019
Published by Springer Nature Switzerland AG 2019
P. Panagiotopoulos et al. (Eds.): ePart 2019, LNCS 11686, pp. 155–166, 2019.
https://doi.org/10.1007/978-3-030-27397-2_13

Considering eParticipation in terms of citizens' capabilities development, it is possible to assess the impact of ICT beyond superficial levels of access and use or its economic benefits [12, 24]. Instead of focusing solely on technological determinants, we adopt Amartya Sen's capability approach (CA) in the ICT for development (ICT4D) context to study eParticipation. This approach to human well-being emphasizesthe importance of freedom of choice as individual empowerment. In Sen's view, the term 'capability' refers to environmental opportunities and the individual abilities a person needs in order to live the life he or she wants [21].

Although Madon's work from 2004 employed CA as a theoretical resource to understand how effectively people benefit from the use of ICT applications and access, is still missing the look at what people can or cannot do with the ICT applications provided [24] ICT use has been supported by the principles of CA in ICT4D research and theoretical exploration regarding the application of CA to ICT and human development [24]. However, Zheng [24] claims that CA in ICT4D studies lacks a theory that provides a balance between Sen's functionings and capabilities. In order to fill this gap, we propose the theory of eParticipation as responsible for the expansion of several human capabilities and freedoms of individuals.

In this study, we considered the eParticipation field as shaped by Sæbø et al. [18] and Medaglia [11] combining the capability approach of Sen [21] and Nussbaum [15]. Although the capability approach is particularly difficult to operationalize in practice [24], we discovered some mechanisms in the eParticipation literature that could be seen as a way to operationalize it.

This paper starts off by reviewing the eParticipation literature, then we discuss the aspects of human development and the capability approach (CA). The relationship between eParticipation categories, CA and ICT4D is discussed in Sect. 5. Final remarks and possibilities for future research are presented in the last section.

2   Electronic Participation

According to Sæbø et al. [18] eParticipation contextualization includes the expansion of transparency and people awareness of government activities and ICT-enabled public services. In addition to making information available, the purpose of eParticipation is to create an online ecosystem to support "citizen involvement in deliberation and decision-making processes" [18 p. 403].

For better understanding those online participatory spaces, Medaglia [11] and Sæbø et al. [18] have designed a eParticipation framework defined by five categories: eParticipation activities (eVoting, online political discussion, online decision-making, eActivism, eConsultation, eCampaigning and ePetitioning) characterized as social activities; eParticipation effects (deliberative, democratic and civic engagement) which includes all outcomes, i.e., the impact of eParticipation activities; Contextual factors (underlying technologies, governmental organization, infrastructure, policy and legal issues), that are not part of eParticipation nature, but have a direct effect on these activities; eParticipation actors (citizens, politicians, government institutions and voluntary organizations), comprised of the main actors involved in eParticipation activities; eParticipation evaluations (transparency and openness, quantity, tone and style, demographics), concentrate on assessing and measuring eParticipation effects, activities and actors, focusing on transparency and openness issues. In this study, we used these five categories to analyze how eParticipation has the potential to increase individual capabilities.

The result of eParticipation activities, considering contextual factors, refers to the impact of these activities in terms of desirable and undesirable outcomes in order to achieve some kind of benefit sought through them [11] The main discussion in this study deals with the effects – viewed as capabilities – which can be chosen by individuals – eParticipation actors – and constitutes a fundamental aspect of Sen's capability approach theory. However, as Medaglia [11] remarks, there is a significant risk of public sphere fragmentation and polarization, as a result from the bad diffusion of Internet-based forms of political participation, what could jeopardize people participation in ICT4D context.

3 Human Development and the Capability Approach

Human development is conceptually founded on the capability approach (CA), which aims to expand people's choices. Sen [21] argues that human development takes place through the expansion of capabilities that individuals consider important to have. The concept of agency – the capacity of individuals to act independently and make their own free choices – is intrinsically linked to the capability approach, since individuals are the agents of their own choices, of what they value. Nussbaum [15], who added on to Sen's concept, regards the capability approach as opportunities created by a combination of personal skills and influences from political, social and economic environments.

Along these lines, Sen [21] believes that well-being achievements should be measured in functionings, whereas well-being freedom is reflected by a person's capability set (a set of capabilities available to be chosen). Furthermore, "[...] the focus on agency will always transcend an analysis in terms of functionings and capabilities, and will take agency goals into account" [17 p. 103].

Sen's reasoning is based on the evaluation of social change in terms of improvement to human life. His approach conceives of human life as a set of activities and ways of being called functionings. He relates the judgment of quality of life to the ability to perform these functionings. So, the capability approach is seen as a theoretical framework that demands the freedom to achieve well-being and agency and that can be understood in terms of people's capabilities [17, 24].

Sen [21] does not specify a list of minimum basic capabilities for quality of life, but addresses the subject by stating that one cannot escape assessment of the problem when defining a class of functionings as important and others as not so important. According to him, in some welfare analyses a few functionings can be established, such as the ability to eat well, live well or partake of community life. Sen [19] argues that the first characteristic of well-being can be seen as a vector of functionings, that is, the set of functionings that a person achieves.

A complementary approach is contained in Nussbaum's ten central capabilities. She considers that these central capabilities are the bare minimum in a widely shared understanding of the task of governments. She also believes that these central capabilities can enable people to lead a dignified and minimally flourishing life and, consequently, are necessary for human development. Additionally, she focuses on a central question that can make the discussion more explicit: Which capabilities are the most important? The ten core capabilities defined by Nussbaum [15] are: (1) life, (2) physical health, (3) physical integrity, (4) senses, imagination and thought, (5) emotions, (6) reason, (7) affiliation, (8) other species, (9) play and (10) control over one's environment.

4   Electronic Participation in the ICT for Development Context

On the one hand, Avgerou [2] acknowledges that research on the developmental potential and impact of ICT is multidisciplinary and involves Information Systems (IS), Human Computer Interaction (HCI), Communication and Development Studies [6]. Focusing on the development issue, Walsham et al. [23 p. 317] believe that ICT can help improving socioeconomic conditions in developing countries. Walsham [23 p. 89] elaborates on this idea affirming that "IS scholars and practitioners should be concerned with how to use ICT to help make a better world, where everybody has the opportunity and capability to use technologies to make better lives for themselves, their communities and the world in general".

On the other hand, Brown and Grant [4] pointed out the duality within the research body and suggested two distinct streams of research: studies focusing on (1) understanding technology "for development" (ICT4D) and (2) understanding technology "in developing" countries (ICTD). In turn, Heeks [7] identified several elements that comprise the disciplinary foundations for development informatics research, in addition to categorizing the theories for ICT4D research. In a complementary approach, Heeks [7 p. 627] notes that "[...] infrastructure and access are only the starting point in understanding ICT's contribution to development; they are inputs whereas our real attention should be focused on outputs".

In an effort to link these two points of view, value chain based on the standard input–process–output model to create a sequence of linked ICT-for-development (ICT4D) resources and processes [7], which Heeks [6 p. 627] divided into four domains: Readiness, Availability, Uptake and Impact.

For discussing eParticipation in the ICT4D context, thinking in Heeks [6] framework, besides guaranteeing technological infrastructure, participatory initiatives must take account citizens' capabilities and limitations to participate and to assess their degree of participation and their role in decision-making. We argue in the next sections that Capability Approach (CA) can be the theoretical lens through which we can better analyze the people's participation in ICT4D context.

5   eParticipation, Capability Approach and ICT4D

The pursuit to eradicate poverty and the realization of Sen's capability approach are accepted by Avgerou [2 p. 2] as important research in ICTD studies. She states that "even if not explicitly acknowledged, every ICTD study makes specific assumptions about the way IT innovation happens in the context of developing countries".

In this sense, the study by Puri and Sahay [16] examines the relationship between participation, ICT use, and rural development processes. By reflecting about who defines the participation agenda in developing countries they identify that in many cases it is externally driven, but in some situations it is shared with communities/IS users, it is a community/user driven agenda, and in a few locations it moves towards empowerment, the agenda set by people. They also address what capabilities people need to be able to participate. established to elicit participation, and (e) the knowledge participants have about the problem domain.

Related to this this context, Puri and Sahay [16] pose the question: "How can local participatory processes be sustained and scaled up?" They search for elements in development theory and information system theory to answer this question. In both, the problems of scale and sustainability are crucial. They conclude that if the success of development is based on effective participation, then sustaining these projects over time requires a deeper institutionalization of participatory processes.

Another contemporary study, closely related to eParticipation in the ICTD context, was conducted by Kock and Gaskins [10]. They examined the relationships between Internet diffusion, voice and accountability, and government corruption. According to these authors, policy-makers in developing countries who desire to increase voice and accountability at the national level, and thus the degree to which their citizens participate in the country's governance, should strongly consider initiatives that broaden Internet access in their countries.

In the literature review, it is possible to note the degree of empowerment promoted by ICT access, enabling citizen participation in virtually any public service, not necessarily only in politics or government-related topics [22]. Zheng [24 p. 76] refers to the perspective of Avgerou [2] of the social embeddedness of IT innovation: "[…] even though ICT is perceived as commodities, it has to be considered in connection with the conversion factors and decision-making mechanisms when applied in the context of development". We bridge this gap by understanding the interplay between eParticipation categories and the central human capabilities of Nussbaum [15]. We contend that eParticipation addresses the expansion of several of these human capabilities through eParticipation activities and heightens the capabilities and freedom of individuals, making them more active in society.

To achieve the paper's objective, we have created a conceptual model that shows the relationship between eParticipation, capability approach and ICT4D. The purpose was to analyze the role of eParticipation increasing individual capabilities in the ICT4D context. We operationalize it by taking the concepts presented by Sæbø et al. [18] and Medaglia [11] work on ePartcipation field, combined to Sen [17] and Nussbaum [15] perspectives of capability approach and taking the ICT4D as context. We argue that eParticipation activities are resources provided by government to expand people's capability set (freedom), allowing them to achieve a functioning.

5.1   eParticipation Activities Versus Central Capabilities

Nussbaum [15] stated that the task of government is to enable people to lead a dignified life, or, as Sen [17] presented in his work, to pursue life as a person of value. Through eParticipation activities, governments can provide a set of opportunities (or freedom) for people to choose from Sæbø et al. [21] and Medaglia [11] describe several eParticipation activities that could be considered as a set of expanded capabilities available to individuals, such as the capability to express one's self, vote and participate in communities, make decisions or be informed, resulting in functionings involving living and participating in groups, expressing one's own opinion, listening, being listened to and having access to information for the decision-making process. These activities represent some of the core capabilities necessary for human development, as mentioned by Nussbaum [15], especially to make political choices and enjoy freedom of expression. In this regard, it is possible to identify central capabilities that are expanded by eParticipation activities directly and indirectly.

The four central capabilities that are directly expanded by eParticipation activities are: (1) control over one's environment, (2) affiliation, (3) reason and (4) senses and imagination. This capability approach view of eParticipation is central to our work, that is, the role of eParticipation in the expansion of individual capabilities. We believe that every eParticipation activity is a new capability created or enhanced in a person. The use of ICT in participation activities increases the comprehensiveness of such activities. By using ICT, particularly the Internet, eParticipation activities can exploit the decision-making process, asking citizens to contribute in certain necessary decisions. Again, if we analyze this participation process from the angle of CA, it is evident that there are now more citizens involved in the overall process. In this sense, by taking a general political dimension, we suggest the Proposition 1: *By providing eParticipation activities governments will enlarge people's opportunities for political participation, directly enhancing aspects as control over one's environment, affiliation, reason and senses and imagination.*

Literature distinguishes between electronic machine voting (in a fixed place) and electronic distance voting (by using ICT from different locations). Sæbø et al. [18] have pointed out, in their review of literature, important issues related to eVoting, like security, trust and also concerns to bridging the digital divide. Additionally, Medaglia [11] remarks that the adoption of eVoting systems has the potential to positively affect democratic deliberation and citizen engagement in politics. Thereby, we suggest the Proposition 1A: *By participating in eVoting activities people will be able to (a) have the right of political participationin the sense of control over one's environment (b) to be treated as a dignified being whose worth is equal to that of others in the sense of affiliation.*

Sæbø et al. [18] 'work highlights the increase of citizens' opportunities for agenda setting and policy making through the use of ICT. They also found some research that demonstrated that online participants are well-educated and already politically active. They also argued that the challenge is how to connect online political discourse to more traditional channels. On the other hand, Medaglia [11] emphasizes that the "ICT environments constitute spaces where participation and deliberation in the political discourse take place" [11 p. 351] and several transformations are ongoing like, for instance, the emergence of new types of parties; an open-source based model of politics that revolves around the role of voters as co-producers of political discourse (e.g. blogs). Thereby, we suggest the Proposition 1B: *By participating in online political discourse activities people will be able to engage in critical reflection about the planning of one's own life in the sense of Reason.*

Both studies, Sæbø et al. [18] and Medaglia [11]'s, agree that online decision-making is focused on the direct link between participants and the political decision-making process. This category implies "...an explicit link with political decision-making through the use of ICT and is seen as a potential avenue for increasing political participation" [18 p. 408]. However, Medaglia [11] points up that the majority of the studies investigated by them focus on platforms for specific decision-making purposes (e.g. parliamentary debates, participatory budgeting, collaborative drafting of policy documents and urban planning). Proposition 1C: *By participating in online decision-making activities people will be able to participate effectively in political choices in the sense of control over one's environment.*

According to Medaglia [11], the term eActivism refers to "all activities carried out by voluntary organizations, interest groups, and individuals to promote viewpoints and interests using ICT tools" [11 p. 351]. Sæbø et al. [18] also call attention to the fact that such groups, organizations and individuals seek to influence the political process by using technological means to promote their interests. These authors are mainly concerned about understanding "to what extend such activities really increase the opportunities of citizens (rather than the activists themselves) to participate may be questioned" [18 p. 409]. For example, in an eActivism activity, people can express themselves to others and engage in important discussions. One might ask: "Is eActivism the only way people can express themselves or engage in discussions?" The answer is no, but with eActivism people can expand their capability of activism, participate in many discussions at the same time and increase their voice. Thereby, we suggest the Proposition 1D: *By participating in eActivism activities people will be able to (a) use one's mind in ways protected by guarantees of freedom of expression with respect to political speech in the sense of senses and imagination, (b) engage in various forms of social interaction in the sense of affiliation and (c) having the right of political participation, free speech and freedom of association in the sense of control over one's environment.*

Medaglia [11] summarizes the concept of eConsultation as follows: "eConsultation is an activity of providing ICT-enabled feedback mechanisms from citizens to governments and public agencies, usually initiated by the latter" [11 p. 352] Sæbø et al. [18] highlight that eConsultation focuses on how to increase input from the different stakeholders in government (from citizens, companies or societal groups). The main point discussed in the literature investigated by them is related to how to increase the level of participation and how to include new societal groups. Another important issue is related to transparency as well as the design of the eConsulation services. In the same way, ePetitions refers to a tool through which citizens could influence decision makers' agendas by proposing themes or decisions to be discussed. In ePetition systems, citizens sign a petition online proposing an issue for consideration by the political system [18 p. 410] Considering that both activities corroborate with a participatory democracy, we suggest the Proposition 1E: *By participating in eConsultation and ePetition activities people will be able to (a) participate effectively in political choices in the sense of control over one's environment, (b) live with and in relation to others, to recognize and show concern for other human beings, to engage in various forms of social interaction; and (c) imagine the situation of another and have compassion for that situation; having the capability for both justice and friendship in the sense of affiliation.*

Medaglia [11] and Sæbø et al. [18] 's research has not found studies focusing on eCampaigning. However, Medaglia [11] recognized that the use of digital tools with participatory objectives by politicians in the context of electioneering is widespread and the use of social media is "...paradoxically found to reflect the one-way communication structures of traditional political campaigning, and not to foster citizen involvement in decision-making" [11 p. 352] In this sense, it might foster transparency, which is closely related to eParticipation, as a way to increase citizens' trust and creating new possibilities of public interaction and participation [13]. Thereby, we suggest the Proposition 1F: *By participating in eCampaigning activities people will be able to (a) imagine, think and reason in an informed way in the sense of senses and imagination and (b) form a conception of the good and to engage in critical reflection in the sense of reason.*

The central capabilities that are indirectly expanded by eParticipation activities are: (1) life, (2) physical health, (3) physical integrity, (4) other species, (5) play and (6) emotions. By taking the capability approach, Kleine [9] states that very often ICT-based resources might represent tools used by individuals to enhance capabilities besides a capability itself. Considering development as the expansion of the capacities of human beings to lead lives they value, ICT should be seen as a means to achieve this objective in the development process, conditioned to a set of conversion factors [24]. Helbig et al. [8] emphasizes the lack of attention on citizens' needs and questions if users actually want, or could they use, what government were given. In this way, we suggest the Proposition 2: *The engagement in eParticipation activities might represent a mean that allow people to express their needs and expectations to achieve what is valued by them (indirectly enhancing aspects as life, physical health, physical integrity, other species, play and emotions).*

5.2 Contextual Factors Versus Internal Capabilities with External Opportunities

Although ICT is a key factor for boosting citizen participation, the technology is not available to the entire population. In this respect, Helbig et al. [8] argue that simply dividing people into two groups – those who have or do not have ICT access – does not encompass all the difficulties posed by digital exclusion, since problems of access and use are also issues that need to be discussed. Before ICT can become a tool for expanding citizen participation that is available to all, governments must address structural problems, such as lack of electricity, Internet costs and training for low-income citizens, among others. Contextual factors, as pointed out by Sæbø et al. [18] and Medaglia [11], constitute resources for achieving increased capabilities. However, if ICT access is not possible, this should be viewed as a deprivation of liberty, a reduction in capabilities and inequality of access. Therefore, contextual factors are resources that influence the set of available capabilities. Thus, we suggest the Proposition 3: *The expansion of individual capabilities through eParticipation activities is conditioned by contextual factors.*

Kleine and Unwin [9] identified many factors that influence people's choices. Some of them, as previously discussed in the realm of eParticipation and ICT4D, are material resources, such as tools, equipment and hardware (computers). If a person does not have any ICT device, or Internet access, or even electricity, participation in electronic activities will be restricted. The author lists human resources as educational and skills as potential influencers of people's capability to partake of a certain opportunity. The inequality created between those who have access to technology and those who do not is, in many cases, driven by inequality of education. If, for example, we recognize that even a person with computer access and basic computer skills may not have the ability to understand a subject in an eVoting activity, there will still be restrictions on the extensive use of this mechanism. In sum, the individual capabilities of people with limited access to eParticipation tools (e.g., Internet) are consequently reduced. Furthermore, even individuals with ICT access may have difficulties developing their knowledge, skills and confidence in the use of ICT. Thereby, we suggest the Proposition 3A: *The digital divide might restrict people's engagement in eParticipation activities constraining the possibility for people to participate effectively in political choices that govern one's life; having the right of political participation, free speech and freedom of association.*

Nussbaum [15] introduces the concept of internal preparedness with external opportunity. According to her, "[…] a society might do well at producing internal capabilities but might cut off the avenues through which people actually have the opportunity to function in accordance with those capabilities". For example, a person who has all the internal capabilities to vote, i.e., political knowledge, a high enough educational level to understand the different proposals, might be prevented from voting in a certain political regime. Therefore, eParticipation activities can promote or expand freedom (external opportunities) to leverage this person's internal capability. One clear example is eActivism, which leverages the internal capability to criticize the government. Another example is if a person with a disability or heath issue wants to join in on any government participation activity, he or she can now do so, from literally anywhere, at home or even in a hospital, instead of going to a central location (government office). In that way, we suggest the Proposition 3B: *The degree of empowerment promoted by ICT access might increase people's engagement in eParticipation activities enlarging the possibility for people to participate effectively in political choices that govern one's life; having the right of political participation, free speech and freedom of association.*

5.3   eParticipation Effects, Actors and Evaluation Versus Individual Realized Functionings

Functionings are ways through which well-being achievements can be evaluated. A personal achievement is a set of functionings that demonstrates human well-being. In this sense, agency – the ability of individuals to make their own free choices – can be seen in eParticipation effects such as civic engagement level, an increased democratic and deliberative level or other social impacts, like community empowerment choice and voice. These effects, as eParticipation outcomes, should be thoughtfully heeded in public policy development.

The opportunity to participate in democratic decisions is a capability provided by government. People's choice to effectively use this capability and participate in a deliberative forum is a functioning. Agency and choice are fundamental issues in this case. For instance, a person chooses to engage or participate in a specific online activity. Sen [20] argues that agency is the ability to act on behalf of what a person values. In the eParticipation context, we use agency to choose in which activities to participate (e.g.: eVoting, eDeliberation and/or eActivism). At this point we can consider the role of governments in eParticipation, specifically, as providing activities for use by citizens. This means the realization of capabilities, at the end the functioning proposed by Sen [20]. Thus, we suggest the Proposition 4: *The individual achievement of functionings, through eParticipation activities, is conditioned by individual's choice in engaging on these activities.*

In eParticipation theory, actors are individuals who are engaged in eParticipation effects, or using CA vocabulary, the functioning. Bearing in mind that the term 'capability' refers to environmental opportunities and individual abilities, actors are those who are directly involved in participation through ICT access: citizens, politicians and government institutions. For instance, whoever is behind the computer (or any other device) taking part in an eConsultation or any other eParticipation activity is an individual. By taking a supply and demand perspective of eGovernment, it is possible to verify the phenomena in terms of eParticipation actors. The supply side focuses on "initiatives that create electronic services and, in many cases, opportunities for participation from citizens, businesses, and other stakeholders". Considering the demand side the focus is on "how different social groups try to take advantage of these services and of the other uses of information and communication technologies within society" [11 p. 93].

Using the capabilities available, the individual achievement of functionings – which is a result of personal choice – can be evaluated by the realized functionings. The main mechanism in eParticipation that can be identified is transparency and openness. Openness makes it possible for people to get involved in the processes of government and create value for both [1]. As more government data is available, it will be easier for citizens to find information about government activities, being able to complain and communicate their opinion, representing an increase in their interest in actively participate in the government process.

6 Final Remarks

The objective of this paper was to understand how eParticipation could contribute to increase individual capabilities in an ICT4D context. We started off with the premise that eParticipation can increase different individual capabilities. Moreover, eParticipation in its various forms of social and political engagement is undoubtedly a breakthrough toward increased individual freedom. We know that technology has the power to engage individuals but, at the same time, it can marginalize those who do not have ICT access or the skills to take advantage of it. Indeed, public policy should be created to benefit all citizens, wherever they live.

In this study, we sought to contribute by proposing to fill the gap identified by Zheng [24] that CA requires additional social theories to evaluate and analyze the ICT4D context. For this reason, we focused on eParticipation to analyze some of its features using Nussbaum's core capabilities and Sen's CA. As a result, we have, to a certain extent, developed a proposal that enables us to implement and comprehend, in a concrete way, the relationship between eParticipation categoriesand CA. We believe that this theoretical contribution could provide support to good management in public affairs.

Nevertheless, this paper is a proposal that could serve to launch a new study. For instance, a case study could be carried out to highlight the insights gained from the relationship between eParticipation categories and CA for public policy-making in the ICT4D context. Other studies could also include institutional analysis and CA in ICT4D [3] from an eParticipation perspective, or ones that focus on Smart Cities, more specifically on the way they represent innovation in management and policy as well as technology [14] and public value [5]. A helpful theoretical approach could be developed to investigate Smart Cities and help governments prevent social, political and organizational problems.

References

1. Agrawal, D., Kettinger, W., Zhang, C.: The openness challenge: why some cities take it on and others don't. In: Proceedings of the 20th Americas Conference on Information Systems (AMCIS 2014), Savannah, Georgia, USA (2014)
2. Avgerou, C.: Discourses on ICT and development. Inf. Technol. Int. Dev. **6**(3), 1–18 (2010)
3. Bass, J.M., Nicholson, B., Subrahmanian, E.: A framework using institutional analysis and the capability approach in ICT4D. Inf. Technol. Int. Dev. **9**(1), 19–35 (2013)
4. Brown, A.E., Grant, G.G.: Highlighting the duality of the ICT and development research agenda. Inf. Technol. Dev. **16**(2), 96–111 (2010)
5. Harrison, T.M., et al.: Open government and e-government: democratic challenges from a public value perspective. Inf. Polity **17**(2), 83–97 (2012)
6. Heeks, R.: Do information and communication technologies (ICTs) contribute to development? J. Int. Dev. **22**(5), 625–640 (2010)
7. Heeks, R., Molla, A.: Impact Assessment of ICT-for-development projects: A Compendium of Approaches. Development Informatics Working Paper No. 36, University of Manchester, UK (2009)
8. Helbig, N., Gil-García, J.R., Ferro, E.: Understanding the complexity of electronic government: implications from the digital divide literature. Gov. Inf. Q. **26**(1), 89–97 (2009)
9. Kleine, D., Unwin, T.: Technological revolution, evolution and new dependencies: what's new about ICT4D? Third World Q. **30**(5), 1045–1067 (2009)
10. Kock, N., Gaskins, L.: The mediating role of voice and accountability in the relationship between internet diffusion and government corruption in Latin America and Sub-Saharan Africa. Inf. Technol. Dev. **20**(1), 23–43 (2014)
11. Medaglia, R.: eParticipation research: moving characterization forward (2006–2011). Gov. Inf. Q. **29**(3), 346–360 (2012)
12. Madon, S.: Evaluating the developmental impact of e-governance initiatives: an exploratory framework. Electron. J. Inf. Syst. Dev. Countries **20**(5), 1–13 (2004)

13. de Miranda, P.R.M., Cunha, M.A., Pugas-Filho, J.M.: eParticipation in smart cities of developing countries: research-based practical recommendations. In: Gil-Garcia, J.R., Pardo, T.A., Nam, T. (eds.) Smarter as the New Urban Agenda. PAIT, vol. 11, pp. 315–332. Springer, Cham (2016). https://doi.org/10.1007/978-3-319-17620-8_17

14. Nam, T., Pardo, T.A.: Smart city as urban innovation: focusing on management, policy, and context. In: Proceedings of the 5th International Conference on Theory and Practice of Electronic Governance September, pp. 185–194. ACM (2011)

15. Nussbaum, M.C.: Creating Capabilities. The Human Development Approach. Harvard University Press, Cambridge (2011)

16. Puri, S.K., Sahay, S.: Role of ICTs in participatory development: an Indian experience. Inf. Technol. Dev. 13(2), 133–160 (2007)

17. Robeyns, I.: The capability approach: a theoretical survey. J. Hum. Dev. 6(1), 93–117 (2005)

18. Sæbø, Ø., Rose, J., Flak, L.S.: The shape of eParticipation: characterizing an emerging research area. Gov. Inf. Q. 25(3), 400–428 (2008)

19. Sen, A.: Well-being, agency and freedom: the dewey lectures. J. Philos. 82(4), 169–221 (1985)

20. Sen, A.: Development as capability expansion. J. Dev. Plan. 19, 41–58 (1989)

21. Sen, A.: Development as Freedom. Oxford University Press, Oxford (1999)

22. Susha, I., Grönlund, Å.: eParticipation research: systematizing the field. Gov. Inf. Q. 29(3), 373–382 (2012)

23. Walsham, G.: Are we making a better world with ICTs? Reflections on a future agenda for the IS field. J. Inf. Technol. 27(2), 87–93 (2012)

24. Zheng, Y.: Different spaces for e-development: what can we learn from the capability approach? Inf. Technol. Dev. 15(2), 66–82 (2009)

Author Index

Printed in the United States
By Bookmasters